Trivia
QUIZ
Book

Trivia QUIZ Book

Over 4,500 new brain-teasing questions to entertain family and friends

ARCTURUS

Published by Arcturus Publishing Limited
For Global Software Publishing Ltd
Meadow Lane
St Ives
Cambridgeshire
PE17 4LG

This edition published 2000

Printed and bound by WS Bookwell in Finland

Cover design by Communique

Special thanks to
Nicola Cottingham, Danny O'Shaughnessy and Madeleine Knibbs

Compiled and designed by
© Western Media Publishing Ltd

© Arcturus Publishing Ltd
1-7 Shand Street
London
SE1 2ES

ISBN 1-84193-011-3

THE TRIVIA QUIZ BOOK

Entertainment

| Your rating: | ● 0-5 | Buy a TV | ● 6-10 | Keep at it |
| | ● 11-15 | Join a quiz team | ● 16-20 | Enter a quiz show |

1. Which Radio 1 DJ was the presenter of *The National Lottery – Winning Lines*?
2. Which 1999 film starred Brendan Fraser as a 1920s adventurer and Rachel Weisz as a librarian?
3. What was the title of the 1970s TV saga based on U.S. author Robert Crichton's tracing of his Scottish ancestry?
4. Which U.S. singer/songwriter's debut album was entitled *On How Life Is*?
5. In which 1988 film did Don Ameche play a shoeshine boy mistaken for a Mafia boss?
6. What was the title of the 1986 number one by the Spitting Image puppets?
7. Which actor played Nick Leeson in the 1999 film about the collapse of Barings Bank, *Rogue Trader*?
8. Who presented ITV's *Eye Spy*, which featured footage of crimes from surveillance cameras?
9. With which George Michael song did Robbie Williams have a top five hit in 1996?
10. Who starred in the 1952 biopic of Australian swimmer Annette Kellerman, as the *Million Dollar Mermaid*?
11. Which vocalist had a 1962 hit with *Ain't That Funny*?
12. Which 1999 action-comedy starred Mark Wahlberg and Lou Diamond Phillips as hitmen?
13. Who was Fred's neighbour and bowling partner in TV's *The Flintstones*?
14. Which actor played the butler Ruggles in the 1935 film version of *Ruggles of Red Gap*?
15. Which Changing Rooms designer joined Quentin Wilson to present the BBC 2 series *All the Right Moves*?
16. Which veteran actor starred as an art thief in the 1999 film *Entrapment*?
17. Which 1999 BBC 1 period drama set in the 18th century charted the true story of the Lennox sisters?
18. Which actress played Queen Christina in the 1933 film?
19. Which sports presenter joined Michael Buerk to present the BBC's coverage of Prince Edward and Sophie Rhys-Jones' wedding in 1999?
20. Who provided the voice of the unseen Charlie in the U.S. TV series *Charlie's Angels*?

ANSWERS: 1 *Simon Mayo*, 2 *The Mummy*, 3 *The Camerons*, 4 *Macy Gray's*, 5 *Things Change*, 6 *The Chicken Song*, 7 *Ewan McGregor*, 8 *Mary Nightingale*, 9 *Freedom*, 10 *Esther Williams*, 11 *Jimmy Justice*, 12 *The Big Hit*, 13 *Barney Rubble*, 14 *Charles Laughton*, 15 *Anna Ryder Richardson*, 16 *Sean Connery*, 17 *Aristocrats*, 18 *Greta Garbo*, 19 *Sue Barker*, 20 *John Forsythe*.

? General Knowledge

Your rating: ● 0-5   Join a library   ● 6-10   Keep at it
               ● 11-15   Join a quiz team   ● 16-20   Join Mensa

1. Which two countries are connected by the Simplon Pass?
2. Where was a women's peace camp set up outside a U.S. airbase near Newbury in 1981?
3. Which popular novelist died at her home in Newcastle-upon-Tyne in 1998?
4. By what title was Antony Armstrong-Jones known after his marriage to Princess Margaret?
5. Which hard silvery metal has the chemical symbol Ni?
6. With which of the senses is the word olfactory connected?
7. Which unit of length is defined as the length of the path travelled by light in a vacuum in 1/299,792,458 of a second?
8. What name is given to the form of ritual suicide practised by Japanese samurai?
9. By what letters were the elite German military corps, the Schutzstaffel, known?
10. Which warlike seafaring Biblical people give their name to people indifferent to artistic or cultural values?
11. What is the largest island of the Outer Hebrides?
12. In which Middle Eastern country did the golden hamster originate?
13. Which London landmark came from Heliopolis in Egypt?
14. Who was the official propagandist of Nazi Germany?
15. Which extreme English Puritan sect was led by John Lilburne?
16. Who was Britain's first Labour prime minister?
17. Who was president of the United States during World War I?
18. Which Australian feminist wrote *The Female Eunuch*?
19. What was the occupation of Jack Ketch?
20. Which Czech-born composer wrote the music for *Rose Marie and The Vagabond King*?

ANSWERS: 1 *Italy and Switzerland*, 2 *Greenham Common*, 3 *Dame Catherine Cookson*, 4 *Earl of Snowdon*, 5 *Nickel*, 6 *Smell*, 7 *Metre*, 8 *Hara-kiri*, 9 *S.S.*, 10 *Philistines*, 11 *Lewis with Harris*, 12 *Syria*, 13 *Cleopatra's Needle*, 14 *Joseph Goebbels*, 15 *Levellers*, 16 *Ramsay MacDonald*, 17 *Woodrow Wilson*, 18 *Germaine Greer*, 19 *Hangman*, 20 *Rudolf Friml*.

THE TRIVIA QUIZ BOOK

 *General Knowledge*

Your rating:	● 0-5	Join a library	● 6-10	Keep at it
	● 11-15	Join a quiz team	● 16-20	Join Mensa

1. Which popular Italian operatic tenor made his debut at La Scala in 1966?
2. What name is given to any animal without a backbone?
3. Which barrister and playwright, who created Rumpole, received a knighthood in 1998?
4. What spice is obtained from the plant *Zingiber officinale*?
5. Which London park contains the Serpentine, Rotten Row and Speakers' Corner?
6. What is the oldest university in the United States?
7. Which British novelist wrote *Brave New World* and *Eyeless in Gaza*?
8. In which English county is the port of Plymouth?
9. Which apostle and martyr was originally known as Saul of Tarsus?
10. What is the capital of Poland?
11. Of which U.S. state is Frankfort the capital?
12. Which chronic disease is caused by the bacillus *Mycobacterium leprae*?
13. Who scored an own goal in the opening match of the 1998 World Cup Finals?
14. Which Italian painter and architect designed the campanile of Florence Cathedral?
15. Who wrote *Zorba the Greek*?
16. Which agency of the United Nations is represented by the initials I.L.O.?
17. In which U.S. state is the city of Paterson?
18. Which country was plunged into political uncertainty when its leader, General Sani Abacha, died suddenly in 1998?
19. By what name is the songbird *Regulus regulus* better known?
20. Which English poet and essayist wrote *Imaginary Conversations of Literary Men and Statesmen*?

ANSWERS: 1 *Luciano Pavarotti*, 2 *Invertebrate*, 3 *John Mortimer*, 4 *Ginger*, 5 *Hyde Park*, 6 *Harvard*, 7 *Aldous Huxley*, 8 *Devon*, 9 *Saint Paul*, 10 *Warsaw*, 11 *Kentucky*, 12 *Leprosy*, 13 *Tommy Boyd of Scotland*, 14 *Giotto*, 15 *Nikos Kazantzakis*, 16 *International Labour Organisation*, 17 *New Jersey*, 18 *Nigeria*, 19 *Goldcrest*, 20 *Walter Savage Landor*.

 *General Knowledge*

1. Of which breed of sledge dog is the Siberian the best known
2. What is the most famous opera by Ruggiero Leoncavallo?
3. Which alcoholic drink is distilled from grain flavoured with juniper berries?
4. Who scored England's first goal in the 1998 World Cup Finals?
5. Which popular name for the Netherlands is actually a low-lying region of the country?
6. What was the name of Napoleon Bonaparte's first wife?
7. Which U.S. president, who succeeded Richard Nixon, was born Leslie King?
8. What name is given to the offspring produced by the mating of two unrelated animals or plants?
9. Which big cat is also called a panther?
10. Which fertiliser is chiefly made up of the excrement of seabirds?
11. Which British author wrote the didactic book *Self-Help*?
12. What name is given to sharp or burning pain originating in a nerve?
13. Which town is the administrative centre of Shetland?
14. What is the heaviest lanthanide element?
15. Which Yorkshire cricketer was the first professional to captain England?
16. Who succeeded Lloyd George as prime minister in 1922?
17. Which naturally-occurring protein that helps to fight viruses was discovered by British virologist Alick Isaacs in 1957?
18. What is the S.I. unit of intensity of illumination?
19. Which British adventure novelist died in June 1998, at the age of 84?
20. In Greek legend, which king of Pylos who served in the Trojan War was noted for his wisdom?

ANSWERS: 1 Husky. 2 I Pagliacci. 3 Gin. 4 Alan Shearer. 5 Holland. 6 Josephine. 7 Gerald Ford. 8 Hybrid. 9 Leopard. 10 Guano. 11 Samuel Smiles. 12 Neuralgia. 13 Lerwick. 14 Lutetium. 15 Len Hutton. 16 Bonar Law. 17 Interferon. 18 Lux. 19 Hammond Innes. 20 Nestor.

Entertainment

Your rating:
- 0-5 Buy a TV
- 11-15 Join a quiz team
- 6-10 Keep at it
- 16-20 Enter a quiz show

1. Which 1999 Woody Allen film starred Kenneth Branagh as failed novelist Lee Simon?
2. Who presented the BBC 1 gameshow *The Other Half*?
3. What was the title of the Chemical Brothers' third album?
4. Which long-running TV drama series of the 1960s and 1970s starred John Stride as a go-getting solicitor?
5. Which actress played a runaway teenage daughter in the 1975 film *Night Moves*?
6. Which Children's BBC series originally featured the pop group S Club 7?
7. Which British group had three number one hits in 1963, including *I Like It*?
8. Which ITV hospital drama series starred Martin Shaw as consultant Robert Kingsford?
9. Which 1999 film set in a Manhattan prep-school starred Reese Witherspoon and Sarah Michelle Gellar?
10. Which BBC 1 docu-soap featured Jackie the trans-sexual prostitute?
11. Who sang about *Sweet Nothin's* in 1960?
12. Who played an escaped convict on his third breakout in the 1985 film *Runaway Train*?
13. Which Essex town provided the setting for Channel 4's documentary series *Soldier Town*?
14. What was the title of the New Seekers' 1973 number one hit?
15. Which actress played a gangster's moll lumbered with a little boy in the 1999 film *Gloria*?
16. Who had a 1999 top five hit with *Beautiful Stranger*?
17. Which 1983 film starred James Fox as a father searching for his missing daughter?
18. What was the name of the *EastEnders* character played by Craig Fairbrass, who made his first appearance in the Square in 1999 as Carol Jackson's boyfriend?
19. Who released his first studio album for 11 years in 1999, entitled *Bad Love*?
20. Which BBC 1 police drama series starred Warren Clarke and Colin Buchanan?

ANSWERS: *1 Celebrity. 2 Dale Winton. 3 Surrender. 4 The Main Chance. 5 Melanie Griffith. 6 Miami 7. 7 Gerry and the Pacemakers. 8 Always and Everyone. 9 Cruel Intentions. 10 Paddington Green. 11 Brenda Lee. 12 Jon Voight. 13 Colchester. 14 You Won't Find Another Fool Like Me. 15 Sharon Stone. 16 Madonna. 17 Runners. 18 Dan Sullivan. 19 Randy Newman. 20 Dalziel and Pascoe.*

THE TRIVIA QUIZ BOOK

⟨?⟩ General Knowledge

Your rating:
- 0-5   Join a library
- 11-15   Join a quiz team
- 6-10   Keep at it
- 16-20   Join Mensa

1. Which founder of Protestantism appeared before the Diet of Worms in 1521?
2. What name is given to a dealer licensed to lend money on the security of an item of movable personal property?
3. Which African statesman received the freedom of the city of Cardiff in a ceremony at Cardiff Castle in 1998?
4. Of which African country is Lusaka the capital?
5. Which Roman god of the sea is identified with the Greek god Poseidon?
6. From which ship did the famous bell hanging in the underwriting room at Lloyd's come?
7. Which British admiral had an affair with Emma Hamilton?
8. Which French chemist and microbiologist devised vaccines for anthrax and rabies?
9. Who directed *The Maltese Falcon*, *The African Queen* and *The Dead*?
10. In which English county is Luton?
11. Which Persian poet, astronomer and mathematician is best known for the poems translated by Edward Fitzgerald and others?
12. Rathlin island, off the north coast of Antrim, was the refuge of which Scottish king?
13. Which revolutionary anthem with music by Pierre Degeyter was the Soviet national anthem until 1944?
14. For what part of the body is C.N.S. an abbreviation?
15. Which American Beat poet established his reputation with *Howl*?
16. What is the third largest city of France?
17. Which king of England married Catherine of Valois?
18. What sort of creature is a pochard?
19. Which alloy of iron contains 36% nickel?
20. In which European country is Neuchâtel?

ANSWERS: *1 Martin Luther. 2 Pawnbroker. 3 Nelson Mandela. 4 Zambia. 5 Neptune. 6 Lutine. 7 Horatio Nelson. 8 Louis Pasteur. 9 John Huston. 10 Bedfordshire. 11 Omar Khayyám. 12 Robert the Bruce. 13 Internationale. 14 Central nervous system. 15 Allen Ginsberg. 16 Lyon. 17 Henry V. 18 A duck. 19 Invar. 20 Switzerland.*

 General Knowledge

Your rating: ● 0-5   Join a library   ● 6-10   Keep at it
                  ● 11-15   Join a quiz team   ● 16-20   Join Mensa

1. What name was used for Germany during Hitler's dictatorship, as a successor to two previous German empires?
2. Who wrote *The Railway Children* and *The Would-be Goods*?
3. Which alloy can be manufactured using the Bessemer process?
4. Who wrote the ragtime tunes *Maple Leaf Rag* and *The Entertainer*?
5. Which legendary Greek hero killed the Minotaur with the help of Ariadne?
6. Of which American city is Beverly Hills a residential suburb?
7. Which London art gallery was built with the financial support of a sugar merchant?
8. What sort of clay takes its name from the Italian for baked earth?
9. In which European city is the Galileo Galilei airport?
10. What did the Thirteen Colonies become in 1776?
11. Which French Rococo artist is noted for paintings such as *The Swing*?
12. What is the largest of the Medway towns?
13. Which film starring Nicolas Cage and Meg Ryan is a remake of Wim Wenders's *Wings of Desire*?
14. Of which ancient kingdom was Croesus the last native king?
15. Which Russian poet and novelist wrote *A Hero of Our Time*?
16. Of which Himalayan country is Thimphu or Thimbu the capital?
17. Which English physician discovered the circulation of the blood?
18. Who wrote the music for *West Side Story* and *On The Town*?
19. What name is given to the 1942 *Report on Social Insurance and Allied Services* that laid the foundations for the welfare state?
20. Which New Zealand-born cartoonist created *Colonel Blimp*?

ANSWERS: 1 *Third Reich*, 2 *Edith Nesbit*, 3 *Steel*, 4 *Scott Joplin*, 5 *Theseus*, 6 *Los Angeles*, 7 *Tate Gallery*, 8 *Terracotta*, 9 *Pisa, Italy*, 10 *United States of America*, 11 *Jean Honoré Fragonard*, 12 *Gillingham*, 13 *City of Angels*, 14 *Lydia*, 15 *Mikhail Lermontov*, 16 *Bhutan*, 17 *William Harvey*, 18 *Leonard Bernstein*, 19 *Beveridge Report*, 20 *Sir David Low*

 *General Knowledge*

Your rating: ● 0-5   Join a library   ● 6-10   Keep at it
          ● 11-15   Join a quiz team   ● 16-20   Join Mensa

1. Which New Zealand soprano sang at the wedding of the Prince and Princess of Wales?
2. What name is given to the soft tissue found in the cavities of bones?
3. Which team beat Scotland 3-0 in their last match of the 1998 World Cup?
4. What is the name for the shaggy-coated wild ox that inhabits mountain pastures of central Asia?
5. Which Tuscan city hosts the annual Palio horse races?
6. Who was beheaded by Herod Antipas at the request of Salome?
7. Which former poet laureate wrote the verse autobiography *Summoned by Bells*?
8. What is the administrative centre of Somerset?
9. Which Imperial unit of length is equal to 0.9144 metre?
10. What was the face value of the commemorative Princess Diana coin issued by the Royal Mint?
11. Which famous American horse race is run at Churchill Downs?
12. What type of tree was Yggdrasil, that was thought to span heaven and hell in Norse mythology?
13. Who designed the Banqueting House in Whitehall?
14. In which English county is the resort of Bexhill-on-Sea?
15. Which transuranic element has the symbol Pu?
16. Who directed the films *Midnight Cowboy* and *Billy Liar*?
17. Which rock and roll pioneer wrote *Johnny B. Goode* and *Roll Over Beethoven*?
18. In Greek mythology, the blood of which centaur, killed by Heracles, caused the hero's death?
19. What name is given to the female part of a flower, comprising one or more carpels?
20. Which Greek poet is traditionally considered to be the inventor of tragedy?

ANSWERS: 1 Dame Kiri Te Kanawa, 2 Marrow, 3 Morocco, 4 Yak, 5 Siena, 6 John the Baptist, 7 Sir John Betjeman, 8 Taunton, 9 Yard, 10 Five pounds, 11 Kentucky Derby, 12 Ash, 13 Inigo Jones, 14 East Sussex, 15 Plutonium, 16 John Schlesinger, 17 Chuck Berry, 18 Nessus, 19 Pistil, 20 Thespis.

Sports

Your rating:	● 0-5	Wooden spoon	● 6-10	Bronze medal
	● 11-15	Silver medal	● 16-20	Gold medal

1. Which Scottish rugby player scored 56 points in the 1995 Five Nations Championship?
2. Which Arsenal player was injured whilst celebrating victory at the League Cup final in 1993?
3. Which city was the first to host the Commonwealth Games twice?
4. How many times did Harry Vardon win the British Open?
5. Which nation hosted and won the 1968 European football championships?
6. Who defeated Goran Ivanisevic in the final of the 1992 Wimbledon men's singles championship?
7. Which city hosted the 1964 Olympic Games?
8. In which country was Lennox Lewis born?
9. Who topped England's group (Group 5) in the Euro 2000 qualifiers?
10. From 1990 to 1994, who was runner-up for five consecutive years in snooker's World Championship?
11. Which jockey won his first 2000 Guineas on Crepello in 1957?
12. In 1999, which rugby league club knocked St. Helens out of the Challenge Cup?
13. In which city can the Edgbaston Test cricket ground be found?
14. Which football team were managed by Paul Jewell during the 1999/2000 season?
15. At the 1992 Winter Olympics, which Italian skier successfully defended his giant slalom title?
16. At which golf course does the Masters take place?
17. In which country can the Estoril Grand Prix circuit be found?
18. Which German striker scored twice in the Euro 96 final?
19. Which British athlete was 1500m champion at the 1978 Commonwealth Games?
20. In which sport might one see an Eskimo roll?

ANSWERS: *1 Gavin Hastings, 2 Steve Morrow, 3 Edinburgh, 4 Six times, 5 Italy, 6 Andre Agassi, 7 Tokyo, 8 Great Britain, 9 Sweden, 10 Jimmy White, 11 Lester Piggott, 12 Leeds Rhinos, 13 Birmingham, 14 Bradford City, 15 Alberto Tomba, 16 Augusta, 17 Portugal, 18 Oliver Bierhoff, 19 David Moorcroft, 20 Canoeing.*

 *General Knowledge*

Your rating:
- 0-5 Join a library
- 11-15 Join a quiz team
- 6-10 Keep at it
- 16-20 Join Mensa

1. Which military corps, popularly known as Beefeaters, have been the sovereign's bodyguard since 1485?
2. What name is given to a mass of soft unconsolidated sand that is unable to support any appreciable weight when saturated?
3. What name is given to an ornamental design made of small coloured pieces or glass, stone or tile?
4. According to legend, who began to investigate gravitation after seeing an apple fall from a tree?
5. Which three Allied leaders attended the Yalta Conference in 1945?
6. Who was elected president of the National Union of Mineworkers in 1981?
7. Which child star of the 1930s won a special Academy Award in 1934?
8. Which Manchester-born painter was famous for his bleak industrial landscapes dotted with matchstick figures?
9. What is the famous geyser in Yellowstone National Park called?
10. Which Friends actress starred in the film *The Object of My Affection*?
11. Which Italian film director made the controversial *Last Tango in Paris*?
12. With which musical instrument was Artur Schnabel associated?
13. Which Chilean poet and ambassador won the 1971 Nobel Prize for literature?
14. The Bay of Plenty is an inlet of the Pacific Ocean on the coast of which country?
15. Which card game is played with two packs of 32 cards, the cards between 2 and 6 having been removed?
16. How many players are there in a netball team?
17. In which country is the city of Ostrava?
18. What are the names of the two contrasting but complementary principles at the root of traditional Chinese cosmology?
19. Which U.S. president died a month after taking office in 1841?
20. What sort of creature is a thickhead?

ANSWERS: *1 Yeomen of the Guard, 2 Quicksand, 3 Mosaic, 4 Sir Isaac Newton, 5 Churchill, Roosevelt and Stalin, 6 Arthur Scargill, 7 Shirley Temple, 8 L. S. Lowry, 9 Old Faithful, 10 Jennifer Aniston, 11 Bernardo Bertolucci, 12 Piano, 13 Pablo Neruda, 14 New Zealand, 15 Bézique, 16 Seven, 17 Czech Republic, 18 Yin and yang, 19 William Henry Harrison, 20 A bird.*

 *General Knowledge*

Your rating:
● 0-5 Join a library
● 11-15 Join a quiz team
● 6-10 Keep at it
● 16-20 Join Mensa

1. Which Swiss hero was reputed to have shot an apple from his son's head?
2. Who was the principal god in Roman mythology?
3. What is the professional governing body of solicitors in England and Wales?
4. What was the nickname of British pirate Edward Teach?
5. Which Labour politician created the National Health Service?
6. What name is given to magma that has erupted from a volcano?
7. Which veteran actress star of *Absolutely Fabulous* was awarded a C.B.E. in the 1998 Queen's Birthday Honours?
8. In poker, what name is given to three cards of one denomination and two of another?
9. Which Irish author wrote *Ulysses* and *Finnigans Wake*?
10. Which pop group recorded the albums *Rubber Soul* and *Revolver*?
11. Which U.S. general commanded the 7th Army in Sicily and the 3rd Army in France in World War II?
12. By what name is the parasitic insect *Pediculus humanus capitis* better known?
13. The Old Believers is a schismatic sect of which church?
14. Which English poet and critic wrote *The Angel in the House*?
15. What name is given to members of a religious movement organised by Charles Taze Russell in the 1870s?
16. In which Indian city did over 2000 people die in an escape of poisonous gas from a Union Carbide factory in 1984?
17. Which Jewish holiday is also known as the Day of Atonement?
18. Which famous reference work was written by Henry Watson Fowler in 1926?
19. Who was the official dressmaker to the Queen who was knighted in 1977?
20. Which Manchester G.P. was found guilty of murdering his female patients in 2000?

ANSWERS: 1 *William Tell*. 2 *Jupiter*. 3 *Law Society*. 4 *Blackbeard*. 5 *Aneurin Bevan*. 6 *Lava*. 7 *June Whitfield*. 8 *Full house*. 9 *James Joyce*. 10 *The Beatles*. 11 *George S Patton*. 12 *Head louse*. 13 *Russian Orthodox Church*. 14 *Coventry Patmore*. 15 *Jehovah's Witnesses*. 16 *Bhopal*. 17 *Yom Kippur*. 18 *Modern English Usage*. 19 *Sir Norman Hartnell*. 20 *Dr Harold Shipman*.

 *General Knowledge*

Your rating:
- 0-5 Join a library
- 11-15 Join a quiz team
- 6-10 Keep at it
- 16-20 Join Mensa

1. Which Somerset village gives its name to a famous cheese?
2. Who was the first Hanoverian king of Great Britain and Ireland?
3. Which high-profile Hollywood couple announced the break-up of their ten-year marriage in 1998?
4. Of which country did Robert Mugabe become president in 1987?
5. Which Nobel prize-winning novelist wrote *A Farewell to Arms*?
6. What name is given to the sterile offspring of a male ass and a female horse?
7. Which of Shakespeare's great tragedies is set in Elsinore?
8. What name is given to the upgrading of a former working class street or district for habitation by the middle classes?
9. In which popular tourist area is the mountain Helvellyn?
10. For which condition did Tory leader William Hague undergo an operation in 1998?
11. Which expanse of sea in the Orkney Islands was the main base of the British Grand Fleet in World War I?
12. What is the S.I. unit of force?
13. Which football team were knocked out of the 1998 World Cup despite scoring six goals in their last match?
14. Who was the 11th U.S. president, who acquired California for the Union?
15. Which English novelist wrote *The Heir of Redclyffe*?
16. By what name are the serfs of ancient Sparta known?
17. Which British actress was the mother of Gordon Craig?
18. What is the chief town of the island of Mull?
19. Which Austrian-born composer wrote *Verklärte Nacht* and *Moses und Aaron*?
20. Which former poet laureate wrote a version of *King Lear* with a happy ending?

ANSWERS: 1 *Cheddar*. 2 *George 1*. 3 *Bruce Willis and Demi Moore*. 4 *Zimbabwe*. 5 *Ernest Hemingway*. 6 *Mule*. 7 *Hamlet*. 8 *Gentrification*. 9 *Lake District*. 10 *Sinusitis*. 11 *Scapa Flow*. 12 *Newton*. 13 *Spain*. 14 *James K. Polk*. 15 *Charlotte M Yonge*. 16 *Helots*. 17 *Ellen Terry*. 18 *Tobermory*. 19 *Arnold Schoenberg*. 20 *Nahum Tate*.

Entertainment

Your rating:
● 0-5   **Buy a TV**
● 6-10   **Keep at it**
● 11-15   **Join a quiz team**
● 16-20   **Enter a quiz show**

1. Which ex-Father Ted star played Eamon Donaghy in ITV's comedy series *Big Bad World*?
2. Which male vocalist and guitarist had top ten hits with *Parisienne Walkways* and *Out in the Fields*?
3. Which 1999 film starred Rupert Penry-Jones as a girl whose mind is trapped inside her ideal man's body?
4. In which BBC 1 drama series did Lenny Henry star as headmaster Ian George?
5. Which girl's name was the title of Gerry Monroe's 1970 top five hit?
6. Which actress played an insecure model in the 1970 film *Puzzle of a Downfall Child*?
7. Which Crimewatch presenter fronted BBC 1's instructional series *So You Think You're a Good Driver*?
8. Which pop group had 1967 top five hits with *A Little Bit Me A Little Bit You* and *Alternate Title*?
9. Which 1950s soap family included a grandmother played by Nancy Roberts?
10. Which comedian was *The Punch and Judy Man* in the 1963 film?
11. Which character got engaged to *Coronation Street* hairdresser Maxine Heavey in 1999?
12. Which Glasgow collective re-released their 1996 album *Tigermilk* in 1999?
13. Who starred as *Barbara* in the ITV comedy series?
14. Which 1999 film set in a Seattle high school was loosely based on Shakespeare's *The Taming of the Shrew*?
15. Which 1980s sitcom starred Ian Lavender and Kim Braden as a couple who haven't decided whether to marry after a seven-year engagement?
16. Which New York dance act released an album entitled *There's A Poison Going On* in 1999?
17. Which 1981 film starred Ryan O'Neal as an English professor recruited into his father's dressmaking firm?
18. What was the title of the BBC 2 cookery and travel series which featured TV chef Ainsley Harriott visiting the Americas?
19. Which actor starred as a Cornish eccentric who buries run-over animals in the 1999 film *All the Little Animals*?
20. Which chef presented BBC 2's cookery series *Fresh Food*?

ANSWERS: 1 *Ardal O'Hanlon,* **2** *Gary Moore,* **3** *Virtual Sexuality,* **4** *Hope & Glory,* **5** *Sally,* **6** *Faye Dunaway,* **7** *Nick Ross,* **8** *The Monkees,* **9** *The Grove Family,* **10** *Tony Hancock,* **11** *Ashley Peacock,* **12** *Belle and Sebastian,* **13** *Gwen Taylor,* **14** *10 Things I Hate About You,* **15** *Have I Got You Where You Want Me?,* **16** *Public Enemy,* **17** *So Fine,* **18** *Ainsley's Big Cook Out,* **19** *John Hurt,* **20** *Rick Stein.*

 # General Knowledge

1. Which disease was deliberately introduced to the UK in the 1950s to control the rabbit population?
2. What is the capital of Finland?
3. Which big cat is the swiftest mammal?
4. What name is given to the ends of the earth's axis, about which it rotates?
5. Which major Indian religion was founded by Nanak?
6. In which Spanish city is the Prado art gallery?
7. Which British prime minister negotiated the Munich Agreement with Hitler, Daladier and Mussolini?
8. On which port was the second atomic bomb used against Japan in World War II dropped?
9. Which game has playing periods called chukkas?
10. Who was the manager who led England to World Cup victory in 1966?
11. Which jazz pioneer was backed by the Red Hot Peppers?
12. In which country was conductor André Previn born?
13. Which team was the first to score a Golden Goal in World Cup?
14. To which English king was Henrietta Maria married?
15. Which British economic historian wrote *Religion and the Rise of Capitalism*?
16. On which river does Preston stand?
17. Which Italian artist sculpted *Apollo and Daphne* for Cardinal Borghese?
18. New London in Connecticut is at the mouth of which river?
19. Who wrote *A House for Mr Biswas* and *A Bend in the River*?
20. Which British air marshal became Eisenhower's deputy in World War II?

ANSWERS: 1 Myxomatosis, **2** Helsinki, **3** Cheetah, **4** North and South Pole, **5** Sikhism, **6** Madrid, **7** Neville Chamberlain, **8** Nagasaki, **9** Polo, **10** Sir Alf Ramsey, **11** Jelly Roll Morton, **12** Germany, **13** France, **14** Charles I, **15** R. H. Tawney, **16** Ribble, **17** Gianlorenzo Bernini, **18** Thames, **19** V. S. Naipaul, **20** Baron Tedder.

(?) General Knowledge

Your rating:	● 0-5 Join a library	● 6-10 Keep at it
	● 11-15 Join a quiz team	● 16-20 Join Mensa

1. Which compound found in tonic water was the first drug used to treat malaria?
2. What name is given to the use in war of toxic substances on humans, animals or plants?
3. Which Hollywood actress played Jane opposite Johnny Weissmuller's Tarzan?
4. What sort of creature is a mamba?
5. Which residential district of London is famous for its Royal Hospital for old soldiers?
6. What was the Roman name for the Scottish tribes living north of the Antonine Wall?
7. Which singer's first big hit was Heartbreak Hotel?
8. Which part of *The Canterbury Tales* by Geoffrey Chaucer contains descriptions of all the pilgrims?
9. What was the name of the English captain whose life was said to have been saved by Pocahontas?
10. Which team knocked England out of the 1998 World Cup after a penalty shoot-out?
11. Which Scottish-born American naval commander in the American Revolution later became a rear admiral in the Russian navy?
12. Who wrote *The Good Companions* and *An Inspector Calls*?
13. What sort of creature is a grouper?
14. What sort of creature transmits lassa fever to humans?
15. Which British civil engineer constructed the Menai road suspension bridge and the Caledonian Canal?
16. What was the language of the Aztecs?
17. Which cavity at the upper end of the trachea contains the vocal cords?
18. Of which U.S. state is Atlanta the capital?
19. In Greek mythology, who was the last king of Troy?
20. Which Charles Dickens novel features the character Wackford Squeers?

ANSWERS: 1 Quinine. 2 Chemical warfare. 3 Maureen O'Sullivan. 4 A snake. 5 Chelsea. 6 Picts. 7 Elvis Presley. 8 The Prologue. 9 John Smith. 10 Argentina. 11 John Paul Jones. 12 J B Priestley. 13 A fish. 14 A rat. 15 Thomas Telford. 16 Nahuatl. 17 Larynx. 18 Georgia. 19 Priam. 20 Nicholas Nickleby.

THE TRIVIA QUIZ BOOK

 *General Knowledge*

Your rating: ● 0-5 Join a library ● 6-10 Keep at it
● 11-15 Join a quiz team ● 16-20 Join Mensa

1. In which English county is the town of Cheltenham?
2. Which prime number is between 11 and 17?
3. What is the official religion of Italy?
4. Which singer and actress married actor James Brolin at her Malibu home?
5. What branch of painting is concerned with the representation of inanimate objects?
6. Which stage of human history came after the Bronze Age?
7. Which British king secretly married Maria Fitzherbert?
8. Who starred in the films *The Glenn Miller Story* and *The Philadelphia Story*?
9. What is the name of the instrument doctors use to listen to sounds within the body?
10. Which hard white substance forms the tusks of elephants and walruses?
11. Which Greek sculptor was famous for his Discus Thrower, known through Roman copies?
12. What name is given to a line on a map joining places of equal temperature?
13. Of which country was Dom Mintoff the prime minister?
14. To which French king was Nicolas Poussin court painter?
15. Which brothers wrote the comic novel *Diary of a Nobody*?
16. What is the largest species of cat in the Americas?
17. Which American amateur golfer won the Grand Slam of both amateur and professional opens of the USA and Britain in 1930?
18. By what name was Namibia known before 1968?
19. Which metallic element has the symbol Be?
20. How many horns does an Indian rhinoceros have?

Entertainment

Your rating:
- **0-5** Buy a TV
- **11-15** Join a quiz team
- **6-10** Keep at it
- **16-20** Enter a quiz show

1. Who was *Svengali* in the 1931 film?
2. Which British male vocalist had a number one hit in 1960 with *Please Don't Tease*?
3. Who was the presenter of ITV's documentary series *Eye of the Storm*?
4. What was the title of the Specials' 1981 number one hit?
5. Who presented the 1970s series *The Hollywood Greats*?
6. Which male vocalist sang the theme song to the 1978 movie *Grease*?
7. Which actress played Susan in the 1940 film *Susan and God*?
8. What was the title of the album released in 1999 by soft rock artist Sophie B. Hawkins?
9. Which ex-Blue Peter presenter hosted the ITV show *Mad About Pets*?
10. Who wrote the novel on which the film *Maybe Baby* is based?
11. Which comedian was the presenter of ITV's talent show *Give Your Mate a Break*?
12. Which Radio 1 dance DJ was behind the album *Essential Selection Ibiza 1999*?
13. Which actor played a young Obi-Wan Kenobi in the Star Wars prequel, *Episode 1: The Phantom Menace*?
14. On which TV talent show did Jim Davidson find fame?
15. Which American band's sixth album, released in 1999, was entitled *Dizzy Up the Girl*?
16. Who played Dolly in the 1969 film musical *Hello, Dolly!*?
17. Who presented *Star Secrets* on BBC 1?
18. What was the title of J.X.'s 1996 top five hit single?
19. Which 1949 Carol Reed film starring Orson Welles was re-released in 1999?
20. Which duo had a 1968 number one with *Cinderella Rockefella*?

ANSWERS: 1 John Barrymore. 2 Cliff Richard, 3 Richard Madeley, 4 Ghost Town, 5 Barry Norman, 6 Frankie Valli, 7 Joan Crawford, 8 Timbre, 9 John Noakes, 10 Ben Elton, 11 Les Dennis, 12 Pete Tong, 13 Ewan McGregor, 14 New Faces, 15 The Goo Goo Dolls, 16 Barbra Streisand, 17 Carol Smillie, 18 There's Nothing I Won't Do, 19 The Third Man, 20 Esther and Abi Ofarim.

 *General Knowledge*

Your rating: ● 0-5   Join a library   ● 6-10   Keep at it
               ● 11-15 Join a quiz team   ● 16-20 Join Mensa

1.   Which French novelist wrote the book translated as *Remembrance of Things Past*?
2.   What does the abbreviation I.R.A. stand for?
3.   Which British golfer won the British Open in 1969 and the U.S. Open in 1970?
4.   What is the capital of Sweden?
5.   With which athletics field event is Jan Zelezny associated?
6.   What is the anatomical name for the lower jawbone?
7.   Which Scottish racing driver was world champion in 1969, 1971 and 1973?
8.   What was the nickname of U.S. Confederate general Thomas Jackson?
9.   Which American author wrote *Rip Van Winkle* and *The Legend of Sleepy Hollow*?
10. In which U.S. state is Las Vegas?
11. Which Old Testament prophet predicted the destruction of Nineveh by the Medes?
12. Who wrote *Goodbye to Berlin* and *Mr Norris Changes Trains*?
13. Which Thomas Hardy novel features the character Michael Henchard?
14. What was the nickname of World War II U.S. General Joseph W Stilwell?
15. Which British chronicler wrote *Historia Regum Britanniae*?
16. What sort of creature is a mugger?
17. Which English cardinal wrote *The Dream of Gerontius*, on which an Elgar oratorio is based?
18. What is the state capital of Mississippi?
19. What name is given to atoms with the same atomic number but different numbers of neutrons in their nuclei?
20. Which Scottish mathematician invented logarithms?

? General Knowledge

Your rating: ● **0-5** Join a library ● **6-10** Keep at it
● **11-15** Join a quiz team ● **16-20** Join Mensa

1. What is the name for the saclike organ between the oesophagus and the duodenum?
2. In which U.S. state is the city of Tampa?
3. What is the capital of Jamaica?
4. Who wrote *The Strange Case of Dr Jekyll and Mr Hyde* and *The Master of Ballantrae*?
5. Which unidentified murderer killed and mutilated prostitutes in the East End of London in 1888?
6. What does the acronym NATO stand for?
7. Which prime minister took the UK into the E.E.C.?
8. In zoology, which order of mammals includes monkeys, apes, prosimians and man?
9. Which market town is the administrative centre of Essex?
10. Which Russian dramatist wrote *The Cherry Orchard*, *The Three Sisters* and *Uncle Vanya*?
11. Which ancient city in the Peloponnese was the home of Agamemnon?
12. What was the name of the extremist republican club in the French Revolution that overthrew the Girondins?
13. For what do the initials I.S.B.N. stand?
14. What name is given to the part of a flower's carpel that receives the pollen grains?
15. Which form of gelatin is obtained from the swim bladders of various fishes?
16. In what year was the Big Bang in the City of London?
17. Which Zimbabwean politician became president of Z.A.P.U. in 1961?
18. What was the first of the new towns to be developed in England after World War II?
19. Which constellation contains the red variable star Mira Ceti?
20. What sort of creature is a jacamar?

ANSWERS: 1 *Stomach*. 2 *Florida*. 3 *Kingston*. 4 *Robert Louis Stevenson*. 5 *Jack the Ripper*. 6 *North Atlantic Treaty Organisation*. 7 *Edward Heath*. 8 *Primates*. 9 *Chelmsford*. 10 *Anton Chekhov*. 11 *Mycenae*. 12 *Jacobins*. 13 *International Standard Book Number*. 14 *Stigma*. 15 *Isinglass*. 16 *1986*. 17 *Joshua Nkomo*. 18 *Stevenage*. 19 *Cetus*. 20 *A bird*.

THE TRIVIA QUIZ BOOK

 *General Knowledge*

| Your rating: | ● 0-5 | Join a library | ● 6-10 | Keep at it |
| | ● 11-15 | Join a quiz team | ● 16-20 | Join Mensa |

1. Which British rock singer recorded the album *Every Picture Tells a Story*?
2. What was sought by Jason and the Argonauts?
3. Which suburb of Liverpool hosts the Grand National annually?
4. Who did Pete Sampras beat in the 1998 men's singles final at Wimbledon?
5. Which British airport was opened to passengers in 1946?
6. What is the world's largest continent?
7. Which noisy black-and-white crow is attracted to bright objects?
8. In which county is the market town of Ashby-de-la-Zouch?
9. What name is given to a naval vessel with a large flat deck for launching and landing warplanes?
10. What name is given to the extensive grasslands of the interior of North America?
11. Which photographer proved that a trotting horse momentarily raises all four legs simultaneously?
12. Who wrote the books commonly called *Tristram Shandy* and *A Sentimental Journey*?
13. Which comic writer created Alf Garnett?
14. On which river does Northampton stand?
15. Which geological period of time extends from the formation of the earth's crust to the beginning of the Palaeozoic era?
16. Who was the Greek goddess of the rainbow?
17. Which English garden designer coined the term landscape gardening?
18. Which metalloid element has the symbol Ge?
19. Which Buckinghamshire village contains the country churchyard immortalised in Thomas Gray's famous *Elegy*?
20. What name is given to marks on the body of a living person resembling the five wounds that Christ received at the crucifixion?

ANSWERS: 1 *Rod Stewart*, 2 *The Golden Fleece*, 3 *Aintree*, 4 *Goran Ivanisevic*, 5 *Heathrow*, 6 *Asia*, 7 *Magpie*, 8 *Leicestershire*, 9 *Aircraft carrier*, 10 *Prairie*, 11 *Eadweard Muybridge*, 12 *Laurence Sterne*, 13 *Johnny Speight*, 14 *River Nene*, 15 *Precambrian period*, 16 *Iris*, 17 *Humphry Repton*, 18 *Germanium*, 19 *Stoke Poges*, 20 *Stigmata*.

Entertainment

Your rating: ● **0-5** Buy a TV ● **6-10** Keep at it
● **11-15** Join a quiz team ● **16-20** Enter a quiz show

1. Which comedian and presenter was *Leaving The 20th Century* on BBC 2 in 1999?
2. Which U.S. group had a number one hit in 1974 with *Ms Grace*?
3. What was the title of the 1950s TV series of Scotland Yard-based police thrillers?
4. The pinnacle of which singer's career was captured on the 1999 double CD *Downtown - The Pye Anthology*?
5. Which *Wayne's World* star appeared in the 1990 film *Opportunity Knocks*?
6. Which Spanish holiday island in the Balearics was the subject of a 1999 Channel 4 documentary series?
7. In 1999, which singer and DJ released a 1996 album of solo recordings entitled *The Unrecoupable One Man Bandit*?
8. Which ex-Soldier Soldier actor starred as police officer Tom McCabe in the BBC drama series Badger?
9. Which actor played Big Boy in the 1999 film *The Hi-Lo Country*?
10. Which BBC 1 consumer series was co-presented by Alice Beer and Dr Mark Porter?
11. Which 1982 3-D monster film set in 1992 featured Demi Moore?
12. Which 1980s British soap opera followed the boardroom intrigues in the family firm of Coleman and Son, dealers in precious stones?
13. Which *EastEnders* actress duetted with Mike Sarne on the 1962 number one hit *Come Outside*?
14. Which Royle Family actor starred as Macca in the 1999 one-off Channel 4 drama Dockers?
15. What was the title of Vanilla Ice's 1990 number one hit?
16. Which ITV comedy series starred Denise Van Outen as Leigh?
17. Which actor played D.H. Lawrence in the 1981 film *Priest of Love*?
18. Which scientist presented the 1999 BBC 1 series *The Secret Life of Twins*?
19. Which Canadian band were *Living on Video* in 1985?
20. Which 1957 Federico Fellini film starring his wife, Giulietta Masina, was re-released in 1999?

ANSWERS: *1 Mark Lamarr, 2 Tymes, 3 Dial 999, 4 Petula Clark, 5 Dana Carvey, 6 Ibiza (Ibiza Uncovered), 7 Boy George, 8 Jerome Flynn, 9 Woody Harrelson, 10 Watchdog Healthcheck, 11 Parasite, 12 Diamonds, 13 Wendy Richard, 14 Ricky Tomlinson, 15 Ice Ice Baby, 16 Babes in the Wood, 17 Ian McKellen, 18 Professor Robert Winston, 19 Trans-X, 20 Nights of Cabiria.*

 *General Knowledge*

Your rating: ● 0-5   Join a library   ● 6-10   Keep at it
            ● 11-15   Join a quiz team   ● 16-20   Join Mensa

1. Which number system uses only the digits 0 and 1?
2. What form of music, characterised by improvisation and syncopated rhythms, originated in New Orleans at the turn of the century?
3. Which famous cowboy actor and singer was associated with the horse Trigger?
4. Cape Agulhas is the southernmost point of which continent?
5. Which light silvery-white metallic element has the symbol Mg?
6. What does AIDS stand for?
7. Which British prime minister unexpectedly resigned in 1976?
8. By what name is the currency of the UK known?
9. Who is Monaco's head of state?
10. Which city in Staffordshire is the centre of the British ceramic industry?
11. Which Hungarian dramatist wrote the play *Liliom*, which was adapted as the musical *Carousel*?
12. Coimbra was formerly the capital of which European country?
13. Which British-born conductor conducted the Philadelphia Orchestra from 1912 to 1938?
14. Who left Barnsley to become manager of Sheffield Wednesday in 1998?
15. Which American poet wrote *The Man with the Blue Guitar*?
16. In which country is the city of Invercargill?
17. Which Egyptian goddess was the sister and wife of Osiris?
18. Which Old Testament book attributed to Jeremiah mourns the fall of Jerusalem?
19. What sort of creature is a stilt?
20. Which Shakespeare play features the characters Banquo and Fleance?

ANSWERS: 1 Binary system, 2 Jazz, 3 Roy Rogers, 4 Africa, 5 Magnesium, 6 Acquired Immune Deficiency Syndrome, 7 Harold Wilson, 8 Sterling, 9 Prince Rainier III, 10 Stoke-on-Trent, 11 Ferenc Molnár, 12 Portugal, 13 Leopold Stokowski, 14 Danny Wilson, 15 Wallace Stevens, 16 New Zealand, 17 Isis, 18 Lamentations, 19 A bird, 20 Macbeth.

 *General Knowledge*

| Your rating: | ● 0-5 | Join a library | ● 6-10 | Keep at it |
| | ● 11-15 | Join a quiz team | ● 16-20 | Join Mensa |

1. Which British actress won an Oscar for her performance in the film *A Passage to India*?
2. What is the capital and chief port of Tasmania?
3. Who won the 1998 women's singles final at Wimbledon?
4. Who was the first boxer to beat Muhammad Ali as a professional?
5. Which Bradford-born artist noted for his pictures of swimming pools was the subject of the 1974 film *A Bigger Splash*?
6. Who wrote *Three Men in a Boat*?
7. Which Charles Dickens novel features the character Fagin?
8. Of which American city is Hollywood a suburb?
9. Which naval administrator is famous for his *Diary* which includes descriptions of the Plague and the Fire of London?
10. Who was the first Christian martyr?
11. Which town on the West Bank of the River Jordan is revered as the burial place of Abraham?
12. In Norse mythology, what was the home of the principal gods, linked to earth by the rainbow bridge Bifrost?
13. Which Scottish psychiatrist wrote *The Divided Self* and *The Politics of Experience*?
14. Of which U.S. state is Bismarck the capital?
15. Which metric unit of volume is equal to one cubic metre?
16. What sort of creature is a moloch?
17. Which English novelist wrote *Anglo-Saxon Attitudes*?
18. With what sort of tests is French psychologist Alfred Binet associated?
19. Which French composer wrote the *Symphonie espagnole*?
20. What is the name of the rocky islet at the mouth of the Firth of Clyde whose rock is used in the manufacture of curling stones?

ANSWERS: *1 Dame Peggy Ashcroft, 2 Hobart, 3 Jana Novotna, 4 Joe Frazier, 5 David Hockney, 6 Jerome K Jerome, 7 Oliver Twist, 8 Los Angeles, 9 Samuel Pepys, 10 Saint Stephen, 11 Hebron, 12 Asgard, 13 R D Laing, 14 North Dakota, 15 Stere, 16 A lizard, 17 Angus Wilson, 18 Intelligence, 19 Edouard Lalo, 20 Ailsa Craig.*

❓ General Knowledge

| Your rating: | ● 0-5 | Join a library | ● 6-10 | Keep at it |
| | ● 11-15 | Join a quiz team | ● 16-20 | Join Mensa |

1. Which Berkshire village has a racecourse which was established by Queen Anne in 1711?
2. Of which South American country is Asunción the capital?
3. Which *Coronation Street* actor lost his court battle to sue his solicitors over an ill-fated libel action?
4. How many cards are in a standard pack of playing cards, excluding jokers?
5. Which black American tennis player won the U.S. Open in 1968 and the Wimbledon title in 1975?
6. What name is given to the first ten amendments to the U.S. Constitution, incorporated in 1791?
7. Of which country was Shimon Peres prime minister?
8. Which fire-retarding fibrous form of certain silicate minerals has white and blue varieties?
9. What is the largest of the Channel Islands?
10. Which alkaline fluid is produced by the liver and stored in the gall bladder?
11. Which French dramatist wrote *Tartuffe*, *Le Misanthrope* and *Le Bourgeois Gentilhomme*?
12. Who became caretaker prime minister of Australia after the dismissal of Gough Whitlam in 1975?
13. Which major religion's name means submission?
14. Who was the detained Nigerian opposition leader who died of a reported heart attack in the midst of negotiations over his release in 1998?
15. Which Scottish mathematician is best known for his formula which gives the approximate value for the factorial of a large number?
16. Of which South American country is the Bio-Bio the longest river?
17. Which metallic element has the symbol Ho?
18. Who painted the *Marriage à la Mode* series of paintings?
19. Which important religious building contains the Kaaba?
20. What is the modern name for the ancient Roman town of Camulodunum?

Entertainment

Your rating: ● 0-5   **Buy a TV**   ● 6-10   **Keep at it**
● 11-15   **Join a quiz team**   ● 16-20   **Enter a quiz show**

1. Which 1999 soundtrack album featured the Melanie C solo track *Ga Ga*?
2. What was the name of Joanna Lumley's character in the TV series *The New Avengers*?
3. Which jazz/soul singer released an album entitled *Snow on the Sahara* in 1999?
4. Who played Selina in the 1953 film *So Big*?
5. The 30th anniversary of which event was marked in 1999 by the two-part Channel 4 documentary *Mission Impossible*?
6. Which Texan girl group had a 1999 hit with the song *Bills Bills Bills*?
7. Which BBC 1 medical drama series featured Richard Wilson and Art Malik?
8. Which actor reprised his roles as both Austin Powers and his arch-enemy Dr Evil in the 1999 film sequel?
9. Which actress starred as Lady Glencora in the Seventies series *The Pallisers*?
10. Which son of a famous Spanish crooner released an album in 1999 entitled *Under My Eyes*?
11. Who played the scientist in the 1967 film *Frankenstein Created Woman*?
12. Who played General MacArthur in the 1981 film *Inchon*?
13. Which U.S. vocalist had a top five hit in 1957 with *Mr. Wonderful*?
14. Who presented the ITV cookery series *Really Good Food*?
15. Which musician has been a member of Depeche Mode, Yazoo and Erasure?
16. Which BBC 1 series of dramatic reconstructions featured the work of the Forensic Science Service?
17. Which newsreader presented the BBC 1 documentary series *Tobacco Wars*?
18. Which British vocalist had a top five hit in 1980 with *Stop the Cavalry*?
19. Which recent black-comedy thriller features Patricia Arquette, Don Johnson and Ellen DeGeneres?
20. Which 1960s comedy series featured Duncan Macrae and Roddy McMillan as the skipper and engineer of a Scottish steamer?

ANSWERS: 1 *Big Daddy.* 2 *Purdey.* 3 *Natalie Cole.* 4 *Jane Wyman.* 5 *The first moon walk.* 6 *Destiny's Child.* 7 *Life Support.* 8 *Mike Myers.* 9 *Susan Hampshire.* 10 *Julio Iglesias Jr.* 11 *Peter Cushing.* 12 *Laurence Olivier.* 13 *Peggy Lee.* 14 *Mary Nightingale.* 15 *Vince Clarke.* 16 *Trail of Guilt.* 17 *Michael Buerk.* 18 *Jona Lewie.* 19 *Goodbye Lover.* 20 *Para Handy.*

THE TRIVIA QUIZ BOOK

 *General Knowledge*

Your rating:	● 0-5	Join a library	● 6-10	Keep at it
	● 11-15	Join a quiz team	● 16-20	Join Mensa

1. Which American diplomat and scientist is famous for flying a kite in a thunderstorm?
2. By what name is the German shepherd dog commonly known?
3. Which British cyclist crashed out of the 1998 Tour de France while wearing the Yellow Jersey?
4. Who is the patron saint of England?
5. Which famous art society is based at Burlington House in London?
6. What is the second book of the Old Testament?
7. Which mock trophy is awarded to the winning team in cricket matches between England and Australia?
8. By what name were the Nazi secret police, formed in 1933, known?
9. What name is given to a straight line that touches a curve at only one point?
10. Which fruit may be eaten dried as prunes?
11. Which 16th century English composer wrote the 40-part motet *Spem in Alium*?
12. What was historian A. J. P. Taylor's first name?
13. Which French footballer scored twice in the 1998 World Cup final?
14. Of which country is Tegucigalpa the capital?
15. Which English ballet dancer and choreographer created Margot Fonteyn's most famous roles?
16. By what name is the small falcon *Falco subbuteo* better known?
17. Which Belgian novelist created the Parisian detective Maigret?
18. Who was president of the U.S.A. from 1849 to 1850?
19. What sort of creature is a Tasmanian devil?
20. Which French philosopher wrote *Du Contrat social* and *Émile*?

ANSWERS: 1 *Benjamin Franklin.* 2 *Alsatian.* 3 *Chris Boardman.* 4 *Saint George.* 5 *Royal Academy.* 6 *Exodus.* 7 *The Ashes.* 8 *Gestapo.* 9 *Tangent.* 10 *Plums.* 11 *Thomas Tallis.* 12 *Alan.* 13 *Zinedine Zidane.* 14 *Honduras.* 15 *Sir Frederick Ashton.* 16 *Hobby.* 17 *Georges Simenon.* 18 *Zachary Taylor.* 19 *A marsupial.* 20 *Jean Jacques Rousseau.*

 *General Knowledge*

Your rating:	● 0-5	Join a library	● 6-10	Keep at it
	● 11-15	Join a quiz team	● 16-20	Join Mensa

1. Which German Jewish girl wrote a diary while hiding from the Nazis in Amsterdam?
2. In which English city is the Ashmolean museum?
3. By what name are third molars better known?
4. Of which sport is sculling a form?
5. Which composer famously transcribed Allegri's *Miserere* from memory at the age of 14?
6. What sort of creature is an oryx?
7. Which highly nutritious substance is fed to larvae that will develop into queen bees?
8. What is the third largest continent in the world?
9. Which star of Japanese monster movies made a comeback in a 1998 Hollywood blockbuster?
10. What is the official language of Austria?
11. Which geological period came between the Ordovician and Devonian periods?
12. Who did the illustrations for Lewis Carroll's *Alice's Adventures in Wonderland*?
13. Which Croatian striker won the Golden Shoe as top scorer in the 1998 World Cup?
14. What is the profession of Kenzo Tange?
15. Which figure of speech differs from a metaphor in being an explicit comparison?
16. What is the capital of Uzbekistan?
17. Which famous impostor claimed to be Edward, Earl of Warwick?
18. Who established an auction house for horses in London in 1766?
19. Which British dramatist wrote *The Fair Penitent* and *The Tragedy of Jane Shore*?
20. Which Indian state was known as Madras until 1968?

ANSWERS: 1 *Anne Frank*, 2 *Oxford*, 3 *Wisdom teeth*, 4 *Rowing*, 5 *Wolfgang Amadeus Mozart*, 6 *An antelope*, 7 *Royal Jelly*, 8 *North America*, 9 *Godzilla*, 10 *German*, 11 *Silurian*, 12 *Sir John Tenniel*, 13 *Davor Suker*, 14 *Architect*, 15 *Simile*, 16 *Tashkent*, 17 *Lambert Simnel*, 18 *Richard Tattersall*, 19 *Nicholas Rowe*, 20 *Tamil Nadu*.

? *General Knowledge*

Your rating:	● 0-5	Join a library	● 6-10	Keep at it
	● 11-15	Join a quiz team	● 16-20	Join Mensa

1. Which substance used as a form of riot control is also called a lachrymator?
2. What name is given to people whose way of life involves movement from place to place?
3. Which armoured military vehicle was invented by Ernest Swinton?
4. At which London church were statues of ten 20th-century martyrs unveiled by the Archbishop of Canterbury in 1998?
5. Which society maintains gardens at Wisley in Surrey that are open to the public?
6. What name is given to the tough fibrous cords that connect muscles to bones?
7. Which Old Testament figure was instructed to build an ark?
8. What is the largest of the Canary Islands?
9. Which four letters often appear on the representation of the cross in Christian art?
10. In which country are the Magyars the largest ethnic group?
11. Which British short-story writer and critic wrote *A Cab at the Door* and *Midnight Oil*?
12. Who became king of France in the July Revolution of 1830?
13. Which of the gifts brought by the three Wise Men is also known as olibanum?
14. In Greek mythology, which king was condemned to stand within reach of fruit and water that moved away when he tried to reach them?
15. Which former England and British Lions scrum half became chairman of the Sports Council in 1978?
16. What sort of creature is a mouthbrooder?
17. Which of the apostles is surnamed Zelotes or the Canaanite?
18. Which French painter was known as Le Douanier?
19. By what name was the Royal Ballet known before 1956?
20. Which English poet and authority on William Blake wrote the volume *Stone and Flower*?

Entertainment

Your rating: ● 0-5   Buy a TV   ● 6-10   Keep at it
● 11-15 Join a quiz team   ● 16-20 Enter a quiz show

1. In which 1971 film did Steve McQueen star as a racing car driver?
2. Who replaced Nick Hancock as presenter of BBC 2's *Room 101*?
3. Which blues/jazz artist's career from 1949 to 1961 was documented by an album in E.M.I.'s *Legends of the 20th Century* series, released in 1999?
4. Which animal-lover was the narrator of the BBC 1 series *Animal People*?
5. Which *X-Files* star played a stage director in the 1999 film *Playing By Heart*?
6. Which Scotsman was the main presenter of the 1970s TV show *People and Politics*?
7. Which H. E. Bates novel was the 1959 film *The Mating Game* based upon?
8. Who presented the ITV documentary series *Tested to Destruction*?
9. Which group had a number one hit in 1971 with *I'd Like To Teach the World To Sing (In Perfect Harmony)*?
10. Which French actress starred as an alcoholic widow in the 1999 film *Place Vendome*?
11. Which docu-soap, featuring Trude Mostue, embarked upon its fifth series in 1999?
12. Which U.S. group had a top ten hit in 1971 with *Run Baby Run*?
13. Which British actor starred as a fumbling private-eye in the 1975 film *Peeper*?
14. Which group had a 1971 number one hit with *Hot Love*?
15. Which Nickelodeon TV cartoon series was made into a 1999 feature film?
16. What was the title of comedian Stanley Baxter's first TV series?
17. Which 1992 film starred Peter O'Toole as a 19th century lord of the manor in dispute with Welsh peasants?
18. Which veteran *EastEnders* character was caught in possession of an illegal substance in 1999?
19. Which U.S. soul singer's fourth album, released in 1999, was entitled *Mary*?
20. Which Channel 4 sci-fi series was a spin-off from a 1994 film about a portal that provides access to various different planets?

ANSWERS: 1 *Le Mans*, 2 *Paul Merton*, 3 *Fats Domino*, 4 *Rolf Harris*, 5 *Gillian Anderson*, 6 *Llew Gardner*, 7 *The Darling Buds of May*, 8 *Carol Vorderman*, 9 *The New Seekers*, 10 *Catherine Deneuve*, 11 *Vets in Practice*, 12 *Newbeats*, 13 *Michael Caine*, 14 *T. Rex*, 15 *Doug (Doug's First Movie)*, 16 *On the Bright Side*, 17 *Rebecca's Daughters*, 18 *Dot Cotton*, 19 *Mary J. Blige's*, 20 *Stargate: SG-1*.

 # General Knowledge

Your rating: ● 0-5   Join a library   ● 6-10   Keep at it
              ● 11-15 Join a quiz team   ● 16-20 Join Mensa

1. Which police force is also known as the Mounties?
2. In the Christian calendar, what is the first day of Lent?
3. By what name is the European freshwater fish Tinca tinca better known?
4. From which former duchy of France did William the Conqueror come?
5. In which South American country did the ballroom dance the tango originate?
6. Which of Britain's armed services is known as the Senior Service?
7. What does E.S.P. stand for?
8. Which organisation for the welfare of ex-servicemen and women was established under the leadership of Douglas Haig in 1921?
9. By what name was American author Samuel Langhorne Clemens better known?
10. In which country was the guitarist John Williams born?
11. Which British dramatist wrote *A Man for All Seasons* and the screenplay for *Lawrence of Arabia*?
12. In which Italian city is the Uffizi art gallery which contains the art treasures of the Medici?
13. Which syndrome is also called myalgic encephalomyelitis, or M.E.?
14. What is the first letter on the bottom row of a typewriter keyboard?
15. Which Ethiopian lake is the source of the Blue Nile?
16. What was the name of T. H. White's tetralogy retelling the Arthurian legend?
17. Which British composer wrote the cantata *The Whale* and the opera *Thérèse*?
18. At which port in Tanzania did Henry Stanley find David Livingstone?
19. Which actor was married to Dulcie Gray?
20. By what collective name were the French composers Auric, Durey, Honegger, Milhaud, Poulenc and Tailleferre known?

 *General Knowledge*

Your rating: ● **0-5** Join a library   ● **6-10** Keep at it
● **11-15** Join a quiz team   ● **16-20** Join Mensa

1. Which scientific organisation was founded in London by Count Rumford in 1799?
2. What is the highest mountain in the world?
3. Which opera did Verdi compose for the opening of the Suez Canal?
4. Which Robert Altman film, starring Kenneth Branagh, is based on a novel by John Grisham?
5. Which radioactive element has the chemical symbol U?
6. Who was Lord Protector of England from 1653 to 1658?
7. Which colourless odourless gas has the chemical symbol O?
8. Who was the mother of Edward VII?
9. Which British amateur golfer finished joint fourth in the 1998 Open at Royal Birkdale?
10. What was the name of King Arthur's magic sword?
11. Which Russian author wrote the novel *Fathers and Sons* and the play *A Month in the Country*?
12. Who commanded the French and Spanish fleet defeated by Nelson at the Battle of Trafalgar?
13. Which African bird is also known as a tickbird?
14. With which academic discipline is Leonhard Euler associated?
15. Which singer and songwriter recorded the 1965 album *Highway 61 Revisited*?
16. What name is given to the young of herrings and sprats?
17. Which Greek philosopher claimed "You cannot step into the same river twice"?
18. Which body advising the British monarch grew out of the Curia Regis?
19. Who was the last king of Rome?
20. What sort of creature is a francolin?

ANSWERS: 1 *Royal Institution*, 2 *Mount Everest*, 3 *Aida*, 4 *The Gingerbread Man*, 5 *Uranium*, 6 *Oliver Cromwell*, 7 *Oxygen*, 8 *Queen Victoria*, 9 *Justin Rose*, 10 *Excalibur*, 11 *Ivan Turgenev*, 12 *Pierre de Villeneuve*, 13 *Oxpecker*, 14 *Mathematics*, 15 *Bob Dylan*, 16 *Whitebait*, 17 *Heraclitus*, 18 *Privy Council*, 19 *Tarquin the Proud (Tarquinius Superbus)*, 20 *A partridge*.

 *General Knowledge*

Your rating:
● 0-5 Join a library
● 11-15 Join a quiz team
● 6-10 Keep at it
● 16-20 Join Mensa

1. Which factory moved from Tower Hill to Llantrisant in 1968?
2. What covenant, delivered to Moses on two stone tablets, is also known as the Decalogue?
3. Which star of fly-on-the-wall TV series *The Cruise* reached the top of the album charts?
4. How many labours were performed by Heracles or Hercules?
5. Which insect is also known as a white ant?
6. In which U.S. state are the Everglades?
7. Which Czech composer is best known for his Ninth Symphony, *From the New World*?
8. What does R.S.P.C.A. stand for?
9. What name is given to the deciduous dentition of young children?
10. Which style of painting was developed by Pablo Picasso and Georges Braque?
11. Which English biblical translator was tried for heresy and executed in Belgium in 1536?
12. Who was the Soviet foreign minister from 1957 to 1985?
13. Which English poet of World War I wrote *Anthem for Doomed Youth*?
14. In which county is the market town of Evesham?
15. Which silvery-white element has the symbol Te?
16. What sort of creature is a bonito?
17. Which 19th century English poet established his reputation with *Morte d'Arthur*?
18. What name is given to the colour purple in heraldic terminology?
19. Which English monarch founded Eton College in 1440?
20. Who was the first man to play golf on the moon?

ANSWERS: 1 *Royal Mint.* 2 *Ten Commandments.* 3 *Jane McDonald.* 4 *Twelve.* 5 *Termite.* 6 *Florida.* 7 *Antonin Dvorak.* 8 *Royal Society for the Prevention of Cruelty to Animals.* 9 *Milk teeth.* 10 *Cubism.* 11 *William Tyndale.* 12 *Andrei Gromyko.* 13 *Wilfred Owen.* 14 *Hereford and Worcester.* 15 *Tellurium.* 16 *A fish.* 17 *Lord Tennyson.* 18 *Purpure.* 19 *Henry VI.* 20 *Alan Shepard.*

Entertainment

Your rating: ● 0-5   **Buy a TV**   ● 6-10   **Keep at it**
           ● 11-15 **Join a quiz team**   ● 16-20 **Enter a quiz show**

1. What was the title of the BBC 1 sports chat show hosted by John Inverdale?
2. Which 1999 film set in 1869 starred Will Smith and Kevin Kline as two U.S. marshals?
3. Who presented BBC 1's *TV's Greatest Hits*?
4. What was the title of Bristolian rapper Tricky's 1999 album release?
5. Which U.S. actor was TV's *Columbo*?
6. Which 1980 film about American teenagers starred Jodie Foster and Scott Baio?
7. What was the title of the BBC 1 series following the fortunes of military recruits at the Winchester and Pirbright army training centres?
8. What was the title of Billy Joel's 1983 number one single?
9. Which 1999 film starred James Woods and Melanie Griffith as criminal drug users?
10. Which actor played Jack Dent in the BBC 1 drama series *Jack of Hearts*?
11. Which Irish singer had a top five hit with *Hold Me Now* in 1987?
12. Which actor starred as a serial murderer of middle-aged women in the 1968 film *No Way to Treat a Lady*?
13. Which character in *The Bill*, played by Karl Collins, originally sported an afro?
14. Who were *Leavin' on a Jet Plane* in the charts in 1970?
15. Which 1999 Robert Altman film starred Glenn Close and Julianne Moore as sisters?
16. Who was the original human presenter of the children's programme *Rainbow*?
17. Which actor played a sheriff compromised by a precocious teenager in the 1970 film I *Walk the Line*?
18. Which Radio 1 duo presented BBC 1's *Match of the 90s*?
19. Which New York rap star released his second album in 1999, entitled *Forever*?
20. Which ex-player presented ITV's football magazine series *On the Ball* with Gabby Yorath?

 # General Knowledge

1. Which alcoholic drink distilled from the agave plant is named after a town in Mexico?
2. By what first name was Harry Lillis Crosby better known?
3. Which member of The Beatles lived at 20 Forthlin Road, Allerton, the most modern building owned by the National Trust?
4. The childhood disease rickets is caused by a deficiency of which vitamin?
5. Which river flows to the North Sea at Berwick, forming part of the border between England and Scotland?
6. What sort of creature is a skink?
7. Which British island was called Vectis by the Romans?
8. Which river flows from the Pennines in Cumbria to the North Sea via Middlesbrough?
9. Who wrote the *Just William* stories?
10. What is the maximum number of sets in a men's tennis match?
11. Which Indian city's harbour is dominated by the Gateway of India?
12. By what name is Roman dramatist Publius Terentius Afer known?
13. Which lanthanide element has the symbol Dy?
14. Who captured his second major of 1998 in winning the Open at Royal Birkdale?
15. Which garden pest is also known as a thunder fly?
16. What name is given to the study of the history of words?
17. At which English racecourse is the Two Thousand Guineas run?
18. Which South American soldier and statesman was known as the Liberator?
19. Which observatory was founded by Charles II in 1675?
20. On which Italian island is the volcano Mount Etna?

 # *General Knowledge*

Your rating: ● **0-5**   Join a library   ● **6-10**   Keep at it
                  ● **11-15** Join a quiz team   ● **16-20** Join Mensa

1. Which popular winter sport has Nordic and Alpine varieties?
2. What was the adopted surname of Russian revolutionary Vladimir Ilyich Ulyanov?
3. In which South American country is the port of Fray Bentos?
4. What is the second largest of the Channel Islands?
5. Which Italian city is famous for its leaning tower?
6. What is the main river of the Midlands?
7. Which Czech-born tennis player won the men's singles at the U.S. Open in 1985, 1986 and 1987?
8. What does R.S.P.B. stand for?
9. By what name was American stripper Rose Louise Hovick known?
10. Which metallic element has the symbol Na?
11. Which c.g.s. unit is equal to the work done when a force of one dyne acts through a distance of one centimetre?
12. Of which African country is Conakry the capital?
13. Which island in the Pacific Ocean was settled by mutineers from the Bounty and Tahitian women in 1790?
14. What is the nickname of British freelance aid worker Sally Becker?
15. Which British dramatist wrote the controversial play *Saved*?
16. In which English county is Charnwood Forest?
17. Which British cartoonist created the schoolgirls of St Trinian's?
18. What name is given to an ionised gas produced at extremely high temperatures?
19. Which English statesman who became first Earl of Chatham was known as the Great Commoner?
20. Whom did Nelson Mandela marry in 1998?

ANSWERS: *Skiing,* 2 *Lenin,* 3 *Uruguay,* 4 *Guernsey,* 5 *Pisa,* 6 *River Trent,* 7 *Ivan Lendl,* 8 *Royal Society for the Protection of Birds,* 9 *Gypsy Rose Lee,* 10 *Sodium,* 11 *Erg,* 12 *Guinea,* 13 *Pitcairn Island,* 14 *The Angel of Mostar,* 15 *Edward Bond,* 16 *Leicestershire,* 17 *Ronald Searle,* 18 *Plasma,* 19 *William Pitt the Elder,* 20 *Graca Machel.*

 *General Knowledge*

Your rating: ● **0-5** Join a library ● **6-10** Keep at it
● **11-15** Join a quiz team ● **16-20** Join Mensa

1. Which political party was formed in 1925 with the aim of achieving Welsh independence?
2. What is the capital of Japan?
3. Which Hungarian composer wrote *The Merry Widow* and *The Land of Smiles*?
4. What is the latitude of the equator?
5. Which precious metal has the symbol Pt?
6. In which U.S. state is the city of Seattle?
7. What name is given to minute or microscopic animals and plants that live in the upper layers of fresh and salt water?
8. What is the fruit of the plant *Citrus limon* called?
9. Which beheading device was used extensively in the French Revolution?
10. What country did the Rottweiler come from originally?
11. Which lanthanide element has the symbol Er?
12. What did the E stand for in the name of U.S. Confederate general Robert E. Lee?
13. What sort of creature is a planarian?
14. What name is given to the tiny disc-shaped structures in blood that help it to clot?
15. Which is the shallowest of the Great Lakes?
16. On which river does Guildford stand?
17. Which German city was the scene of Napoleon's defeat at the Battle of the Nations in 1813?
18. Of which former Soviet republic is Nagorno-Karabakh an autonomous region?
19. Which British actor, dramatist and raconteur wrote the play *Romanoff and Juliet*?
20. Which pope caused controversy with his failure to condemn fascism during World War II?

ANSWERS: 1 Plaid Cymru, 2 Tokyo, 3 Franz Lehár, 4 Zero degrees, 5 Platinum, 6 Washington, 7 Plankton, 8 Lemon, 9 Guillotine, 10 Germany, 11 Erbium, 12 Edward, 13 A flatworm, 14 Platelets, 15 Lake Erie, 16 River Wey, 17 Leipzig, 18 Azerbaijan, 19 Peter Ustinov, 20 Pius XII.

THE TRIVIA QUIZ BOOK

Entertainment

Your rating: ● 0-5 **Buy a TV** ● 6-10 **Keep at it**
● 11-15 **Join a quiz team** ● 16-20 **Enter a quiz show**

1. Which actor played Hugh Grant's father-in-law in the 1999 film *Mickey Blue Eyes*?
2. Which 1999 BBC 2 feature-length drama was based on a Melvyn Burgess novel about two teenagers who run away from home?
3. Previously unreleased tracks from which pop artist featured on the 1999 album *The Vault... Old Friends 4 Sale*?
4. Who were the original writers of TV's *Comedy Playhouse*?
5. Who played Betty Mahmoody in the 1991 film about her life, *Not Without My Daughter*?
6. Which member of the Mitchell family returned to *EastEnders* during 1999?
7. What was Marty Robbins' top five 1962 hit called?
8. Which actor played millionaire art thief Thomas Crown in the 1999 remake of *The Thomas Crown Affair*?
9. Which presenter undertook an *Animal Odyssey* on BBC 1?
10. Which group had a 1974 number one with *Sugar Baby Love*?
11. What was the title of the 1977 Disney animation featuring two heroic mice?
12. Which U.S. gangster drama series, which was nominated for 16 Emmys, came to Channel 4 in 1999?
13. What was the title of Thin Lizzy's 1976 top ten hit?
14. What was the title of the 1999 film featuring Bill Murray, which follows the story of a 15-year-old boy's crush on his teacher?
15. Who starred as *The Likely Lads* in the 1960s comedy series?
16. Which band released *Six-Track EP* to mark their appearances at the 1999 Reading and Leeds festivals?
17. Which comic duo starred in the 1942 film *Rio Rita*?
18. Which *Coronation Street* character returned to Weatherfield in 1999 to visit his father, who had undergone a triple heart by-pass operation?
19. What was the subtitle of the 1999 *South Park* movie?
20. Which profession came under the spotlight in the Channel 4 series *Masters of the Universe*?

THE TRIVIA QUIZ BOOK

 *General Knowledge*

Your rating: ● 0-5   Join a library   ● 6-10   Keep at it
● 11-15   Join a quiz team   ● 16-20   Join Mensa

1. Which actress played Scarlett O'Hara in the 1939 film *Gone With The Wind*?
2. What name is given to a pottery jug or mug shaped like a stout man in 18th-century dress?
3. Which Swiss ski resort is famous for the Cresta Run?
4. What name for an irregular soldier or freedom-fighter comes from the Spanish for 'small war'?
5. On which river does Leeds stand?
6. What is the usual date of the vernal, or spring, equinox?
7. Which French city is famous for its annual 24-hour race?
8. Who wrote *Far From the Madding Crowd*?
9. The disease scurvy is caused by a deficiency of which vitamin?
10. What name was given to the outer garment worn by citizens of ancient Rome?
11. Which Italian city is famous for the remains of Hadrian's villa and the Renaissance Villa d'Este and gardens?
12. By what name was Swiss-born French architect Charles-Édouard Jeanneret known?
13. Which portrait painter produced the famous 'warts and all' painting of Oliver Cromwell?
14. What is the chief ore of uranium?
15. Which American poet and novelist married Ted Hughes in 1956?
16. What name is given to the placenta when it is expelled following the delivery of a baby?
17. Which Norwegian explorer was the father of Leif Eriksson?
18. What sort of creature is a screamer?
19. What was the first name of Argentinian revolutionary Che Guevara?
20. Which Shakespeare play features the characters Helena and Bertram?

ANSWERS: 1 *Vivien Leigh.* 2 *Toby jug.* 3 *St Moritz.* 4 *Guerrilla.* 5 *River Aire.* 6 *March 21st.* 7 *Le Mans.* 8 *Thomas Hardy.* 9 *Vitamin C.* 10 *Toga.* 11 *Tivoli.* 12 *Le Corbusier.* 13 *Sir Peter Lely.* 14 *Pitchblende.* 15 *Sylvia Plath.* 16 *Afterbirth.* 17 *Eric the Red.* 18 *A bird.* 19 *Ernesto.* 20 *All's Well That Ends Well.*

 # General Knowledge

Your rating: ● 0-5   Join a library   ● 6-10   Keep at it
● 11-15   Join a quiz team   ● 16-20   Join Mensa

1. Which fortified wine takes its name from Jerez de la Frontera, where it was originally made?
2. Of which North American mountain system is Mount Elbert the highest peak?
3. Which chess piece can only move diagonally?
4. How many tentacles do squid have?
5. Which Derbyshire town is famous for its church with a crooked spire?
6. What sort of creature is a guillemot?
7. Which island group was officially known as Zetland until 1974?
8. What was the stage name of actress Harlean Carpentier, the original Blonde Bombshell?
9. What name is given to a Welsh assembly in which bards and minstrels compete for prizes?
10. Of which fruit is morello a variety?
11. In which American city was the convention of legionnaires at which legionnaires' disease was first identified?
12. Which fibrous protein is the major constituent of hair, nails, feathers, beaks and claws?
13. Whose 45-year-old conviction for murdering a policeman was overturned in 1998?
14. Which Irish novelist wrote *Uncle Silas* and *In a Glass Darkly*?
15. What was the name of the oil company founded by John D. Rockefeller in 1870?
16. Which king of England succeeded his father King John?
17. Which presidential retreat in the Appalachian mountains was the venue for peace agreements between Israel and Egypt in the 1970s?
18. By what name was world champion welterweight and middleweight boxer Walker Smith known?
19. In what country was composer César Franck born?
20. Which industrial port on the River Seine has a ferry link with Britain?

ANSWERS: *1* Sherry, *2* The Rockies, *3* Bishop, *4* Ten, *5* Chesterfield, *6* A bird, *7* Shetland Islands, *8* Jean Harlow, *9* Eisteddfod, *10* Cherry, *11* Philadelphia, *12* Keratin, *13* Derek Bentley, *14* Sheridan Le Fanu, *15* Standard Oil, *16* Henry III, *17* Camp David, *18* Sugar Ray Robinson, *19* Belgium, *20* Le Havre.

 *General Knowledge*

Your rating:
- 0-5   Join a library
- 11-15   Join a quiz team
- 6-10   Keep at it
- 16-20   Join Mensa

1. Which unorthodox American chess player beat Boris Spassky in Reykjavik in 1972 to become world champion?
2. What was the nickname of American president Dwight D. Eisenhower?
3. What sort of beans are used to make baked beans?
4. By what name is the mouth organ also known?
5. The Shiites and Sunnites are sects of which religion?
6. Of which mineral is alabaster a form?
7. Which famous basketball team was founded by Abraham Saperstein in 1927 to play exhibition matches?
8. What name is given to procedures that can be carried out by a medically unqualified person immediately after injury?
9. Which rare antelope is the national emblem of South Africa?
10. For which of the security services did David Shayler work?
11. Which Liberal politician was prime minister from 1905 to 1908?
12. In Greek mythology, who was the daughter of Agamemnon who helped her brother Orestes to kill her mother Clytemnestra?
13. Which novel features the character Hetty Sorrel?
14. For which English county did West Indian cricketer Gary Sobers play?
15. Which famous invention did James Hargreaves name after his daughter?
16. In which industrial town in Greater Manchester was the Cooperative Movement founded?
17. Which Algerian-born French novelist won the 1957 Nobel Prize for literature?
18. By what name is Italian monk Giovanni di Bernardone better known?
19. Of which Athenian philosopher were Plato and Xenophon disciples?
20. Which British pilot and philanthropist married Sue Ryder in 1959?

ANSWERS: 1 Bobby Fischer. 2 Ike. 3 Haricot beans. 4 Harmonica. 5 Islam. 6 Gypsum 7 Harlem Globetrotters. 8 First aid. 9 Springbok. 10 MI5. 11 Sir Henry Campbell-Bannerman. 12 Electra. 13 Adam Bede. 14 Nottinghamshire. 15 Spinning jenny. 16 Rochdale. 17 Albert Camus. 18 St Francis of Assisi. 19 Socrates. 20 Leonard Cheshire.

Entertainment

Your rating: ● 0-5   Buy a TV   ● 6-10   Keep at it
              ● 11-15 Join a quiz team ● 16-20 Enter a quiz show

1. Which Texan country trio released their second album, *Fly*, in 1999?
2. Which actress starred as a 25-year-old copy editor who goes back to high school in the 1999 film *Never Been Kissed*?
3. Which series of the 1960s and 1970s starred Edward Woodward as a secret service agent?
4. What was the title of Lyle Lovett's 1999 live album?
5. In which 1964 film did Debbie Reynolds play the reincarnation of a murdered Hollywood writer Lothario?
6. Which female singer had a 1955 top ten hit with *Under the Bridges of Paris*?
7. Which rock singer's death was the subject of the 1999 Channel 4 documentary *In Excess*?
8. Which U.S. pop group had a 1980 hit with *Celebration*?
9. Which actor played John Candy's brother-in-law in the 1988 film *The Great Outdoors*?
10. Which city did *EastEnders'* Bianca Butcher visit in 1999 for her art college interview?
11. Which vocalist featured on Coolio's 1995 number one *Gangsta's Paradise*?
12. Which 1999 film starred Eddie Murphy as a pickpocket and bootlegger in the Prohibition era?
13. Which *Coronation Street* character was played by Violet Carson?
14. Which guitarist released an album of collaborations in 1999 entitled *Supernatural*?
15. Which 1960 western satire about a travelling theatre company in the wilds of Wyoming starred Sophia Loren and Anthony Quinn?
16. Who did *Coronation Street*'s Kevin Webster propose to in 1999?
17. Which ex-EastEnder released her debut album, *You Me & Us*, in 1999?
18. Who hosted the ITV game show *Would I Lie to You*?
19. Which actor/singer played a soldier who falls in love with a mixed race girl in the 1958 film *Kings Go Forth*?
20. Who co-presented the BBC's review and preview show of the 1999 Edinburgh festival, *Edinburgh Uncovered*, with Alan Tyler?

ANSWERS: *1 The Dixie Chicks, 2 Drew Barrymore, 3 Callan, 4 Live in Texas, 5 Goodbye Charlie, 6 Eartha Kitt, 7 Michael Hutchence's, 8 Kool and the Gang, 9 Dan Ackroyd, 10 Manchester, 11 LV, 12 Life, 13 Ena Sharples, 14 Carlos Santana, 15 Heller in Pink Tights, 16 Alison, 17 Martine McCutcheon, 18 Steve Penk, 19 Frank Sinatra, 20 Mariella Frostrup.*

 *General Knowledge*

Your rating: ● 0-5   Join a library   ● 6-10   Keep at it
               ● 11-15   Join a quiz team   ● 16-20   Join Mensa

1. Which stock character of the commedia dell'arte and lover of Columbine was known as Arlecchino in Renaissance Italy?
2. Of which U.S. state is Richmond the capital?
3. In what year did Margaret Thatcher succeed Edward Heath as leader of the Conservative Party?
4. By what name was Scottish outlaw Robert MacGregor better known?
5. Of which Asian country, formerly known as Ceylon, is Colombo the capital?
6. What was the name of the dog carried into space by Sputnik 2?
7. Which ancient forest is associated with the legends of Robin Hood?
8. What is the smallest of the four main islands of Japan?
9. Who was the last Anglo-Saxon king of England?
10. Which Jane Austen novel features the character Fitzwilliam Darcy?
11. Which Spanish Jesuit missionary was known as the Apostle of the Indies?
12. Who was the leader of the Jacobins in the French Revolution who instigated the Reign of Terror?
13. Which ancient region between the Mediterranean and the Dead Sea was the Promised land of the Israelites?
14. In which play by Sheridan does the character Mrs Malaprop appear?
15. Which bay, bordered by Virginia and Maryland, is the largest inlet on the U.S.A.'s Atlantic coast?
16. By what name was Romanian-born film actor Emanuel Goldenberg better known?
17. Which British author wrote the novels *Clarissa* and *Pamela*?
18. Who wrote *One Flew Over the Cuckoo's Nest*?
19. Which sculptor created the statue of Peter Pan in Kensington Gardens?
20. Which English furniture designer made his name with his 1791 *Cabinet-maker and Upholsterer's Drawing Book*?

ANSWERS: 1 Harlequin, **2** Virginia, **3** 1975, **4** Rob Roy, **5** Sri Lanka, **6** Laika, **7** Sherwood Forest, **8** Shikoku, **9** Harold II, **10** Pride and Prejudice, **11** St Francis Xavier, **12** Maximilien Robespierre, **13** Canaan, **14** The Rivals, **15** Chesapeake Bay, **16** Edward G Robinson, **17** Samuel Richardson, **18** Ken Kesey, **19** George Frampton, **20** Thomas Sheraton.

General Knowledge

Your rating: ● 0-5 Join a library   ● 6-10 Keep at it
● 11-15 Join a quiz team   ● 16-20 Join Mensa

1. Which navigational instrument has an arc of a sixth of a circle?
2. What is the fastest swimming stroke?
3. Which city in South Yorkshire is famous for its steel?
4. In which European country is the port of Ostend?
5. Which giant planet between Saturn and Neptune orbits the sun every 84 earth years?
6. What name is given to substances used to kill insects by chemical action?
7. Which specialised agency of the United Nations is known by the initials I.M.F.?
8. What is the name of the force of volunteer soldiers that supplements the regular army?
9. What name is given to the seven brightest stars of Ursa Major?
10. Which Charles Dickens novel features the character Uriah Heep?
11. Which English artist is best remembered for his illustrations for *Winnie-the-Pooh* and *The Wind in the Willows*?
12. What name is given to the maximum velocity that can be attained by an object moving through a fluid?
13. Which Italian cyclist won the 1998 Tour de France?
14. In Greek mythology, which beautiful youth was chosen as cupbearer to Zeus?
15. Which king of England was buried in the newly-consecrated Westminster Abbey in 1066?
16. What is the main ingredient of guacamole?
17. Which British poet made his name with *Poems and Ballads* in 1866?
18. On which Italian river does the city of Turin stand?
19. By what name was President Theodore Roosevelt's programme for economic and social reform known?
20. Which French statesman and cardinal founded the French Academy?

ANSWERS: 1 Sextant. 2 Front crawl. 3 Sheffield. 4 Belgium. 5 Uranus. 6 Insecticides. 7 International Monetary Fund. 8 Territorial Army. 9 The Plough. 10 Great Expectations. 11 E. H. Shepard. 12 Terminal velocity. 13 Marco Pantani. 14 Ganymede. 15 Edward the Confessor. 16 Avocado. 17 Algernon Swinburne. 18 Po. 19 Square Deal. 20 Cardinal Richelieu.

THE TRIVIA QUIZ BOOK

 *General Knowledge*

Your rating:
- 0-5   Join a library
- 11-15   Join a quiz team
- 6-10   Keep at it
- 16-20   Join Mensa

1. Which sweet syrup is produced by bees from the nectar of flowers?
2. What name was given to the coalition of Germany, Italy and Japan in World War II?
3. Which British racing motorcyclist won the 500cc world championship in 1976?
4. Who was the 'rogue trader' whose dealings led to the collapse of Barings bank?
5. Which Wiltshire town developed around the workshops of the Great Western Railway?
6. What is the capital of Uruguay?
7. What was the name of the Celtic paradise to which King Arthur was taken after his final battle?
8. Which former England cricket captain played for Somerset, Worcestershire, Queensland and Durham?
9. What name is given to a slip of the tongue in which the first letters of words are transposed?
10. What name is given to the scientific study of plants?
11. Which Swiss-born member of Les Six wrote *King David* and *Pacific 231*?
12. What name is given to a substance that is a poor conductor of electricity and therefore has a high resistivity?
13. Which ventriloquist was associated with the hand puppet Lamb Chop?
14. In which U.S. state is the Garden of the Gods?
15. Which pope proclaimed the First Crusade at the Council of Clermont in 1095?
16. What sort of creature is a numbat?
17. Which metallic element has the symbol Os?
18. In Greek mythology, what sort of spirits were naiads, dryads and nereids?
19. Which British actor and theatre manager became a stage idol after playing Richard III in 1741?
20. Which American composer wrote *Imaginary Landscape No 4* for randomly tuned radio sets?

ANSWERS: 1 *Honey,* 2 *Axis Powers,* 3 *Barry Sheene,* 4 *Nick Leeson,* 5 *Swindon,* 6 *Montevideo,* 7 *Avalon,* 8 *Ian Botham,* 9 *Spoonerism,* 10 *Botany,* 11 *Arthur Honegger,* 12 *Insulator,* 13 *Shari Lewis,* 14 *Colorado,* 15 *Urban II,* 16 *A marsupial,* 17 *Osmium,* 18 *Nymphs,* 19 *David Garrick,* 20 *John Cage.*

Entertainment

| Your rating: | ● 0-5 | Buy a TV | ● 6-10 | Keep at it |
| | ● 11-15 | Join a quiz team | ● 16-20 | Enter a quiz show |

1. Which British actor made his directorial debut with the 1999 film *The War Zone*?
2. Which British actor played the philanderer in the comedy show *Casanova '73*?
3. What was the title of the 1999 number one single by Latin artist Lou Bega?
4. Which ex-racing driver presented the ITV series *Great Escapes*?
5. What was the title of the Marcels' 1961 number one hit?
6. Which 1999 Viking action adventure film starred Antonio Banderas as an Arab poet?
7. Which late sports presenter was the 1999 TV tribute *The Bravest Fight* dedicated to?
8. Which Canadian group had a 1980 hit with *Echo Beach*?
9. What was the name of Cher's character in the 1990 film *Mermaids*?
10. Which BBC 2 meteorological series was presented by Ian McCaskill, Simon King, Isobel Lang and Howie Watkins?
11. Which Italian musician and producer had a 1996 top five hit with *Children*?
12. Which 1999 film by Swingers director Doug Liman follows three intertwining stories?
13. Behind what type of shop were the Manhattan headquarters of the spy organisation in TV's *The Man From UNCLE*?
14. Which 1980s pop group released the 1999 revival album *Lexicon of Live*?
15. Which 1992 film set in an Irish town visited by a troupe of travelling actors starred Albert Finney, Aidan Quinn and Robin Wright?
16. Which 1999 BBC 1 psychological drama starred Clive Owen as a lawyer who kills a cyclist in a road rage incident?
17. Which Birmingham quartet released their fourth album, *One From the Modern*, in 1999, marking their tenth anniversary?
18. Which Radio 1 DJ's 60th birthday was marked in 1999 by a night of programming on BBC 2?
19. In which 1999 film did Robert Carlyle star as a 19th century cannibal?
20. Who duetted with Mick Jagger on the 1985 number one *Dancing in the Street*?

ANSWERS: 1 *Tim Roth*, 2 *Leslie Phillips*, 3 *Mambo No. 5 (A Little Bit of)*, 4 *Martin Brundle*, 5 *Blue Moon*, 6 *The 13th Warrior*, 7 *Helen Rollason*, 8 *Martha and the Muffins*, 9 *Mrs Flax*, 10 *The Essential Guide to Weather*, 11 *Robert Miles*, 12 *Go*, 13 *Del Floria's tailor shop*, 14 *ABC*, 15 *The Playboys*, 16 *Split Second*, 17 *Ocean Colour Scene*, 18 *John Peel's*, 19 *Ravenous*, 20 *David Bowie*.

 *General Knowledge*

Your rating:	● 0-5	Join a library	● 6-10	Keep at it
	● 11-15	Join a quiz team	● 16-20	Join Mensa

1. Which Swedish-born actress starred in *Grand Hotel*, *Anna Karenina* and *Ninotchka*?
2. What name is given to a device in which a moving fluid drives a wheel or motor?
3. Which Old Testament character was banished to the land of Nod, on the east of Eden?
4. In which Hollywood blockbuster did Bruce Willis play an oil driller attempting to save the world from being destroyed by an asteroid?
5. Which event in American history led the British Government to pass the Intolerable Acts?
6. What name is given to a rapid movement of snow and ice, and sometimes rock debris, down a steep slope?
7. Which Italian island was Napoleon's first place of exile?
8. What name is given to vines or shrubs of the genus *Lonicera*?
9. Which Scottish town is at the head of the Moray Firth?
10. Of which country did Mario Soares become president in 1986?
11. Which protein hormone is secreted by the islets of Langerhans in the pancreas in response to a high concentration of glucose in the blood?
12. What was the former name of the Istanbul suburb Uskudar, site of Florence Nightingale's hospital in the Crimean War?
13. Which Surrey and England batsman made his maiden Test century against South Africa at Headingley in 1998?
14. In which county is the village of Borstal which gave its name to institutions for young offenders?
15. Which king of England was murdered at Corfe Castle in 978 and canonised in 1001?
16. To which French town was the papacy removed for much of the 14th century?
17. Which former vaudeville singer and dancer played a gangster in the 1931 film *The Public Enemy*?
18. Of which Polynesian kingdom is Nuku'alofa the capital?
19. Which pop group recorded the album *Meat is Murder*?
20. Which D H Lawrence novel features the character Rupert Birkin?

ANSWERS: *1 Greta Garbo, 2 Turbine, 3 Cain, 4 Armageddon, 5 Boston Tea Party, 6 Avalanche, 7 Elba, 8 Honeysuckle, 9 Inverness, 10 Portugal, 11 Insulin, 12 Scutari, 13 Mark Butcher, 14 Kent, 15 Edward the Martyr, 16 Avignon, 17 James Cagney, 18 Tonga, or the Friendly Islands, 19 The Smiths, 20 Women in Love.*

 *General Knowledge*

Your rating:	● 0-5	Join a library	● 6-10	Keep at it
	● 11-15	Join a quiz team	● 16-20	Join Mensa

1. Which German-born physicist was famous for his theories of relativity?
2. What was the last battle of the Wars of the Roses?
3. Which comedy actress created Mrs Merton?
4. What name is given to any animal without a backbone?
5. Which Swiss city is the location of the headquarters of the International Red Cross and the World Health Organisation?
6. What sort of creature is an eland?
7. Which Buckinghamshire country house has been the official country residence of British prime ministers since 1921?
8. What is the capital of Canada?
9. What fruit did actress and royal mistress Nell Gwyn sell in Drury Lane?
10. Which American Beat novelist wrote *On the Road* and *Big Sur*?
11. Which Basque town's bombing by German planes inspired a famous painting by Picasso?
12. On which Antarctic island is Mount Erebus, the world's southernmost active volcano?
13. Which Roman soldier and martyr was supposedly sentenced to be executed by archers?
14. Who was the first woman to be appointed Government Chief Whip?
15. Which small prosimian primate of Madagascar has a ring-tailed variety?
16. In which U.S. state is the city of Pittsburgh?
17. Which Roman Catholic order founded by Saint Angela Merici in 1535 was the first women's teaching order?
18. Who wrote an acclaimed biography of Samuel Johnson which was published in 1791?
19. What is the capital of the Republic of Seychelles?
20. Which Scottish winter sports resort is between the Monadhliath and Cairngorm mountains?

ANSWERS: 1 *Albert Einstein.* 2 *The Battle of Bosworth Field.* 3 *Caroline Aherne.* 4 *Invertebrate.* 5 *Geneva.* 6 *An antelope.* 7 *Chequers.* 8 *Ottawa.* 9 *Oranges.* 10 *Jack Kerouac.* 11 *Guernica.* 12 *Ross Island.* 13 *Saint Sebastian.* 14 *Ann Taylor.* 15 *Lemur.* 16 *Pennsylvania.* 17 *Ursulines.* 18 *James Boswell.* 19 *Victoria.* 20 *Aviemore.*

 *General Knowledge*

Your rating:
- 0-5   Join a library
- 11-15   Join a quiz team
- 6-10   Keep at it
- 16-20   Join Mensa

1. Which former prime minister became the first Earl of Avon?
2. Who was the famous heroine who helped her lighthouse keeper father to rescue five people from the Forfarshire?
3. Which Labour MP played Elizabeth I in a 1971 television series?
4. On which island off the coast of Kent is the port of Sheerness?
5. Which British film director made the films *Oliver!* and *The Third Man*?
6. In what year was the state of Israel established?
7. Which industrial town in Kent is linked to Purfleet in Essex by a tunnel and road bridge?
8. Who painted the *Mona Lisa*?
9. Across which stream did Julius Caesar lead his army to precipitate civil war with Pompey?
10. Which ship carried the Pilgrim Fathers to America?
11. Which English author and traveller wrote *Lavengro* and *Romany Rye*?
12. In which region of Russia did the Samoyed dog originate?
13. Which husband of Mary Queen of Scots was the father of James I of England?
14. United States embassies in which two African countries were bombed by terrorists in 1998?
15. Which British three-day-event horse rider won gold medals at the 1968 and 1972 Olympics?
16. Who wrote *The Scarlet Letter* and *The House of the Seven Gables*?
17. Which Dutch artist painted *The Garden of Earthly Delights*?
18. High Willhays is the highest point of which moorland area of Britain?
19. What name is given to a contraction of the heart?
20. Which journalist and founder of Punch wrote *London Labour and the London Poor*?

ANSWERS: 1 *Anthony Eden.* 2 *Grace Darling.* 3 *Glenda Jackson.* 4 *Isle of Sheppey.* 5 *Sir Carol Reed.* 6 *1948.* 7 *Dartford.* 8 *Leonardo da Vinci.* 9 *The Rubicon.* 10 *The Mayflower.* 11 *George Borrow.* 12 *Siberia.* 13 *Lord Darnley.* 14 *Kenya and Tanzania.* 15 *Richard Meade.* 16 *Nathaniel Hawthorne.* 17 *Hieronymus Bosch.* 18 *Dartmoor.* 19 *Systole.* 20 *Henry Mayhew.*

Entertainment

Your rating:	● 0-5	Buy a TV	● 6-10	Keep at it
	● 11-15	Join a quiz team	● 16-20	Enter a quiz show

1. Which late 1950s TV comedy show starred Mandy Miller as a girl looking after her widowed mother?
2. What was the title of Gomez's follow-up to 1998's Mercury Music Prize-winning album *Bring It On*?
3. Which wrestler starred in the 1991 sci-fi spoof *Suburban Commando*?
4. Which 1999 BBC 1 drama starred Nick Berry, Neil Pearson, Warren Clarke and Robert Daws as four friends?
5. What was the title of Australian group New World's 1971 top ten hit?
6. Which 1999 film was the last to be directed by Stanley Kubrick?
7. Which hypnotist attempted to *Hyp the Streets* on Channel 4?
8. Which song provided both Herman's Hermits and Sam Cooke with top ten hits?
9. Which actress starred as a waitress who shares a cop's lottery winnings as a tip in the 1994 film *It Could Happen To You*?
10. Who presented the updated Channel 5 version of *It's a Knockout*?
11. Which U.S. group had two top ten hits with *Tracy* and *When Julie Comes Around*?
12. Which chat show presenter was All Talk on BBC 1?
13. Which *Dawson's Creek* actor was the star of the 1999 American football film *Varsity Blues*?
14. Which British comedy actor starred as a butler opposite Elaine Stritch in the 1970s series *Two's Company*?
15. Which British boy band released their second album, *Nexus*, in 1999?
16. Which actress played Mrs March in the 1994 film version of *Little Women*?

17. Which ITV drama series starred Emily Woof, Geraldine Somerville, Michelle Collins and Lesley Sharp as gun-toting thieves?
18. Which veteran singer released an album of collaborations entitled *Reload* in 1999?
19. Which *EastEnders* character left for Manchester in 1999 after a disastrous affair with her mother's boyfriend?
20. Which British band had a 1999 top ten single with *Moving*?

ANSWERS: 1 *Sunday's Child*, 2 *Liquid Skin*, 3 Hulk Hogan, 4 *The Mystery of Men*, 5 Tom Tom Turnaround, 6 *Eyes Wide Shut*, 7 Paul McKenna, 8 *Wonderful World*, 9 Bridget Fonda, 10 Keith Chegwin, 11 *Cufflinks*, 12 Clive Anderson, 13 James Van Der Beek, 14 Donald Sinden, 15 *Another Level*, 16 Susan Sarandon, 17 *Daylight Robbery*, 18 Tom Jones, 19 Bianca Butcher, 20 Supergrass.

 # General Knowledge

Your rating: ● 0-5　Join a library　　● 6-10　Keep at it
　　　　　　　● 11-15　Join a quiz team　　● 16-20　Join Mensa

1. Which English scientist was the most famous passenger on HMS Beagle from 1831 to 1836?
2. What name is given to the most prestigious U.S. universities such as Harvard, Yale and Princeton?
3. With which car manufacturer did Charles Stewart Rolls go into partnership?
4. What is the capital of Spain?
5. Which Austrian physician who pioneered psychoanalysis wrote *The Interpretation of Dreams*?
6. What name is given to the larvae of houseflies and blowflies?
7. Which shrub is also known as may?
8. What breed of dog was developed from the fox terrier by the Rev John Russell?
9. Which Oscar-winning Welsh actor pledged £1 million to the National Trust for the purchase of part of Mount Snowdon?
10. Of which U.S. state is Boston the capital?
11. Which American film producer founded MGM with Sam Goldwyn?
12. What is the main river of Vietnam, also called Song Hong?
13. Which historic house saw a 30% increase in visitors following the release of the film *Mrs Brown*?
14. Under what name did former Lord Chancellor Baron Hailsham of St Marylebone become a Conservative MP?
15. Which Indian city is the capital of Rajasthan?
16. What sort of creature is a dasyure?
17. Which American-born British inventor invented the first fully automatic machine gun?
18. In which seaport near Plymouth was the Royal Naval College established in 1905?
19. Which Old Testament prophet was the last of the judges who led the Israelites before the establishment of the monarchy?
20. With which American oil company did BP merge?

ANSWERS: *1 Charles Darwin. 2 Ivy League. 3 Sir Henry Royce. 4 Madrid. 5 Sigmund Freud. 6 Maggots. 7 Hawthorn. 8 Jack Russell terrier. 9 Sir Anthony Hopkins. 10 Massachusetts. 11 Louis B. Mayer. 12 Red River. 13 Osborne House. 14 Quintin Hogg. 15 Jaipur. 16 A marsupial. 17 Sir Hiram Maxim. 18 Dartmouth. 19 Samuel. 20 Amoco.*

 *General Knowledge*

Your rating: ● 0-5 Join a library   ● 6-10 Keep at it
● 11-15 Join a quiz team   ● 16-20 Join Mensa

1. Which religious and political movement in 16th-century Europe led to the establishment of Protestant churches?
2. On which notorious fracture in the earth's crust was the city of San Francisco built?
3. Which French author, famous for her love affair with Frédéric Chopin, wrote the novel *Indiana*?
4. What is the name of the famous whirlpool off the Norwegian Lofoten Islands?
5. Which strait separates European and Asian Turkey and connects the Black Sea with the Sea of Marmara?
6. For which infectious disease is rubella the technical name?
7. Which former music hall comedian starred in the films *Oh, Mr Porter!* and *Ask a Policeman*?
8. In what year was John Lennon shot dead?
9. Which arm of the Indian Ocean is connected to the Mediterranean Sea by the Suez Canal?
10. With which musical instrument were Anton and Artur Rubinstein associated?
11. Which Yorkshire village was the home of the Brontës from 1820?
12. Under the French Revolutionary calendar, what day became 1 Vendémiaire, the first day of the year?
13. Which Russian word meaning self-publication described clandestinely distributed writings in the former Soviet Union?
14. Of which zodiacal constellation is Regulus the brightest star?
15. Which Texas city was the scene of the Mexican attack on the Alamo in 1836?
16. What name is given to the pilgrimage to Mecca prescribed as a religious duty for Muslims?
17. Which former Labour MP presented more budgets than any other chancellor?
18. What sort of creature is an axolotl?
19. Which American journalist wrote *Ten Days That Shook The World*, an account of the Russian Revolution?
20. A pulmonary artery conveys blood from the heart to which organs?

ANSWERS: *1 The Reformation, 2 San Andreas fault, 3 George Sand, 4 Maelstrom, 5 The Bosporus, 6 German measles, 7 Will Hay, 8 1980, 9 Red Sea, 10 Piano, 11 Haworth, 12 September 22, 13 Samizdat, 14 Leo, 15 San Antonio, 16 Hajj, 17 Denis Healey, 18 A salamander, 19 John Reed, 20 The lungs.*

 **General Knowledge**

Your rating: ● 0-5   Join a library   ● 6-10   Keep at it
            ● 11-15   Join a quiz team   ● 16-20   Join Mensa

1. Which nocturnal flightless bird is the national symbol of New Zealand?
2. What name is given to a thick-skinned mammal such as an elephant, rhinoceros or hippopotamus?
3. Which Sicilian criminal organisation is known as Cosa Nostra in the United States?
4. Which Poet Laureate was appointed a member of the Order of Merit in 1998?
5. Which spirit is distilled from molasses derived from sugar cane?
6. What is the Islamic name for God?
7. Which inlet of the Tasman Sea was the site of Captain Cook's first landing in Australia?
8. Of which group of islands, famous for a fortified wine, is Funchal the capital?
9. Which cult TV series was adapted for a film starring Ralph Fiennes and Uma Thurman?
10. By what name was the Russian city of St Petersburg known from 1924 to 1991?
11. Which American newspaper publisher was said to be the model for Orson Welles's *Citizen Kane*?
12. Who succeeded to the U.S. presidency after the assassination of Abraham Lincoln?
13. Which French composer wrote the operas *Manon*, *Thais* and *Werther*?
14. Pilot Peter Dimond was jailed for flying which fugitive businessman out of Britain in 1993?
15. Which U.S. poet is best known for his *Spoon River Anthology*?
16. What sort of creature is an alewife?
17. Which king of Macedon won the Battle of Issus in 333 B.C.?
18. What name is given to the technique of painting in which water-based paints are applied to wet plaster?
19. Which African country was formerly known as Zaire?
20. What is the largest of the Japanese Volcano Islands, captured by U.S. Marines in 1945?

ANSWERS: 1 *Kiwi*, 2 *Pachyderm*, 3 *The Mafia*, 4 *Ted Hughes*, 5 *Rum*, 6 *Allah*, 7 *Botany Bay*, 8 *Madeira*, 9 *The Avengers*, 10 *Leningrad*, 11 *William Randolph Hearst*, 12 *Andrew Johnson*, 13 *Jules Massenet*, 14 *Asil Nadir*, 15 *Edgar Lee Masters*, 16 *A fish*, 17 *Alexander the Great*, 18 *Fresco*, 19 *Democratic Republic of Congo*, 20 *Iwo Jima*.

Entertainment

Your rating:	● 0-5 Buy a TV	● 6-10 Keep at it
	● 11-15 Join a quiz team	● 16-20 Enter a quiz show

1. Which 1999 black comedy film featuring Kirstie Alley and Ellen Barkin satirised American beauty pageants?

2. In which 1950s TV series were figures of authority in London challenged by a Manchester audience via a live link-up?

3. Which pioneering dance music duo released an album in 1999 entitled *Rhythm and Stealth*?

4. Which 1995 comedy film about the relationships of a group of siblings and friends starred Sarah Jessica Parker, Antonio Banderas and Mia Farrow?

5. Which 1999 BBC 1 1960s drama followed the escapades of 18-year-old twins Ellie and Arden Brookes?

6. Which song provided both David Bowie and Amii Stewart with top ten hits?

7. Which actor starred as an army cop investigating the murder of a captain in the 1999 film *The General's Daughter*?

8. Which comedy duo starred in the BBC 1 period sitcom *Let Them Eat Cake*?

9. Who starred in and directed the 1995 film *Mighty Aphrodite*?

10. Who had a number one hit with *Good Timin'* in 1960?

11. Which former *EastEnders* actor starred in the 1999 World War I film *The Trench*?

12. Which Prohibition criminal was played by Neville Brand in the U.S. TV series *The Untouchables*?

13. What was the title of Tori Amos' 1999 double CD album release?

14. Who played a mute Scottish widow in the 1993 film *The Piano*?

15. Which Liverpool and England footballer displayed his Soccer Skills in a BBC 2 series?

16. Which *Star Wars: Episode I* actor played a scientist in the 1999 film *The Haunting*?

17. Which ex-EastEnder was *Alive in Alaska* in a 1999 BBC 1 documentary?

18. In which 1999 film did Billy Crystal play a psychiatrist who treats a Mafia boss played by Robert De Niro?

19. In which UK city was the BBC 2 black comedy drama series *Eureka Street* set?

20. What was the title of Everything But The Girl's 1999 album release?

ANSWERS: 1 Drop Dead Gorgeous. 2 Under Fire. 3 Leftfield. 4 Miami Rhapsody. 5 Sex, Chips & Rock 'n' Roll. 6 Knock On Wood. 7 John Travolta. 8 French & Saunders. 9 Woody Allen. 10 Jimmy Jones. 11 Paul Nichols. 12 Al Capone. 13 To Venus and Back. 14 Holly Hunter. 15 Michael Owen. 16 Liam Neeson. 17 Ross Kemp. 18 Analyze This. 19 Belfast. 20 Temperamental.

 *General Knowledge*

Your rating: ● 0-5   **Join a library**   ● 6-10 **Keep at it**
            ● 11-15 **Join a quiz team**   ● 16-20 **Join Mensa**

1. Which king of Wessex was said to have allowed a peasant housewife's cakes to burn?
2. By what name is Karol Wojtyla better known?
3. Which market town in Northern Ireland was devastated by a terrorist bomb in August 1998?
4. Who succeeded to the U.S. presidency after the assassination of John F. Kennedy?
5. Which medical specialty is concerned with the problems and illnesses of children?
6. What is the capital of New Zealand?
7. Which popular holiday destination is the southernmost province of Portugal?
8. By what name is Reg Dwight better known?
9. Which Dutch courtesan and dancer was shot by the French on espionage charges in 1917?
10. With whom did Bill Clinton confess to having a relationship that was 'not appropriate'?
11. Which English essayist and critic wrote *The Spirit of the Age*?
12. What was the first name of the actor father of Daniel and Anna Massey?
13. Which Russian city is the home of the Kirov Ballet?
14. In which event in the 1998 European Championships did British athletes win all three medals?
15. Which Italian virtuoso violinist inspired works by Rachmaninov, Brahms and others?
16. What nationality was the painter and etcher Paul Klee?
17. Which lyricist collaborated with Frederick Loewe on the musicals *Brigadoon*, *My Fair Lady* and *Camelot*?
18. Of which U.S. state is Madison the capital?
19. Which British field marshal was appointed secretary of state for war on the outbreak of World War I?
20. Which American novelist wrote *The Man with the Golden Arm*?

ANSWERS: 1 *Alfred the Great.* 2 *Pope John Paul II.* 3 *Omagh.* 4 *Lyndon B Johnson.* 5 *Paediatrics.* 6 *Wellington.* 7 *Algarve.* 8 *Sir Elton John.* 9 *Mata Hari.* 10 *Monica Lewinsky.* 11 *William Hazlitt.* 12 *Raymond.* 13 *St Petersburg.* 14 *Men's 200m.* 15 *Niccolo Paganini.* 16 *Swiss.* 17 *Alan Jay Lerner.* 18 *Wisconsin.* 19 *Lord Kitchener of Khartoum.* 20 *Nelson Algren.*

 *General Knowledge*

Your rating: ● 0-5   Join a library   ● 6-10   Keep at it
           ● 11-15   Join a quiz team   ● 16-20   Join Mensa

1. Which Old Testament character maintained his faith in God despite losing his family, property and health?
2. What is the largest city in the United States?
3. Which TV series stars David Duchovny and Gillian Anderson?
4. In what year did Margaret Thatcher become the first woman prime minister of the United Kingdom?
5. Which Indian city gives its name to a style of riding breeches?
6. What is the capital of Algeria?
7. Which French patriot was known as the Maid of Orléans?
8. What sort of animal is a mastiff?
9. Which tree's edible nuts are also known as cobnuts?
10. In which country are spaniels thought to have originated?
11. What is the largest city in South Africa?
12. Who was President Nixon's national security adviser who was awarded the 1973 Nobel peace prize?
13. Of which African country is Matabeleland a part?
14. What name is given to the European blister beetle once used in powder form as a supposed aphrodisiac?
15. Which Portuguese explorer was associated with the ship *Trinidad*?
16. What is the capital of American Samoa?
17. Which Flemish artist painted the ceiling of the Banqueting Hall in Whitehall?
18. What is astronaut Buzz Aldrin's first name?
19. In which European country is the ski resort Kitzbühel?
20. Which king of England was known as Lackland?

ANSWERS: *1 Job. 2 New York City. 3 The X-Files. 4 1979. 5 Jodhpur. 6 Algiers. 7 Joan of Arc. 8 A dog. 9 Hazel. 10 Spain. 11 Johannesburg. 12 Henry Kissinger. 13 Zimbabwe. 14 Spanish fly. 15 Ferdinand Magellan. 16 Pago Pago. 17 Peter Paul Rubens. 18 Edwin. 19 Austria. 20 King John.*

 *General Knowledge*

1. Which village in northeast Scotland is the traditional destination for walkers from Land's End?
2. What is the English name for the movement in French cinema called Nouvelle Vague?
3. Which French footballer played both for and against Manchester United in a match to raise money for the survivors of the Munich air disaster?
4. What is the technical name for short-sightedness?
5. Which British aviator established records with solo flights to Australia, Tokyo and the Cape of Good Hope in the 1930s?
6. What is the name of the character who personifies the U.S. government and people?
7. On which street is the New York Stock Exchange?
8. Which acute viral infection passed on by animal bites is also called hydrophobia?
9. Where in Cheshire is the site of the Nuffield Radio Astronomy Laboratories of the University of Manchester?
10. What was the original name of heavyweight boxer Muhammad Ali?
11. Which fortified palace on a rocky hill in Granada is an outstanding example of moorish architecture?
12. Who was the fourth son of Edward III who became Duke of Lancaster in 1340?
13. Which French artist and sculptor was regarded as the leader of the Fauvists?
14. Of which country was Mohammed Ali Jinnah the first governor general?
15. What does the acronym UNICEF stand for?
16. How long, in feet, is a table tennis table?
17. Which French humanist and satirist wrote *Gangantua* and *Pantagruel*?
18. Which English philosopher wrote the *Essay concerning Human Understanding*?
19. Who directed the films *The Leopard*, *The Damned* and *Death in Venice*?
20. Which trade unionist was general secretary of the Transport and General Workers' Union from 1968 to 1978?

ANSWERS: 1 *John O'Groats,* **2** *New Wave,* **3** *Eric Cantona,* **4** *Myopia,* **5** *Amy Johnson,* **6** *Uncle Sam,* **7** *Wall Street,* **8** *Rabies,* **9** *Jodrell Bank,* **10** *Cassius Clay,* **11** *Alhambra,* **12** *John of Gaunt,* **13** *Henri Matisse,* **14** *Pakistan,* **15** *United Nations International Children's Emergency Fund,* **16** *Nine feet,* **17** *Francois Rabelais,* **18** *John Locke,* **19** *Luchino Visconti,* **20** *Jack Jones.*

Entertainment

Your rating: ● 0-5   Buy a TV   ● 6-10   Keep at it
           ● 11-15   Join a quiz team   ● 16-20   Enter a quiz show

1. Which children's series depicting secondary school life was devised by Phil Redmond in 1980?
2. Which 1992 science-fiction film featuring Pierce Brosnan used virtual reality simulation?
3. Which *Inspector Morse* actor played cheated husband Geoff Meadows in the BBC 1 drama series *Pure Wickedness*?
4. Which British group had a number one with *Firestarter* in 1996?
5. Which actress played Queen of the Fairies Titania in the 1999 film version of *A Midsummer Night's Dream*?
6. In which zoo was the BBC 1 series *Molly's Zoo* set?
7. Which saxophonist duetted with David A. Stewart on the 1990 top ten hit *Lily Was Here*?
8. What was the subtitle of the 1991 film *Terminator 2*?
9. Who presented the BBC 1 series *Mysteries*?
10. What was the title of Whigfield's 1994 number one hit?
11. In which 1999 film did Helena Bonham Carter portray a victim of motor-neurone disease?
12. Which 1970s drama series about a stately home starred Gerald Harper as a landowner?
13. Which U.S. singer released an album entitled *Amen* in 1999?
14. Which Oscar-winning actress starred as a meteorologist in the 1996 film *Twister*?
15. What was the title of the late-night Channel 4 entertainment series presented by Denise van Outen?
16. Which rock star released an album entitled *Hours...* in 1999?
17. Which *Coronation Street* character's tragic death coincided with Maxine and Ashley Peacock's 1999 wedding?
18. Which U.S. vocalist had a 1992 top ten hit with *One Shining Moment*?
19. Which Channel 4 series followed the fortunes of the Bowlers, who took part in an experiment recreating the domestic life of a Victorian family?
20. In which 1999 film did Adam Sandler play a surrogate father?

58

THE TRIVIA QUIZ BOOK

(?) General Knowledge

Your rating: ● 0-5   Join a library   ● 6-10   Keep at it
● 11-15 Join a quiz team ● 16-20 Join Mensa

1. Which gas used in advertising signs has the symbol Ne?
2. What is the name of the small transverse flute that is accompanied by drums in military bands?
3. Which branch of mathematics uses symbols to represent unknown quantities?
4. What surname was assumed by Russian dictator Joseph Dzhugashvili?
5. Which British field marshal gave his name to a sleeve that extends to the neck without shoulder seams?
6. What does the abbreviation RAF stand for?
7. Which American national holiday is observed on July 4?
8. In what year did Edmund Hillary and Tenzing Norgay become the first mountaineers to reach the summit of Mount Everest?
9. Of which landlocked Asian country is Katmandu the capital?
10. What name is given to the use of live animals for experiments?
11. Which English colonial administrator secured the transfer of Singapore to the East India Company in 1819?
12. *Blind Fireworks* was the first published volume of poems by which Irish-born poet?
13. Which Conservative politician was secretary of state for education and science between 1981 and 1986?
14. Who wrote the novel *The Horse Whisperer*?
15. Viti Levu is the largest island of which country?
16. In which African country is Owen Falls?
17. Which Charles Dickens novel features the character Gabriel Varden?
18. What is the highest mountain in North America?
19. Which Irish painter is best known for *The Death of Nelson*?
20. A loganberry is a cross between which two fruits?

ANSWERS: 1 Neon, 2 Fife, 3 Algebra, 4 Stalin, 5 Baron Raglan, 6 Royal Air Force, 7 Independence Day, 8 1953, 9 Nepal, 10 Vivisection, 11 Sir Thomas Stamford Raffles, 12 Louis MacNeice, 13 Sir Keith Joseph, 14 Nicholas Evans, 15 Fiji, 16 Uganda, 17 Barnaby Rudge, 18 Mount McKinley, 19 Daniel Maclise, 20 Raspberry and blackberry.

 # General Knowledge

1. Which spectacular cave on the Hebridean island of Staffa inspired an overture by Mendelssohn?
2. Who wrote *The Guns of Navarone* and *Where Eagles Dare*?
3. Of which African country is Rabat the capital?
4. What is the state capital of Indiana?
5. Which British postal expert invented the adhesive stamp?
6. What does the acronym U.F.O. stand for?
7. Which American actor starred in the films *The Magnificent Seven*, *Bullitt* and *Papillon*?
8. Do stalagmites grow upwards or downwards?
9. Which radioactive element, discovered by Pierre and Marie Curie, has the symbol Ra?
10. Who replaced Kenny Dalglish as manager of Newcastle United in 1998?
11. Which German admiral rebuilt the German navy before World War II in spite of the Treaty of Versailles?
12. What name is given to the male reproductive organ of a flower that contains an anther?
13. What name is given to books printed before the 16th century?
14. What name was given to the followers of religious reformer John Wycliffe?
15. Which organ is inflamed in a case of nephritis or Bright's disease?
16. Who replaced David Owen as leader of the S.D.P.?
17. Who wrote the short novel on which Bizet's opera *Carmen* was based?
18. What was the nom de plume of the French man of letters François-Marie Arouet?
19. Which Dutch city is the country's main radio and television broadcasting centre?
20. Who took his last bow as principal conductor of the City of Birmingham Symphony Orchestra in 1998?

ANSWERS: *1 Fingal's Cave, 2 Alistair MacLean, 3 Morocco, 4 Indianapolis, 5 Sir Rowland Hill, 6 Unidentified flying object, 7 Steve McQueen, 8 Upwards, 9 Radium, 10 Ruud Gullit, 11 Erich Raeder, 12 Stamen, 13 Incunabula, 14 Lollards, 15 The kidney, 16 Robert Maclennan, 17 Prosper Mérimée, 18 Voltaire, 19 Hilversum, 20 Sir Simon Rattle.*

 *General Knowledge*

Your rating:
- 0-5   **Join a library**
- 11-15   **Join a quiz team**
- 6-10   **Keep at it**
- 16-20   **Join Mensa**

1. Which notoriously cruel Roman emperor is said to have been responsible for the deaths of two wives and of his mother?
2. By what name was Russian-born entertainer Asa Yoelson, star of *The Jazz Singer*, better known?
3. Which wooden 'religious offering' allowed the Greeks to get inside the walls of Troy?
4. By what initials is the high explosive trinitrotoluene better known?
5. Which Olympic event takes place over a course 26 miles 385 yards long?
6. What name is given to the closure of a workplace by an employer to prevent employees from working?
7. Which parade takes place on the sovereign's official birthday?
8. Which Scottish loch is associated with sightings of a monster?
9. By what name is the ozonosphere commonly known?
10. Which corrosion-resistant alloy of iron, chromium and nickel is widely used for making cutlery and kitchen utensils?
11. Which British spy defected to the Soviet Union in 1951 with Guy Burgess?
12. To which class of nymphs did Amphitrite, wife of Poseidon, and Thetis, mother of Achilles, belong in Greek mythology?
13. Which British novelist wrote *Sinister Street* and *Whisky Galore*?
14. What name is given to the fruit of the Chinese tree *Prunus persica*?
15. Which British poet and dramatist wrote *Every Man in his Humour* and *The Alchemist*?
16. What is the highest mountain in Canada?
17. Which German Nazi leader became head of the S.S. in 1929?
18. Which British poet and novelist wrote *Modern Love* and *The Egoist*?
19. What was the full name of the charity represented by the acronym Oxfam?
20. Of which African country is Lomé the capital?

 # *Sports*

Your rating: ● 0-5   Wooden spoon   ● 6-10   Bronze medal
● 11-15   Silver medal   ● 16-20   Gold medal

1. Which sport is played by the Boston Red Sox?
2. According to the new rule enforced for the first time in Euro 2000, what is the maximum length of time a goalkeeper can control the ball with his hands?
3. Which Dutch striker is scared of flying?
4. What country does the athlete Noureddine Morceli represent?
5. What is the nickname of South Africa's rugby union team?
6. Who did Tommy Docherty succeed as manager of Manchester United?
7. At which venue did Nick Faldo win his first British Open in 1987?
8. Which city hosted the 1992 Olympic Games?
9. Which motor racing driver was Formula One world champion in 1972 and 1974?
10. Who topped the Republic of Ireland's group (Group 8) in the Euro 2000 qualifiers?
11. Which rugby league player was voted 1985 Man of Steel?
12. Which club signed Justin Fashanu from Norwich City?
13. Which female tennis player beat Bobby Riggs in the 'Battle of the Sexes' of 1973?
14. At which event did the Italian athlete Gelindo Bordin win gold at the 1988 Olympics?
15. In 1969, which heavyweight boxer was awarded the O.B.E.?
16. Which batsman scored a record Test innings of 375?
17. Who won snooker's World Championship for the third time in 1977?
18. In 1989, which horse won the Cheltenham Gold Cup?
19. In the 1991 Ryder Cup, which German golfer missed a critical 8-foot putt against Hale Irwin?
20. Which nation beat the U.S.S.R. in the final of the 1988 European championships?

ANSWERS: *1 Baseball. 2 Six seconds. 3 Dennis Bergkamp. 4 Algeria. 5 The Springboks. 6 Frank O'Farrell. 7 Muirfield. 8 Barcelona. 9 Emerson Fittipaldi. 10 Yugoslavia. 11 Ellery Hanley. 12 Nottingham Forest. 13 Billie Jean King. 14 Marathon. 15 Henry Cooper. 16 Brian Lara. 17 John Spencer. 18 Desert Orchid. 19 Bernhard Langer. 20 Holland.*

 *General Knowledge*

Your rating: ● 0-5   Join a library   ● 6-10   Keep at it
              ● 11-15 Join a quiz team   ● 16-20   Join Mensa

1. Which British actress married Laurence Olivier in 1961?
2. In Arthurian legend, what was the name of the wizard who counselled King Arthur?
3. Which country beat England at the Oval in 1998 thanks to the 16 wickets taken by off-spinner Muttiah Muralitharan?
4. What is the name of the official residence of the U.S. president in Washington, D.C.?
5. Which heavy metal has the chemical symbol Pb?
6. What is the capital of Thailand?
7. Which international organisation formed after World War I was superseded by the United Nations?
8. What is the innermost planet in our solar system?
9. Which swashbuckling film star was married to Mary Pickford?
10. Which sedative drug developed in the 1950s was withdrawn after causing thousands of fetal malformations?
11. Which English racing driver won the world driver's championship in 1962 and 1968?
12. What name is given to the middle value of a set of numbers arranged in order of magnitude?
13. Which Australian novelist, author of *The Tree of Man*, won the 1973 Nobel Prize for literature?
14. What are the names of Princess Diana's sisters?
15. Which Irish churchman was the last Roman Catholic to be martyred in England?
16. What does the abbreviation L.P.G. stand for?
17. Of which sultanate is Bandar Seri Begawan the capital and chief port?
18. What name is given to the first six tricks won by partners in a game of bridge or whist?
19. Which English naturalist wrote *The Natural History and Antiquities of Selborne*?
20. Which epoch of geological time is between the Pliocene and Holocene epochs?

ANSWERS: 1 Joan Plowright. 2 Merlin. 3 Sri Lanka. 4 The White House. 5 Lead. 6 Bangkok. 7 League of Nations. 8 Mercury. 9 Douglas Fairbanks. 10 Thalidomide. 11 Graham Hill. 12 Median. 13 Patrick White. 14 Lady Sarah McCorquodale and Lady Jane Fellowes. 15 Saint Oliver Plunket. 16 Liquefied petroleum gas. 17 Brunei. 18 The book. 19 Gilbert White. 20 Pleistocene.

 *General Knowledge*

| Your rating: | ● 0-5 | Join a library | ● 6-10 | Keep at it |
| | ● 11-15 | Join a quiz team | ● 16-20 | Join Mensa |

1. Which American national holiday is celebrated on the fourth Thursday in November?
2. For which highly infectious disease of children is rubeola the technical name?
3. Which London street, associated with government offices, contains the Cenotaph?
4. What is the commercial name of the anti-impotence drug developed by Pfizer Labs?
5. On which temperature scale is the boiling point of water 212 degrees under standard conditions?
6. In what year was the first test-tube baby born?
7. Which mythical animal resembled a white horse with one long horn on its forehead?
8. What is the longest river in France?
9. Which English author and lexicographer was famous for his *Dictionary*, first published in 1755?
10. What sort of creature is a bandicoot?
11. Of which territory of Canada, associated with a famous gold rush, is Whitehorse the capital?
12. What was the name of the family that dominated Florence for most of the 15th, 16th and 17th centuries?
13. In which country did the Sealyham terrier originate?
14. Who wrote the novels *Lost Horizon* and *Goodbye, Mr Chips*?
15. Which open star cluster in the constellation Taurus is named after the seven daughters of Atlas?
16. What sort of drug is tetracycline?
17. Of which African country was Hastings Banda named president for life in 1971?
18. What name was given to Roman citizens who did not belong to the privileged class of the patricians?
19. What was the name of the programme of social reform pursued by President Harry S. Truman?
20. Which American painter wrote *The Gentle Art of Making Enemies*?

ANSWERS: 1 *Thanksgiving Day*, 2 *Measles*, 3 *Whitehall*, 4 *Viagra*, 5 *Fahrenheit*, 6 *1978*, 7 *Unicorn*, 8 *River Loire*, 9 *Samuel Johnson*, 10 *A marsupial*, 11 *Yukon*, 12 *Medici*, 13 *Wales*, 14 *James Hilton*, 15 *Pleiades*, 16 *An antibiotic*, 17 *Malawi*, 18 *Plebeians*, 19 *Fair Deal*, 20 *James McNeill Whistler*.

 *General Knowledge*

1. Which British financial institution was founded in 1694?
2. By what name is the pain-relieving drug acetylsalicylic acid better known?
3. Who led the parliamentary campaign that resulted in the abolition of slavery in the British Empire?
4. At which famous public school did Prince Harry join his elder brother William?
5. Which acute disease affects the muscles of the jaw, hence the popular name lockjaw?
6. What is the capital of Hungary?
7. Which mineral, of which ruby and sapphire are forms, is the second hardest after diamond?
8. What is the name of the tubes that lead from the ovaries to the uterus?
9. Which port and resort in North Yorkshire has associations with Captain Cook and *Dracula*?
10. Which Italian town in Umbria was the birthplace of Saint Francis?
11. Which Conservative politician died in office as chancellor of the Exchequer in 1970?
12. In Greek mythology, what was the name of the sorceress who helped Jason to acquire the Golden Fleece?
13. Which English actor, who specialised in sinister roles, played the tramp in Harold Pinter's *The Caretaker*, filmed in 1963?
14. What sort of creature is a white-eye?
15. Which metallic element has the symbol Tl?
16. In which English county is the market town of Fareham?
17. Which English literary critic wrote *The Great Tradition*?
18. Which U.S. president died in 1901 shortly after being shot by an anarchist?
19. Which Thomas Hardy novel features the character Giles Winterbourne?
20. Of which island group is Thorshavn the capital?

ANSWERS: 1 *The Bank of England*, 2 *Aspirin*, 3 *William Wilberforce*, 4 *Eton College*, 5 *Tetanus*, 6 *Budapest*, 7 *Corundum*, 8 *Fallopian tubes*, 9 *Whitby*, 10 *Assisi*, 11 *Ian MacLeod*, 12 *Medea*, 13 *Donald Pleasence*, 14 *A bird*, 15 *Thallium*, 16 *Hampshire*, 17 *F. R. Leavis*, 18 *William McKinley*, 19 *The Woodlanders*, 20 *Faeroe Islands*.

THE TRIVIA QUIZ BOOK

Entertainment

Your rating:	● 0-5	Buy a TV	● 6-10	Keep at it
	● 11-15	Join a quiz team	● 16-20	Enter a quiz show

1. What was the name of Ron Howard's character in TV's *Happy Days*?
2. What was the title of S Club 7's debut album?
3. In which city was the 1997 film *Twin Town* set?
4. The 1999 series of which BBC 1 medical drama opened with a character recovering from a fall from a balcony?
5. What was Helen Shapiro's first number one hit, released in 1961?
6. Which ITV police drama starred Samantha Janus as D.C. Isobel de Pauli?
7. Which U.S. vocalist had top ten hits in the Eighties with *We Don't Have To... and Say It Again*?
8. Which 1988 film starred River Phoenix as a teenager whose parents are political activists wanted by the F.B.I.?
9. Which comedy-writing duo were behind the BBC 1 twentysomething comedy series *Starting Out*?
10. What was the title of Jimmy Nail's 1992 number one hit?
11. Which 1999 film starred Kate Capshaw, Tom Selleck and Blythe Danner?
12. What was the title of the 1960s series about a 19th-century police detective played by John Barrie?
13. What was the title of Sting's 1999 album release?
14. Which 1992 remake of a 1950 film about a crooked sports promoter starred Robert De Niro and Jessica Lange?
15. Which character was played by Caroline Aherne in the BBC 1 comedy drama *The Royle Family*?
16. Which British pop duo had a 1999 hit single with *New York City Boy*?
17. Which BBC 1 comedy drama series followed the fortunes of London taxi firm Cresta Cabs?
18. Which 1999 film reunited director Garry Marshall with the two stars of his film *Pretty Woman*, Julia Roberts and Richard Gere?
19. Which comedian/actor played Pete Gifford in the ITV romantic comedy drama *Cold Feet*?
20. The 1999 album *Northern Star* was the first solo album by which Spice Girl?

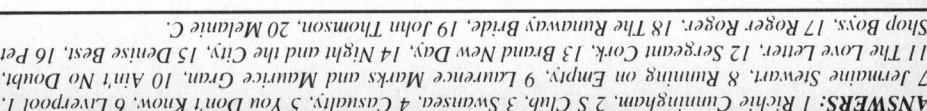

? *General Knowledge*

Your rating:
- **0-5**   Join a library
- **11-15**   Join a quiz team
- **6-10**   Keep at it
- **16-20**   Join Mensa

1. Which alcoholic drink's name is derived from the Gaelic *uisge beatha*, meaning the water of life?
2. After which English scientist is the S.I. unit of electrical capacitance, the farad, named?
3. What is the longest river in England?
4. What name is given to the set of magical beliefs and practices particularly associated with Haiti?
5. Which musical instrument with a circular drumlike body and a guitar-like neck was popular in minstrel shows?
6. What sort of snake was said to have caused the death of Cleopatra?
7. Which island group is called Islas Malvinas by Argentina?
8. In which industry did U.S. president Ronald Reagan work before he entered politics?
9. What was the name of the artificial language invented by L L Zamenhof in 1887?
10. What name is given to a dilute solution of acetic acid used to flavour food and as a preservative?
11. Which Greek biographer and essayist wrote *Parallel Lives*, an important source for Shakespeare's Roman plays?
12. Who directed the films *Some Like It Hot*, *Sunset Boulevard* and *The Front Page*?
13. Who was the Roman god of fire?
14. By what name was blues and folk singer Huddie Ledbetter known?
15. Which Argentinian racing driver won the world driver's championship a record five times in the 1950s?
16. What sort of creature is a sea butterfly?
17. What name is given to the movement for reunification of the various branches of the Christian church?
18. Which Jane Austen novel features the character Anne Elliott?
19. Which Swiss-based organisation is represented by the letters B.I.S.?
20. Who was prime minister of Great Britain when World War I began?

ANSWERS: 1 *Whisky*, 2 *Michael Faraday*, 3 *River Thames*, 4 *Voodoo*, 5 *Banjo*, 6 *An asp*, 7 *Falkland Islands*, 8 *Film industry*, 9 *Esperanto*, 10 *Vinegar*, 11 *Plutarch*, 12 *Billy Wilder*, 13 *Vulcan*, 14 *Leadbelly*, 15 *Juan Manuel Fangio*, 16 *A mollusc*, 17 *Ecumenical movement*, 18 *Persuasion*, 19 *Bank for International Settlements*, 20 *Herbert Asquith*.

(?) *General Knowledge*

Your rating:	● 0-5	Join a library	● 6-10	Keep at it
	● 11-15	Join a quiz team	● 16-20	Join Mensa

1. Which American golfer has won more major championships than any other?
2. By what name was Scottish king Robert I known?
3. Which Italian city is called Firenze in Italian?
4. Who wrote the operas *The Marriage of Figaro* and *Don Giovanni*?
5. Which British order of chivalry is represented by the letters O.M.?
6. What sort of creature is a blenny?
7. Which term meaning 'lightning war' was used to describe military tactics used by Germany in World War II?
8. What is Australia's largest city?
9. Who was the Greek god of love, identified with the Roman Cupid?
10. Which sign of the zodiac is represented by a bull?
11. Which French chef who worked at the Savoy Hotel in London was made a member of the Légion d'Honneur in 1920?
12. What word for a killer is derived from the Arabic for hashish-eaters?
13. Which Japanese film director died in 1998, at the age of 88?
14. In Greek mythology, who was the Muse of comedy?
15. Which German city, famous as the site of the Krupp steelworks, is the administrative centre of the Ruhr?
16. What sort of creature is a noctule?
17. Which American novelist wrote *Slaughterhouse Five* and *Breakfast of Champions*?
18. What name was given to the Church of England clergy who were deprived of their livings for refusing to swear allegiance to William III and Mary?
19. What was the historical name for Anatolia?
20. Which George Bernard Shaw play features the character Bluntschli?

General Knowledge

Your rating: ● **0-5** Join a library   ● **6-10** Keep at it
    ● **11-15** Join a quiz team   ● **16-20** Join Mensa

1. Which former leader of the Liberal Party was acquitted of the charge of incitement to murder?
2. Of which country did Hosni Mubarak become president in 1981?
3. By what name were the Norsemen who raided much of Europe from about 800 A.D. known?
4. What name is given to swollen and twisted veins, especially in the legs?
5. Which port and resort in Suffolk is Britain's biggest container port?
6. What is the capital of Scotland?
7. Who directed the films *On the Waterfront* and *East of Eden*?
8. Who was the god of thunder in Norse mythology?
9. Which French composer wrote *Boléro* and the ballet *Daphnis et Chloë*?
10. Of which African country is Asmara the capital?
11. Which monastery and palace near Madrid, built for Philip II, houses a famous art collection?
12. What name was given to the Chinese students organised to eliminate revisionism during the Cultural Revolution?
13. In which European country is the port of Esbjerg?
14. What is Esher's famous racecourse called?
15. Which blood cells are also known as erythrocytes?
16. Who was the first president of Zambia?
17. Which leading Nazi rocket engineer was taken to the United States after the war and worked for NASA?
18. What is the judicial capital of South Africa?
19. What does the name of the computer programming language FORTRAN stand for?
20. Which religious movement was founded by Mary Baker Eddy?

ANSWERS: *1 Jeremy Thorpe. 2 Egypt. 3 Vikings. 4 Varicose veins. 5 Felixstowe. 6 Edinburgh. 7 Elia Kazan. 8 Thor. 9 Maurice Ravel. 10 Eritrea. 11 El Escorial. 12 Red Guards. 13 Denmark. 14 Sandown Park. 15 Red blood cells. 16 Kenneth Kaunda. 17 Wernher von Braun. 18 Bloemfontein. 19 Formula translation. 20 Christian Science.*

THE TRIVIA QUIZ BOOK

Entertainment

Your rating:	● 0-5	Buy a TV	● 6-10	Keep at it
	● 11-15	Join a quiz team	● 16-20	Enter a quiz show

1. Which 1970s sitcom starred Irene Handl and Wilfred Pickles as two pensioners who fall in love and marry?
2. What is the title of James' tenth album, released in 1999?
3. In which 1976 film did Peter Falk and John Cassavetes star as two old friends whose relationship falls apart?
4. Which U.S. group asked *What's the Frequency, Kenneth?* with a 1994 hit single?
5. Which 1999 bad taste U.S. teen comedy film centred on the lives of four high-school boys?
6. Which character in ITV's *Heartbeat* was played by Derek Fowlds?
7. Which comic actor played a frustrated Welsh librarian in the 1962 film *Only Two Can Play*?
8. Which late actor played Quigley in BBC 1's *Ballykissangel*?
9. Which U.S. vocalist had top ten hits in the Eighties with *Saturday Love* and *Criticize*?
10. Which actor played a Birmingham serial-killer in the 1999 film *Felicia's Journey*?
11. In which Hanna-Barbera cartoon series were a gang of four teenage ghost-hunters hindered by their cowardly dog?
12. Which veteran soul singer released an album in 1999 entitled *No Ordinary World*?
13. Who directed 1959's *Operation Petticoat*, starring Cary Grant and Tony Curtis?
14. Which American teenager had a 1999 number one hit with *Genie in a Bottle*?
15. Which ambitious 1999 BBC documentary series recreated the sights and sounds of prehistoric Earth?
16. Which rap star played a parrot-loving cook in the 1999 film *Deep Blue Sea*?
17. Which *Animal Hospital* presenter did Christa Hart replace?
18. In which 1980 film did Faye Dunaway play Frank Sinatra's wife?
19. Which former TV drama series, forerunner of Kessler, followed the work of the Belgian resistance to help Allied agents and P.o.W.s in World War II?
20. Which female singer collaborated with East 17 on the 1996 hit song *If You Ever*?

ANSWERS: 1 *For the Love of Ada.* **2** *Millionaires.* **3** *Mikey and Nicky.* **4** R.E.M.. **5** *American Pie.* **6** Oscar Blaketon. **7** Peter Sellers. **8** Tony Doyle. **9** Alexander O'Neal. **10** Bob Hoskins. **11** Scooby Doo, Where are You?. **12** Joe Cocker. **13** Blake Edwards. **14** Christina Aguilera. **15** Walking with Dinosaurs. **16** LL Cool J. **17** Shauna Lowry. **18** The First Deadly Sin. **19** Secret Army. **20** Gabrielle.

 *General Knowledge*

Your rating: ● 0-5   Join a library   ● 6-10   Keep at it
              ● 11-15 Join a quiz team   ● 16-20 Join Mensa

1. Which Oxfordshire mansion was a gift from Queen Anne to the Duke of Marlborough and the birthplace of Winston Churchill?
2. Of which Central American country is Managua the capital?
3. What name is given to horses bred for racing that are descended from three Arab stallions brought into England?
4. Who became First Minister of Northern Ireland in 1998?
5. Which continent comprises the land around the South Pole?
6. What name is given to a stoat in its white winter coat?
7. Which Norwegian explorer beat Captain Scott to the South Pole in 1911?
8. Who wrote the detective novels *Murder on the Orient Express* and *Death on the Nile*?
9. What name is given to a shrub or tree trained to grow flat against a wall or trellis?
10. Which actor starred in the films *All The President's Men* and *Out Of Africa*?
11. Which South African writer wrote *The Hunter And The Whale*?
12. Who wrote the autobiographical work *Goodbye To All That*?
13. Which Bavarian town is famous for its passion play, performed every ten years?
14. Which actor starred in *The Witches Of Eastwick* and *One Flew Over The Cuckoo's Nest*?
15. Which Argentinian mountain in the Andes is the highest point in the western hemisphere?
16. What is the second largest city in Zimbabwe?
17. Which Irish politician was known as the Liberator?
18. What was the name of the driver of the car in which Princess Diana was killed?
19. What was the pen name of English composer Philip Heseltine?
20. Which Charles Dickens novel features the character Bella Wilfer?

ANSWERS: 1 *Blenheim Palace*, 2 *Nicaragua*, 3 *Thoroughbreds*, 4 *David Trimble*, 5 *Antarctica*, 6 *Ermine*, 7 *Roald Amundsen*, 8 *Dame Agatha Christie*, 9 *Espalier*, 10 *Robert Redford*, 11 *Sir Laurens van der Post*, 12 *Robert Graves*, 13 *Oberammergau*, 14 *Jack Nicholson*, 15 *Mount Aconcagua*, 16 *Bulawayo*, 17 *Daniel O'Connell*, 18 *Henri Paul*, 19 *Peter Warlock*, 20 *Our Mutual Friend*.

 # General Knowledge

Your rating: ● 0-5 Join a library   ● 6-10 Keep at it
              ● 11-15 Join a quiz team   ● 16-20 Join Mensa

1. Which light gas is used for inflating airships and balloons and in scientific research involving low temperatures?
2. In what year did Elizabeth II become Queen?
3. Which French port was the scene of a major evacuation of allied troops after the fall of France in 1940?
4. Who was the first actress to win an Emmy and an Oscar in the same year?
5. Which skin condition is caused by overactivity and inflammation of the sebaceous glands?
6. What name is given to an area of a desert where water is available?
7. Which Irish novelist wrote *Dracula*?
8. What sort of creature is a red admiral?
9. What is the capital of the Netherlands?
10. Which Shakespeare play features the characters Shylock and Antonio?
11. Which Missouri-born writer wrote the plays *Murder In The Cathedral* and *The Cocktail Party*?
12. Who was Archbishop of Westminster from 1963 to 1975?
13. Which British cellist was married to the pianist and conductor Daniel Barenboim?
14. Which British author wrote the children's story *The Witches*, filmed by Nicolas Roeg?
15. Which radioactive metallic element has the symbol Th?
16. What is the shortest book of the Old Testament?
17. In which Massachusetts city is Arthur Miller's play *The Crucible* set?
18. Which founding father of sociology wrote *The Division Of Labour In Society*?
19. Of which mountain range extending from British Columbia to California is Mount Rainier the highest peak?
20. Who wrote the novel *Love On The Dole*?

ANSWERS: 1 *Helium.* 2 *1952.* 3 *Dunkirk.* 4 *Helen Hunt.* 5 *Acne.* 6 *Oasis.* 7 *Bram Stoker.* 8 *A butterfly.* 9 *Amsterdam.* 10 *The Merchant of Venice.* 11 *T. S. Eliot.* 12 *Cardinal Heenan.* 13 *Jacqueline du Pré.* 14 *Roald Dahl.* 15 *Thorium.* 16 *The Book of Obadiah.* 17 *Salem.* 18 *Emile Durkheim.* 19 *Cascade Range.* 20 *Walter Greenwood.*

 *General Knowledge*

Your rating: ● 0-5   Join a library   ● 6-10   Keep at it
             ● 11-15 Join a quiz team   ● 16-20 Join Mensa

1. Which British naturalist, writer and zoo curator wrote *My Family And Other Animals*?
2. What is the largest inland sea in the world?
3. Which Australian tennis player won the men's title at the U.S. Open in 1997 and 1998?
4. What name is given to the rounded underground base of the stem of a daffodil, tulip or onion?
5. Which Moroccan port hosted a conference between Churchill and Roosevelt in 1943?
6. What is the fifth book of the New Testament?
7. Which American sharpshooter who performed in Buffalo Bill's Wild West Show inspired the musical *Annie Get Your Gun*?
8. What name is given to the science of map and chart making?
9. In Greek mythology, whose elopement with Paris precipitated the Trojan War?
10. Which American president came from a family of peanut farmers?
11. Which double-reeded woodwind instrument is derived from the ancient shawm?
12. What name is given to the side of bacon that can be claimed by a couple in a village in Essex who have not repented of their marriage within a year and a day?
13. What sort of number is used as a measure of a petrol's ability to resist knocking?
14. In which U.S. state is the city of Buffalo?
15. Which distinguished British actress was married to the actor Sir Lewis Casson?
16. By what name was Haitian president François Duvalier known?
17. What name is given to the shrub *Hamamelis virginiana* whose bark yields a solution used in pharmacy?
18. Which German philosopher and Nazi sympathiser wrote *Being And Time*?
19. In which country is the Black Sea port of Odessa?
20. Which George Eliot novel features the character Dunstan Cass?

ANSWERS: *1 Gerald Durrell, 2 Caspian Sea, 3 Pat Rafter, 4 Bulb, 5 Casablanca, 6 Acts of the Apostles, 7 Annie Oakley, 8 Cartography, 9 Helen of Troy, 10 Jimmy Carter, 11 Oboe, 12 Dunmow Flitch, 13 Octane number, 14 New York, 15 Dame Sybil Thorndike, 16 Papa Doc, 17 Witch hazel, 18 Martin Heidegger, 19 Ukraine, 20 Silas Marner.*

Entertainment

Your rating: ● 0-5   **Buy a TV**   ● 6-10   **Keep at it**
● 11-15   **Join a quiz team**   ● 16-20   **Enter a quiz show**

1. Which actor reprised his role as Gregory in Bill Forsyth's 1999 sequel *Gregory's Two Girls*?
2. Which *Looking Good* presenter fronted the BBC 1 show *D.I.Y. S.O.S.*?
3. What was the title of Gerry and the Pacemakers' first number one hit?
4. Which 1951 film musical starred Doris Day and Gene Nelson?
5. Who wrote the ITV dramas entitled *Trial & Retribution*?
6. What was the title of Hot Chocolate's 1977 number one hit?
7. In which 1970s TV series did Peter Barkworth and Hannah Gordon star as a couple separated by their respective jobs in a bank and in showbiz?
8. What was the title of the second album by girl group B*Witched?
9. Where did Herbie the Volkswagen Beetle go to in a 1977 Disney film?
10. On BBC 2, whose *Garden Army* attacked areas of wasteland?
11. What was the title of dance-pop band Steps' 1999 album release?
12. Which BAFTA-winning BBC 2 police drama series returned for a second series in 1999?
13. Which English actress provided the voice of Jane in the 1999 Disney version of *Tarzan*?
14. Who was the original presenter of the quiz show *University Challenge*?
15. Which 1980s pop group released a 1999 comeback album entitled *Wonderful*?
16. Who played Mr Hobbs in the 1962 film *Mr Hobbs Takes a Vacation*?
17. Which former Conservative Prime Minister's years in leadership were the subject of a 1999 BBC 1 documentary series?
18. Who collaborated with Youssou N'Dour on the 1994 top five hit *7 Seconds*?
19. Which 1999 horror film became the most profitable movie ever made?
20. Which UK group asked *Can You Feel the Force* in 1979?

ANSWERS: 1 *John Gordon-Sinclair.* 2 *Lowri Turner.* 3 *How Do You Do It?.* 4 *Lullaby of Broadway.* 5 *Lynda La Plante.* 6 *So You Win Again.* 7 *Telford's Change.* 8 *Awake and Breathe.* 9 *Monte Carlo.* 10 *Charlie Dimmock.* 11 *Steptacular.* 12 *The Cops.* 13 *Minute Driver.* 14 *Bamber Gascoigne.* 15 *Madness.* 16 *James Stewart.* 17 *John Major (The Major Years).* 18 *Neneh Cherry.* 19 *The Blair Witch Project.* 20 *The Real Thing.*

THE TRIVIA QUIZ BOOK

 *General Knowledge*

Your rating:
- 0-5   Join a library
- 11-15   Join a quiz team
- 6-10   Keep at it
- 16-20   Join Mensa

1. Which soft fabric is made from the undercoat of the Kashmir goat?
2. What type of elephant has larger ears, the Indian or the African?
3. Which British athlete won the gold medal in the heptathlon at the 1998 Commonwealth Games in Kuala Lumpur?
4. By what name is American singer/songwriter Robert Allen Zimmerman known?
5. Which Australian tennis player won the men's singles at Wimbledon in 1987?
6. How many arms does an octopus have?
7. Which Irish novelist wrote *The Country Girls*, *Night* and *Returning*?
8. What name is given to a substance that cannot be broken down into simpler fragments by chemical means and that appears in a periodic table?
9. Which two actors star in the *Lethal Weapon* films?
10. What name is given to a mathematician employed by an insurance company to calculate premiums?
11. Which Flemish painter served as the diplomatic envoy of Philip the Good, Duke of Burgundy?
12. What name is given to a line of blank verse consisting of five iambs?
13. Which European bird is also known as the hedge sparrow?
14. Which book of the Old Testament contains the injunction "Thou shalt not suffer a witch to live"?
15. Which member of Scott's expedition to the Antarctic walked out into a blizzard to die?
16. In computing, what does O.C.R. stand for?
17. Who wrote the novel *Bonfire of the Vanities*?
18. Which English navigator was set adrift by a mutinous crew in a bay that now bears his name?
19. What was the first battle of the American Revolution?
20. Which 4th-century Christian martyr gave her name to a firework that spins as it burns?

ANSWERS: *1 Cashmere. 2 African. 3 Denise Lewis. 4 Bob Dylan. 5 Pat Cash. 6 Eight. 7 Edna O'Brien. 8 Element. 9 Mel Gibson and Danny Glover. 10 Actuary. 11 Jan van Eyck. 12 Iambic pentameter. 13 Dunnock. 14 Exodus. 15 Lawrence Oates. 16 Optical character recognition. 17 Tom Wolfe. 18 Henry Hudson. 19 Battle of Lexington and Concord. 20 Saint Catherine of Alexandria.*

 # General Knowledge

Your rating:	● 0-5	Join a library	● 6-10	Keep at it
	● 11-15	Join a quiz team	● 16-20	Join Mensa

1. Which 18th-century Italian adventurer and spy was famous for his many romantic liaisons, recorded in his memoirs?
2. By what name is the contentious collection of sculptures from the Parthenon in the British Museum that the nation acquired in 1816 known?
3. Which Irish dramatist wrote *The Shadow of a Gunman* and *Juno and the Paycock*?
4. What is the national sport of Spain?
5. With which musical instrument was Pablo Casals chiefly associated?
6. What is the fruit of the oak tree called?
7. Which great Italian operatic tenor died in 1921?
8. Which figure in Greek mythology unwittingly killed his father and married his mother?
9. Which British rock group had a 1968 number one with *Jumping Jack Flash*?
10. What name is given to creatures of the family *Formicidae*?
11. In Greek mythology, what was the name of the river of the underworld which caused amnesia in those who drank its waters?
12. Which contemplative Roman Catholic religious order was founded by Saint Bruno in 1084?
13. In what year did the Gunpowder Plot take place?
14. Which highly radioactive metallic element has the symbol Ac?
15. Who was Chancellor of the Exchequer from 1979 to 1983?
16. In which South American country are the Angel Falls?
17. Of which French king was Madame de Pompadour a mistress?
18. Which Armenian composer wrote the ballets *Gayaneh* and *Spartacus*?
19. What was the nickname of the Prussian statesman Prince Otto Eduard Leopold von Bismarck?
20. In a poll to mark the 75th anniversary of the Radio Times, what was chosen as the best ever comedy show?

ANSWERS: *1 Casanova, 2 Elgin marbles, 3 Sean O'Casey, 4 Bullfighting, 5 Cello, 6 An acorn, 7 Enrico Caruso, 8 Oedipus, 9 The Rolling Stones, 10 Ants, 11 Lethe, 12 Carthusians, 13 1605, 14 Actinium, 15 Geoffrey Howe, 16 Venezuela, 17 Louis XV, 18 Aram Ilich Khachaturian, 19 The Iron Chancellor, 20 Morecambe and Wise.*

THE TRIVIA QUIZ BOOK

(?) *General Knowledge*

Your rating:	● 0-5	Join a library	● 6-10	Keep at it
	● 11-15	Join a quiz team	● 16-20	Join Mensa

1. By what name are the Royal Botanic Gardens in Surrey known?
2. Which British actor starred in *Brief Encounter*, *Mutiny on the Bounty* and *Ryan's Daughter*?
3. What is the name of Madonna's first child?
4. Which Queen of England was known as the Virgin Queen?
5. What name is given to a computer software package used to create letters and documents?
6. Which French composer wrote the opera *Carmen*?
7. Which British archaeologist discovered the tomb of Tutankhamen in collaboration with Lord Carnarvon?
8. Who was the fifth wife of Henry VIII and the second to be beheaded?
9. In which sport do riders compete on motorcycles without brakes on dirt tracks?
10. Which former Poet laureate who lived in the Lake District wrote *The Prelude*?
11. Which Russian chess player was world champion from 1969 to 1972?
12. In which former crown colony did E.O.K.A. fight for independence from Britain?
13. Which actress was famous for her portrayal of *Edna, the Inebriate Woman* in a TV drama?
14. What was the name of Mark Antony's wife, whom he divorced when he returned to Cleopatra?
15. Which Nazi politician and diplomat was German ambassador to Britain from 1936 to 1938?
16. For which vinyl resin is P.V.A. an abbreviation?
17. What was the nickname of the soldiers recruited by the British Government to fight Irish nationalists in Ireland in 1920-21?
18. Which American abstract expressionist artist invented action painting?
19. Which American dramatist wrote the play *Waiting for Lefty*?
20. In what year was the first F.I.F.A. World Cup held?

ANSWERS: *1 Kew Gardens, 2 Trevor Howard, 3 Lourdes, 4 Elizabeth I, 5 Word processor, 6 Georges Bizet, 7 Howard Carter, 8 Catherine Howard, 9 Speedway, 10 William Wordsworth, 11 Boris Spassky, 12 Cyprus, 13 Patricia Hayes, 14 Octavia, 15 Joachim von Ribbentrop, 16 Polyvinyl acetate, 17 Black and Tans, 18 Jackson Pollock, 19 Clifford Odets, 20 1930.*

Entertainment

Your rating: ● 0-5   Buy a TV   ● 6-10   Keep at it

● 11-15   Join a quiz team   ● 16-20   Enter a quiz show

1. Which gardening challenge series featured the skills of Alan Titchmarsh, Charlie Dimmock and Tommy Walsh?
2. Which country does Shirley Valentine escape to in the 1989 film?
3. What was the title of Sade's 1984 top ten hit?
4. Which actor wrote and starred in the title role of the 1999 film *Bowfinger*?
5. Which 1960s U.S. series followed the adventures of a group of rich holidaymakers marooned on an uninhabited island?
6. Which British soul singer released an album entitled *Rise* in 1999?
7. Who played Sinbad the Sailor in the 1947 film?
8. Who married Paddy the vet in ITV's *Emmerdale* in 1999?
9. Which U.S. soul diva released an album entitled *Rainbow* in 1999?
10. Which TV traveller's *Hemingway Adventure* was the subject of a BBC 1 series?
11. What was the profession of John Cusack and Billy Bob Thornton's characters in the 1999 film *Pushing Tin*?
12. Which 1999 Channel 4 documentary series followed children neglected by society?
13. What was the title of Simply Red's 1999 album, their seventh studio collection?
14. Which actress was *The Girl from UNCLE* in the 1960s U.S. series?
15. Which comic actor starred in the title role of the Eighties films *Fletch* and *Fletch Lives*?
16. Which BBC 1 drama series starred Michelle Collins as Susie and Pauline Quirke as Mandy?
17. Which UK group had top five hits in the 1960s with *For Your Love*, *Heart Full of Soul* and *Shapes of Things*?
18. Which British actress played Maddy, an Australian single mother, in the 1999 film *Mad Cows*?
19. Which group had a top ten hit in 1979 with *The Logical Song*?
20. Which 1982 film about political corruption starred Glenda Jackson and Jon Finch?

ANSWERS: 1 *Ground Force*. 2 *Greece*. 3 *Your Love is King*. 4 *Steve Martin*. 5 *Gilligan's Island*. 6 *Gabrielle*. 7 *Douglas Fairbanks Jr*. 8 *Mandy Dingle*. 9 *Mariah Carey*. 10 *Michael Palin's*. 11 *Air-traffic controllers*. 12 *Staying Lost*. 13 *Love and the Russian Winter*. 14 *Stefanie Powers*. 15 *Chevy Chase*. 16 *Real Women*. 17 *The Yardbirds*. 18 *Anna Friel*. 19 *Supertramp*. 20 *Giro City*.

? General Knowledge

| Your rating: | ● 0-5 | Join a library | ● 6-10 | Keep at it |
| | ● 11-15 | Join a quiz team | ● 16-20 | Join Mensa |

1. In which European country is the city of Antwerp?
2. What was the name of the zealous but incompetent police force that featured in silent films made by Mack Sennett?
3. Which record-breaking American sprinter died in 1998 at the age of 38?
4. By what name was painter Domenikos Theotokopoulos known?
5. What is the largest artery in the human body?
6. From which desert does the khamsin wind that blows over Egypt come?
7. Which composer wrote the *Music for the Royal Fireworks*?
8. Which fabric used especially for military uniforms gets its name from a Hindi word meaning dust-coloured?
9. What is the second longest river in Europe after the River Volga?
10. What name was given to the great epidemic of plague that ravaged Europe and Asia in the 14th century?
11. Which ancient African city near modern Tunis is said to have been founded by Dido and exiles from Tyre?
12. What is the name of the small flap that prevents food and fluid from entering the windpipe?
13. Which influential British economist wrote *General Theory of Employment, Interest and Money*?
14. Which German Social Democrat leader who ended Helmut Kohl's 16-year reign as Chancellor?
15. Which American theatre workshop associated with method acting was directed by Lee Strasberg?
16. What name is given to the compilation of dictionaries?
17. Of which constellation is the red supergiant Antares the brightest star?
18. What name is given to the positive electrode of an electrolytic cell?
19. Which Jane Austen novel features the character Catherine Morland?
20. Who was the leader of the Gunpowder Plot?

ANSWERS: 1 *Belgium.* **2** *Keystone Kops.* **3** *Florence Griffith-Joyner.* **4** *El Greco.* **5** *The aorta.* **6** *Sahara.* **7** *George Frederick Handel.* **8** *Khaki.* **9** *River Danube.* **10** *Black Death.* **11** *Carthage.* **12** *Epiglottis.* **13** *John Maynard Keynes.* **14** *Gerhard Schröder.* **15** *Actors Studio.* **16** *Lexicography.* **17** *Scorpius.* **18** *Anode.* **19** *Northanger Abbey.* **20** *Robert Catesby.*

 # General Knowledge

Your rating:
- 0-5   Join a library
- 11-15   Join a quiz team
- 6-10   Keep at it
- 16-20   Join Mensa

1. Which American track and field athlete won four gold medals at the 1984 Olympics?
2. Of which European country was Enver Hoxha leader from 1954 to 1985?
3. Which specialised agency of the United Nations is known by the initials W.H.O.?
4. What did the Queen autograph during her visit to Malaysia in 1998 in a break with tradition?
5. Who was the Greek goddess of love, identified with the Roman goddess Venus?
6. What colour is a female blackbird?
7. Which island off the coast of Wales is called Ynys Môn in Welsh?
8. What is the motto of the S.A.S.?
9. Which D. H. Lawrence novel features the character Mellors?
10. In which European city did Princess Diana die?
11. Which breed of terrier takes its name from a character in Walter Scott's novel *Guy Mannering*?
12. What was the name of the line that was confirmed as the border between Poland and Germany at the Potsdam Conference in 1945?
13. Which French composer wrote the opera *Giselle*?
14. Who plays Mary in the film *There's Something About Mary*?
15. Which American novelist wrote *Babbitt* and *Elmer Gantry*?
16. By what name was Italian painter and monk Guido di Pietro known?
17. Which operatic soprano was known as the Swedish nightingale?
18. In Egyptian mythology, what was the name of the jackal-headed god of the dead?
19. Which American baseball player hit himself into the history books with his 70th home run of the season in 1998?
20. What name is given to the outermost layer of cells on animals and plants?

ANSWERS: 1 *Carl Lewis*, 2 *Albania*, 3 *World Health Organisation*, 4 *A football*, 5 *Aphrodite*, 6 *Brown*, 7 *Anglesey*, 8 *Who dares wins*, 9 *Lady Chatterley's Lover*, 10 *Paris*, 11 *Dandie Dinmont terrier*, 12 *Oder-Neisse Line*, 13 *Adolphe Adam*, 14 *Cameron Diaz*, 15 *Sinclair Lewis*, 16 *Fra Angelico*, 17 *Jenny Lind*, 18 *Anubis*, 19 *Mark McGwire*, 20 *Epidermis*.

 *General Knowledge*

Your rating:	● 0-5 Join a library	● 6-10	Keep at it
	● 11-15 Join a quiz team	● 16-20	Join Mensa

1. Which widely-cultivated plant has leafstalks which are edible when cooked and poisonous leaves?
2. By what initials were the Committee of State Security secret police of the Soviet Union known?
3. Against which British novelist was a fatwa issued by Ayatollah Khomeini in 1989 calling for his death?
4. What is the name of the seat in the House of Lords used by the Lord Chancellor?
5. Which of the Apollo space missions made the first manned lunar landing?
6. How many pairs of ribs are there in the human body?
7. In what year did World War I end?
8. Which important vitamin is also called ascorbic acid?
9. By what name is an elk known in North America?
10. Which cricket club has voted to admit women members for the first time in its 211-year history in 1998?
11. Which channel in the central Mediterranean separates Sicily from the mainland of Italy?
12. What name was given to the group of disaffected Liberal MPs who voted against the 1866 Reform Bill?
13. Which U.S. president acquired Florida for the Union and issued a foreign policy doctrine that bears his name?
14. Which Italian poet wrote *The Divine Comedy*?
15. Which metallic element has the symbol Rh?
16. What is the highest mountain in England?
17. What is the longest river of Poland?
18. Which legendary Trojan leader is the hero of Virgil's most famous work?
19. What was the surname of the British Royal Family until it was changed to Windsor in 1917?
20. Which former Sheffield Wednesday player pushed referee Paul Alcock over after being sent off?

ANSWERS: 1 *Rhubarb.* 2 *K.G.B.* 3 *Salman Rushdie.* 4 *The woolsack.* 5 *Apollo 11.* 6 *Twelve.* 7 *1918.* 8 *Vitamin C.* 9 *Moose.* 10 *Marylebone Cricket Club.* 11 *Strait of Messina.* 12 *Adullamites.* 13 *James Monroe.* 14 *Dante Alighieri.* 15 *Rhodium.* 16 *Scafell Pike.* 17 *River Vistula.* 18 *Aeneas (The Aeneid).* 19 *Saxe-Coburg-Gotha.* 20 *Paolo Di Canio.*

Entertainment

Your rating:	● 0-5	Buy a TV	● 6-10	Keep at it
	● 11-15	Join a quiz team	● 16-20	Enter a quiz show

1. Which interior designer fronted the BBC 2 series *Fantasy Rooms*?
2. What was the title of Van Halen's 1984 top ten hit?
3. Which actor played Arthur Winslow in the 1999 filmic adaptation of *The Winslow Boy*?
4. Which 1950s U.S. series starred William Boyd as a black-clad cowboy?
5. Which Irish boy band had a 1999 number one with *Flying Without Wings*?
6. Who played the villain to Tony Curtis' hero in the 1965 film *The Great Race*?
7. Which newsreader hosted The National Television Awards in 1999?
8. Which British boy band had their first number one hit in 1999 with *Keep On Moving*?
9. Which thrice-weekly topical comedy series originally featured Ali G?
10. Which 1999 British film featured an Anglo-Pakistani family living in Salford in 1971?
11. In which 1970s TV series did Barry Foster play a Dutch police inspector?
12. Which American diva released an album entitled *Every Day Is A New Day* in 1999?
13. Which 1956 film starring Richard Attenborough was a light-hearted satire on British army life during World War II?
14. Which former child actors and pop stars were originally known as PJ and Duncan?
15. In which 1999 film did Bruce Willis play a child psychiatrist?
16. Which 1999 ITV post-Cold War thriller starred John Thaw as solicitor's clerk Joshua Mantle?
17. What was the title of the German group the Scorpions' 1991 top five hit?
18. Which actor played Virgil Tibbs, the San Francisco homicide lieutenant in the 1971 film *The Organization*?
19. Who played *Buffy the Vampire Slayer* in the BBC 2 series?
20. Which U.S. vocalist had a number one hit in 1958 with *It's Only Make Believe*?

ANSWERS: 1 *Laurence Llewelyn-Bowen*, 2 *Jump*, 3 *Nigel Hawthorne*, 4 *Hopalong Cassidy*, 5 *Westlife*, 6 *Jack Lemmon*, 7 *Trevor McDonald*, 8 *Five*, 9 *The 11 O'Clock Show*, 10 *East is East*, 11 *Van der Valk*, 12 *Diana Ross*, 13 *Private's Progress*, 14 *Ant and Dec*, 15 *The Sixth Sense*, 16 *The Waiting Time*, 17 *Wind of Change*, 18 *Sidney Poitier*, 19 *Sarah Michelle Gellar*, 20 *Conway Twitty*.

 *General Knowledge*

Your rating:	● 0-5 Join a library	● 6-10 Keep at it
	● 11-15 Join a quiz team	● 16-20 Join Mensa

1. Which alcoholic drink is used to make the drinks Bloody Mary and Screwdriver?
2. What name is given to an industry in which the market is supplied by only one supplier?
3. Which two metals are the principal constituents of brass?
4. Who presented the talk show *Sarah... Surviving Life*?
5. Which Austrian city, twice venue for the Winter Olympics, is the capital of the Tirol?
6. In the Old Testament, who was the first king of Israel?
7. What name is given to scurf that forms on the scalp and comes off in small white scales?
8. Which American novelist wrote *The Bostonians* and *The Turn of the Screw*?
9. What sort of creature is a mandrill?
10. Which Thracian gladiator led a revolt against Rome in 73 BC?
11. Which English poet, famous for his war poems, wrote *The Old Huntsman*?
12. By what name is propanone, used as a solvent in nail varnish remover, commonly known?
13. Which actor played *The Expert* in the 1960s BBC TV series?
14. What name is given to the land between the Tigris and Euphrates rivers?
15. Which French composer is best known for his piano works such as *Trois Gymnopédies*?
16. What was the nickname of the Anglican churchman William Ralph Inge?
17. What nationality is the novelist Chinua Achebe, author of *Things Fall Apart*?
18. What is the S.I. unit of electric potential or electromotive force?
19. Which city, on the River Vienne, is the centre of the French porcelain industry?
20. What sort of creature is an accentor?

ANSWERS: *1 Vodka. 2 Monopoly. 3 Copper and zinc. 4 The Duchess of York. 5 Innsbruck. 6 Saul. 7 Dandruff. 8 Henry James. 9 A monkey. 10 Spartacus. 11 Siegfried Sassoon. 12 Acetone. 13 Marius Goring. 14 Mesopotamia. 15 Erik Satie. 16 The Gloomy Dean. 17 Nigerian. 18 Volt. 19 Limoges. 20 A bird.*

? *General Knowledge*

1. Which actress starred in the films *Gentlemen Prefer Blondes* and *The Misfits*?
2. How many teeth should a human adult have?
3. Which football manager left Leeds United to take over at Tottenham Hotspur?
4. What is the Queen Mother's maiden name?
5. Which city replaced Rio de Janeiro as capital of Brazil in 1960?
6. What is the second largest planet in our solar system?
7. Which sweet yellow liqueur consisting chiefly of brandy and eggs originated in the Netherlands?
8. What name is given to vents or fissures in the earth's surface through which magma rises?
9. Which comedian wrote the play *Mum* for his actress daughter Charlotte?
10. For what sort of sweet is the French town of Montélimar famous?
11. Which section of the Mediterranean Sea contains the Cyclades, Dodecanese and Northern Sporades island groups?
12. Who wrote the libretti for Mozart's operas *The Marriage of Figaro*, *Don Giovanni* and *Cosi fan tutte*?
13. Which actress played the title role in the 1998 film *Elizabeth*?
14. What name is given to the rate of change of the velocity of a moving body?
15. Which English crime writer created Lord Peter Wimsey?
16. By what collective name are the poets John Donne, George Herbert and Andrew Marvell known?
17. Who founded the Royal College of Physicians in 1518?
18. What was the ancient name for the Dardanelles, the strait separating European and Asian Turkey?
19. In Greek mythology, which daughter of Demeter was carried off by Hades, who made her queen of the underworld?
20. Who wrote the novel *The Cruel Sea*, based on his naval experiences in World War II?

ANSWERS: *1 Marilyn Monroe, 2 32, 3 George Graham, 4 Bowes-Lyon, 5 Brasilia, 6 Saturn, 7 Advocaat, 8 Volcanoes, 9 Ronnie Barker, 10 Nougat, 11 Aegean Sea, 12 Lorenzo Da Ponte, 13 Cate Blanchett, 14 Acceleration, 15 Dorothy L. Sayers, 16 Metaphysical poets, 17 Thomas Linacre, 18 Hellespont, 19 Persephone, 20 Nicholas Monsarrat.*

 *General Knowledge*

1. Which American actor starred in *On the Waterfront*, *The Godfather* and *Apocalypse Now*?
2. By what name is the sodium salt of glumatic acid, used as a flavour enhancer in foods, known?
3. Which wind instrument was invented by Adolphe Sax?
4. Of which alcoholic drink are Cognac and Armagnac varieties?
5. Which American president was assassinated by John Wilkes Booth while watching a play?
6. What is the longest river in Europe?
7. On what day in August does the grouse-shooting season begin?
8. What is the capital of Western Australia?
9. Which entrepreneur founded the Virgin record company in 1969?
10. What name is given to rain that has absorbed sulphur dioxide and nitrogen oxides from the atmosphere?
11. Which stretch of water between Wales and S.E. Ireland links the Irish Sea with the Atlantic Ocean?
12. In Greek mythology, who was the father of the Titans?
13. What gives the white sauce soubise its distinctive flavour?
14. What nationality was United Nations secretary general Dag Hammarskjöld?
15. Which tax replaced capital transfer tax in the UK in 1986?
16. What sort of creature is a hairstreak?
17. Which British author wrote *Of Human Bondage*, *The Moon and Sixpence* and *Cakes and Ale*?
18. What name is given to the sea route along the coast of North America between the Atlantic and Pacific Oceans?
19. Which British field marshal was commander-in-chief of the British Expeditionary Force from 1915 to 1918?
20. Which French composer wrote the *Turangalîla symphony*?

ANSWERS: 1 *Marlon Brando*, 2 *Monosodium glutamate*, 3 *Saxophone*, 4 *Brandy*, 5 *Abraham Lincoln*, 6 *River Volga*, 7 *Twelfth*, 8 *Perth*, 9 *Richard Branson*, 10 *Acid rain*, 11 *Saint George's Channel*, 12 *Uranus*, 13 *Onion*, 14 *Swedish*, 15 *Inheritance tax*, 16 *A butterfly*, 17 *Somerset Maugham*, 18 *Northwest Passage*, 19 *Douglas Haig*, 20 *Olivier Messiaen*.

 # *Entertainment*

Your rating: ● 0-5   **Buy a TV**   ● 6-10   **Keep at it**
             ● 11-15   **Join a quiz team**   ● 16-20   **Enter a quiz show**

1. Who played *Buffy the Vampire Slayer* in the BBC 2 series?
2. Who directed the 1999 Western epic *Ride With the Devil*?
3. In which cartoon series did Dick Dastardly try to outdo the other competitors in cross country car races?
4. What was the title of Will Smith's 1999 album release?
5. Which 1984 film was set in Waxahachie, Texas, and starred Sally Field as a widowed mother?
6. Who married Pc Mike Bradley in ITV's *Heartbeat* in 1999?
7. Which dance group covered Adamski's 1990 number one hit *Killer*?
8. Who hosted the ITV series *Kids Say the Funniest Things*?
9. Which actor starred as Tyler Durden in the 1999 film *Fight Club*?
10. Which 1960s series followed the exploits of the occupants of a rocketship which crashed on a planet ruled by very large people?
11. Whose controversial single, *Millennium Prayer*, entered the charts at number two in 1999?
12. Which 1961 film starred John Mills as a trade unionist and Sylvia Syms as his school teacher daughter?
13. Which actor played Jack Green in BBC 1's Sunday family drama *The Magician's House*?
14. What was the title of the Two Cowboys' only hit, in 1994?
15. In which 1999 film did Robin Williams star as a Polish pancake-maker in World War II?
16. Who was the presenter of the Channel 4 series *Lost Gardens*?
17. Which female rap duo had a 1994 top ten hit with *Whatta Man*?
18. Which real-life brothers starred in the title roles of the 1990 film *The Krays*?
19. With whom did Elton John duet on the 1991 number one single *Don't Let the Sun Go Down On Me*?
20. Which actress starred as Steve Martin's wife in the 1999 film *The Out-of-Towners*?

 *General Knowledge*

Your rating: ● 0-5   Join a library   ● 6-10   Keep at it
               ● 11-15 Join a quiz team   ● 16-20   Join Mensa

1. What name is given to the molten rock that may be extruded from a volcano as lava?
2. Who wrote children's stories about the land of Narnia?
3. What is the second planet from the sun?
4. What is the highest mountain in the Alps?
5. What was the nom de plume of British short-story writer Hector Hugh Munro?
6. Of which Caribbean country is Port-au-Prince the capital?
7. Which German city is associated with the legend of the Pied Piper?
8. What name is given to the wind pattern that brings heavy rain to South Asia from April to September?
9. Which French composer wrote *Danse macabre* and *Carnival of the Animals*?
10. What is the first book of the New Testament?
11. Which British composer wrote the music for the hymn *Jerusalem*?
12. What name is given to the time taken for half the atoms in a sample of a radioactive isotope to decay?
13. Who was president of Kenya from 1964 to 1978?
14. In the Old Testament, who was the father of Rehoboam?
15. Which German author wrote the anti-war novel *All Quiet on the Western Front*?
16. In which U.S. state is the volcano Mount St Helens?
17. Which American city and seaport is best known as the site of Yale University?
18. What is a manometer used to measure?
19. What was the name of the legislative assembly of the Weimar Republic which was burnt out when Hitler came to power?
20. Which Italian city is the capital of Umbria?

ANSWERS: 1 *Magma,* **2** *C. S. Lewis,* **3** *Venus,* **4** *Mont Blanc,* **5** *Saki,* **6** *Haiti,* **7** *Hamelin, or Hameln,* **8** *Monsoon,* **9** *Camille Saint-Saëns,* **10** *The Gospel according to Saint Matthew,* **11** *Sir Hubert Parry,* **12** *Half-life,* **13** *Jomo Kenyatta,* **14** *Solomon,* **15** *Erich Maria Remarque,* **16** *Washington,* **17** *New Haven,* **18** *Pressure,* **19** *Reichstag,* **20** *Perugia.*

 *General Knowledge*

Your rating: ● 0-5   Join a library   ● 6-10   Keep at it
                ● 11-15   Join a quiz team   ● 16-20   Join Mensa

1. Which English clergyman and novelist wrote *Alton Locke*, *Westward Ho!*, and the children's story *The Water Babies*?
2. Of which South American country is Lima the capital?
3. Which comic actor starred in the film *The Truman Show*?
4. Who was the famous mistress of English admiral Lord Nelson?
5. Which distinctive pyramidal mountain on the Swiss-Italian border is known as Mont Cervin in French?
6. What name is given to the scientific study of language?
7. Which Indian-born British poet and author wrote *The Jungle Book* and *Kim*?
8. What is fermented to make the Japanese drink sake?
9. By what name was Russian tsar Peter I known?
10. Which breed of tail-less short-haired cat was originally bred on the Isle of Man?
11. Which former director of the Royal Shakespeare Company and The National Theatre was married to actress and dancer Leslie Caron?
12. What name is given to a substance that retards a chemical reaction, also called a negative catalyst or anticatalyst?
13. Which American actor starred in *Lassie Come Home* and *Planet of the Apes*?
14. At which archaeological site in Suffolk was a Saxon ship burial excavated in 1939?
15. Which horse race run at Doncaster is the oldest of the English classics?
16. On which river does the city of Peterborough stand?
17. Which Italian composer wrote the operas *Otello* and *Falstaff*?
18. Which French fashion designer succeeded Christian Dior as designer for Dior in 1957 before establishing his own label in 1962?
19. What was the name of the prison that stood on the site presently occupied by the Old Bailey?
20. Which Charles Dickens novel features the character Captain Cuttle?

ANSWERS: *1 Charles Kingsley, 2 Peru, 3 Jim Carrey, 4 Lady Emma Hamilton, 5 Matterhorn, 6 Linguistics, 7 Rudyard Kipling, 8 Rice, 9 Peter the Great, 10 Manx cat, 11 Sir Peter Hall, 12 Inhibitor, 13 Roddy McDowall, 14 Sutton Hoo, 15 St Leger, 16 River Nene, 17 Giuseppe Verdi, 18 Yves Saint-Laurent, 19 Newgate 20 Dombey and Son.*

THE TRIVIA QUIZ BOOK

 *General Knowledge*

Your rating: ● 0-5   Join a library   ● 6-10   Keep at it
            ● 11-15   Join a quiz team   ● 16-20   Join Mensa

1. Which European country was ruled by António de Oliveira Salazar from 1932 to 1968?
2. What name is given to the season of the church year that begins on the Sunday nearest to Saint Andrew's Day?
3. Which British author wrote the novels *Animal Farm* and *Nineteen Eighty-Four*?
4. What is Disney's full-length animated film set in Imperial China called?
5. In which county is the royal residence Sandringham House?
6. Which region of the U.S.A. comprises the states of Maine, New Hampshire, Vermont, Massachusetts, Rhode Island and Connecticut?
7. For which party was Robert Maxwell an MP from 1964-70?
8. On what date is Armistice Day celebrated?
9. Which five-line form of comic verse was popularised by Edward Lear in the 19th century?
10. Of which African country is Accra the capital?
11. Which Australian tennis player won the men's singles at Wimbledon in 1967, 1970 and 1971?
12. What is the brightest star in the constellation Orion?
13. Which former Chilean dictator was arrested in London in 1998?
14. By what name was American-born Nazi propagandist William Joyce known?
15. Which astronomical unit of distance is greater, a parsec or a light year?
16. What is the capital of Malawi?
17. What does the acronym O.P.E.C. stand for?
18. Which Carthaginian general was the father of Hannibal?
19. Of which Canadian province is Winnipeg the capital?
20. Which Shakespeare play features the characters Mercutio and Tybalt?

ANSWERS: *1 Portugal, 2 Advent, 3 George Orwell, 4 Mulan, 5 New England, 6 Norfolk, 7 Labour, 8 November 11, 9 Limerick, 10 Ghana, 11 John Newcombe, 12 Rigel, 13 General Augusto Pinochet, 14 Lord Haw-Haw, 15 A parsec, 16 Lilongwe, 17 Organisation of Petroleum-Exporting Countries, 18 Hamilcar Barca, 19 Manitoba, 20 Romeo and Juliet.*

Entertainment

Your rating:	● 0-5	Buy a TV	● 6-10	Keep at it
	● 11-15	Join a quiz team	● 16-20	Enter a quiz show

1. Who hosted the TV show *That's Life*?
2. Whose greatest hits featured on the 1999 album *All the Way... A Decade of Song*?
3. Which actress played Burt Reynolds' psychiatrist in the 1983 film *The Man Who Loved Women*?
4. Which seaside town was the setting for the second series of ITV's *Grafters*?
5. Which Irish band had a 1999 hit with *Radio*?
6. Who presented BBC 1's *Holiday Guides 99*?
7. What was the title of U.S. singer/songwriter Beck's eighth album, released in 1999?
8. Which ITV comedy-drama series about the life and loves of an office worker featured Letitia Dean and Gwyneth Strong?
9. Which 1962 film starred Kirk Douglas as a misfit cowboy and Walter Matthau as a sheriff?
10. Which 1960s TV anthology of science-fiction thrillers was created by Leslie Stevens?
11. With whom did Queen collaborate on the 1981 number one hit *Under Pressure*?
12. Which Channel 4 sitcom about a group of under-achieving twenty-somethings starred Tommy Tiernan as video store employee Ed Hewitt?
13. Which 1999 film starred Claire Danes and Kate Beckinsale as two girls wrongly accused of drug smuggling in Thailand?
14. In which 1999 BBC 1 series did an investigative journalist reveal some shocking realities of the fashion world?
15. Which 1981 film pitched Sylvester Stallone, as a New York cop, against Rutger Hauer, as a murderous terrorist?
16. Which actor starred as Neil Byrne, a convicted murderer who escapes from custody, in the ITV drama series *Extremely Dangerous*?
17. Which UK group had a 1973 number one hit with *See My Baby Jive*?
18. Which 1999 Ron Howard film starred Matthew McConaughey, Woody Harrelson and Elizabeth Hurley?
19. Which 1970s U.S. series featured David Cassidy as one of the five singing children of a widowed mother?
20. Which Liverpool band released an album entitled *Tilt* in 1999?

ANSWERS: 1 *Esther Rantzen*, 2 *Celine Dion*, 3 *Julie Andrews*, 4 *Brighton*, 5 *The Corrs*, 6 *Craig Doyle*, 7 *Midnite Vultures*, 8 *Lucy Sullivan is Getting Married*, 9 *Lonely Are the Brave*, 10 *The Outer Limits*, 11 *David Bowie*, 12 *small potatoes*, 13 *Brokedown Palace*, 14 *MacIntyre Undercover*, 15 *Nighthawks*, 16 *Sean Bean*, 17 *Wizzard*, 18 *EDTV*, 19 *The Partridge Family*, 20 *Lightning Seeds*.

 *General Knowledge*

1. Which Dutch artist painted *The Anatomy Lesson of Dr Tulp* and *The Night Watch*?
2. Who succeeded Michael Foot as leader of the Labour Party in 1983?
3. Which footballer starred in the film *Lock, Stock and Two Smoking Barrels*?
4. With which meat is mint sauce traditionally served?
5. Which reclusive American author is best known for his novel *The Catcher in the Rye*?
6. In which U.S. state is the city of San Diego?
7. Which New Testament apostle was martyred on an X-shaped cross?
8. What substance is dissolved in water and fermented to make the alcoholic drink mead?
9. Which two Northern Ireland politicians were awarded the Nobel Peace Prize in 1998?
10. What name is given to the stiffening of a body after death?
11. Which Hungarian composer wrote *Duke Bluebeard's Castle* and *The Miraculous Mandarin*?
12. Who was the Greek goddess of war and wisdom?
13. Which channel separates the Orkney Islands from the mainland of Scotland?
14. What is the brightest star in the constellation Ursa Minor?
15. Which country was formerly known as the Malagasy Republic?
16. To which genus of bushes and trees does the lilac belong?
17. In which country was British ballet dancer and teacher Dame Marie Rambert born?
18. What was American jazz pianist and band leader Count Basie's first name?
19. Which actress found fame late in life playing Miss Marple on TV?
20. What is the official language of the principality of Liechtenstein?

 *General Knowledge*

Your rating: ● 0-5   Join a library   ● 6-10   Keep at it
                ● 11-15   Join a quiz team   ● 16-20   Join Mensa

1. Which French sculptor is famous for works such as *The Burghers of Calais*, *The Kiss* and *The Thinker*?
2. Of which ancient country was Hatshepsut queen?
3. Which adult male singing voice is lower than tenor and higher than bass?
4. Celebrations marking the 40th anniversary of which children's TV programme were marred by the sacking of one of its presenters?
5. Which defensive fortification in China is approximately 1500 miles long?
6. What does the abbreviation R.N.L.I. stand for?
7. Which Test cricket team was captained by Viv Richards?
8. What name is given to gnawing mammals such as rats, mice, squirrels and beavers?
9. Which Turkish city was formerly known as Byzantium and Constantinople?
10. To whom was Anne Hathaway married?
11. In Greek mythology, what was the name of Odysseus's wife who remained faithful during his long absence?
12. From which former province of Spain did Cervantes's *Don Quixote* come?
13. Which organisation was founded in 1935 to promote conservation of the countryside?
14. On which river does the city of Manchester stand?
15. Which Irish river flows from the Wicklow Mountains to Dublin Bay?
16. Who was the first governor general of India?
17. Which market town and resort in S.W. Cornwall is a seaport for the Scilly Isles?
18. To which French statesman was Père Joseph, the original Éminence Grise, secretary and adviser?
19. Which opera by Wagner was about the legendary son of Parsifal?
20. Which English nun was known as the Maid Of Kent?

 *General Knowledge*

Your rating: ● 0-5   Join a library   ● 6-10   Keep at it
              ● 11-15 Join a quiz team   ● 16-20   Join Mensa

1. Which American sport involves such skills as calf roping and steer wrestling?
2. What is the capital of Greece?
3. Which former Spice Girl was appointed as a Goodwill Ambassador for the U.N. Population Fund?
4. The sulphate of which metallic element is given as a 'meal' to patients before certain X-ray photographs are taken?
5. What was the Roman name for London?
6. In which English county is the town of Basingstoke?
7. What is the world's second largest ocean?
8. Which American composer is famous for his writing partnerships with Lorenz Hart and Oscar Hammerstein II?
9. The Court of Tynwald is the Parliament of which dependency of the British crown?
10. Which scale is commonly used to measure the intensity of earthquakes?
11. Which English jockey was champion on the flat a record 26 times between 1925 and 1953?
12. What name is given to any surgical device used to tie a blood vessel to stop it bleeding?
13. Which Australian batsman gave up the chance to break the world record for a Test innings for the sake of his team in 1998?
14. What is the capital of Equatorial Guinea, formerly known as Santa Isabel?
15. In the Old Testament, who succeeded Moses as leader of the Israelites?
16. Which king of the Franks was the father of Charlemagne?
17. What sort of creature is a rifleman?
18. Who wrote the musical on which the Oscar-winning film *Oliver!* was based?
19. What is the last book of the Old Testament?
20. With what sort of reference book is Peter Mark Roget chiefly associated?

ANSWERS: *1 Rodeo. 2 Athens. 3 Geri Halliwell. 4 Barium. 5 Londinium. 6 Hampshire. 7 Atlantic. 8 Richard Rodgers. 9 Isle of Man. 10 Richter Scale. 11 Sir Gordon Richards. 12 Ligature. 13 Mark Taylor. 14 Malabo. 15 Joshua. 16 Pepin the Short. 17 A bird. 18 Lionel Bart. 19 Malachi. 20 Thesaurus.*

Entertainment

Your rating: ● **0-5**   **Buy a TV**   ● **6-10**   **Keep at it**

               ● **11-15**   **Join a quiz team**   ● **16-20**   **Enter a quiz show**

1. Which actor played *Onegin* in the 1999 British film adaptation?
2. Which singer co-presented the BBC 1 National Lottery show *Red Alert*?
3. Which 1960 film about a group of ex-war buddies starred Rat Pack actors Frank Sinatra, Dean Martin, Sammy Davis Jr. and Peter Lawford?
4. Which *Absolutely Fabulous* star played actress Donna Sinclair in the ITV comedy series *Dr Willoughby*?
5. Which guitarist/composer released an album in 1999 entitled *The Millennium Bell*?
6. Which British actor played the villain Reynard in the 1999 Bond film, *The World Is Not Enough*?
7. Who wrote the 1978 TV series *Pennies from Heaven*, starring Bob Hoskins and Gemma Craven?
8. What was the title of Michael Bolton's 1999 compilation of classic tracks of the 1960s, 1970s and 1980s?
9. Which actor starred as baseball player Lou Gehrig in the 1942 film *The Pride of the Yankees*?
10. Which actor played Captain Frank Beck in the 1999 World War I BBC drama *All the King's Men*?
11. Which U.S. vocalist sang the theme song to the 1995 Bond film *GoldenEye*?
12. Which actor played the astronaut in the 1999 film *The Astronaut's Wife*?
13. Which ITV panel gameshow was presented by comedy duo Mel and Sue?
14. Which actor/singer had a 1956 number one with *Memories Are Made of This*?
15. Which 1982 remake of a 1951 Howard Hawks sci-fi classic starred Kurt Russell as the hero?
16. Which BBC 1 sitcom followed the exploits of the Porter family?
17. What was the UK entry in the 1995 Eurovision Song Contest?
18. In which 1999 film did British actress Samantha Morton play Eva, a country girl in 1958 Somerset?
19. Which 1970s TV series set in a world ruled by primates starred Roddy McDowall?
20. In which 1988 film set against the Russian invasion of Czechoslovakia did Daniel Day Lewis star as Tomas, a top surgeon?

ANSWERS: *1 Ralph Fiennes, 2 Lulu, 3 Ocean's Eleven, 4 Joanna Lumley, 5 Mike Oldfield, 6 Robert Carlyle, 7 Dennis Potter, 8 Timeless Vol. 2, 9 Gary Cooper, 10 David Jason, 11 Tina Turner, 12 Johnny Depp, 13 Casting Couch, 14 Dean Martin, 15 The Thing, 16 2point4 children, 17 Love City Groove, by Love City Groove, 18 Dreaming of Joseph Lees, 19 Planet of the Apes, 20 The Unbearable Lightness of Being.*

 # General Knowledge

1. Which infectious tropical disease is transmitted by the female Anopheles mosquito?
2. What name is given to the protective outer layer of the stems and roots of woody plants?
3. Which Christmas carol concerns the plants *Ilex aquifolium* and *Hedera helix*?
4. What was the former name of Ciudad Bolivar, associated with bitters used to make pink gin?
5. Which French actress starred in the films *And God Created Woman* and *Shalako*?
6. The Knight brothers and Donnie Wahlberg were three of the members of which band?
7. Which battle took place on October 14th, 1066?
8. In which city were the 1948 Summer Olympics held?
9. Which estate in East Sussex is the site of an international festival of opera?
10. By what name was Yugoslav statesman Josip Broz known?
11. Which American actress starred in the films *Birth of a Nation* and *Duel in the Sun*?
12. On which of the Iles de Salut off French Guiana was Alfred Dreyfus imprisoned?
13. Which battle of the English Civil War took place on July 2nd, 1644?
14. What sort of creature is a devil's coach horse?
15. Which Assyrian queen was the legendary founder of Babylon with her husband, Ninus?
16. How many symphonies did Johannes Brahms write?
17. Which British novelist wrote New Grub Street and The Private Papers of Henry Ryecroft?
18. What name is shared by the third largest cities in Spain and Venezuela?
19. Who was chief conductor of the London Promenade Concerts from 1957 to 1967?
20. Which nonmetallic element has the symbol I?

 # General Knowledge

Your rating: ● **0-5** Join a library ● **6-10** Keep at it
● **11-15** Join a quiz team ● **16-20** Join Mensa

1. Which Warwickshire market town was the birthplace of William Shakespeare?
2. Who was the Roman god of war, identified with the Greek Ares?
3. Which actor provided the voice for Chip Hazard in the film *Small Soldiers*?
4. What name is given to the ninth month of the Muslim year?
5. Which tuned percussion instrument takes its name from the German for bell play?
6. What sort of antibiotic was first isolated by Sir Alexander Fleming?
7. Which U.S. state was founded by English Quaker William Penn?
8. What is the central colour of a rainbow?
9. Which French city is a meeting place for the European Parliament?
10. What name is given to animals such as kangaroos, wallabies, bandicoots and opossums?
11. Which Russian composer wrote the operas *A Life for the Tsar* and *Russlan and Ludmilla*?
12. What part of the body consists of the duodenum, the jejunum and the ileum?
13. What percentage of agricultural produce or income was payable as a tithe?
14. By what name was Venetian painter Jacopo Robusti known?
15. Which famous Welsh poet had the middle name Marlais?
16. What was the popular name for Ronald Reagan's Strategic Defense Initiative?
17. What name is given to the burial place of Egyptian pharaohs such as Tutankhamen near Thebes?
18. Which Romanian-born French dramatist wrote *The Bald Prima Donna* and *Rhinoceros*?
19. What is the fifth book of the Old Testament?
20. In Norse mythology, in which great hall of Asgard do warriors slain in battle feast with Odin?

ANSWERS: 1 *Stratford-on-Avon.* **2** *Mars.* **3** *Tommy Lee Jones.* **4** *Ramadan.* **5** *Glockenspiel.* **6** *Penicillin.* **7** *Pennsylvania.* **8** *Green.* **9** *Strasbourg.* **10** *Marsupials.* **11** *Mikhail Glinka.* **12** *Small intestine.* **13** *Ten per cent.* **14** *Tintoretto.* **15** *Dylan Thomas.* **16** *Star Wars.* **17** *Valley of the Kings.* **18** *Eugene Ionesco.* **19** *Deuteronomy.* **20** *Valhalla.*

 *General Knowledge*

1. Which composer wrote the ballets *The Firebird* and *The Rite of Spring*?
2. What name was given to the policy of increased openness in the Soviet Union introduced by Mikhail Gorbachev in 1986?
3. Of which small European country is Valletta the capital?
4. Who replaced George Graham as manager of Leeds United?
5. Which flightless black-and-white bird has emperor and fairy varieties?
6. What is the capital of Bosnia and Hercegovina?
7. In what year did the Titanic sink?
8. Which mountain chain is known as the backbone of England?
9. What is the largest city in Scotland?
10. Which Shakespeare play features the characters Polonius and Ophelia?
11. Which German composer wrote the operas *Salome*, *Elektra* and *Der Rosenkavalier*?
12. In Greek mythology, by what name were the giant children of Uranus and Gaea known?
13. Which film set in the glam rock era featured Ewan McGregor and Eddie Izzard?
14. What can a corundum gem of any colour except red be called?
15. Which famous ballet dancer and choreographer was born Edris Stannus?
16. Of which U.S. state is Des Moines the capital?
17. What is the name of the American horse-breaker who inspired the book *The Horse Whisperer*?
18. Which eye disease is marked by increased pressure within the eye?
19. Which American actress starred in *Kramer vs Kramer* and *Out of Africa*?
20. What is a weight on a pendulum or plumb line called?

ANSWERS: 1 *Igor Stravinsky*, 2 *Glasnost*, 3 *Malta*, 4 *David O'Leary*, 5 *Penguin*, 6 *Sarajevo*, 7 *1912*, 8 *The Pennines*, 9 *Glasgow*, 10 *Hamlet*, 11 *Richard Strauss*, 12 *Titans*, 13 *Velvet Goldmine*, 14 *Sapphire*, 15 *Dame Ninette de Valois*, 16 *Iowa*, 17 *Monty Roberts*, 18 *Glaucoma*, 19 *Meryl Streep*, 20 *A bob*.

Entertainment

Your rating: ● 0-5 Buy a TV ● 6-10 Keep at it
● 11-15 Join a quiz team ● 16-20 Enter a quiz show

1. Which 1999 BBC 1 drama about a group of British soldiers sent to Bosnia in 1992 on a peacekeeping mission starred Ioan Gruffudd?
2. Which U.S. singer/songwriter released an album entitled *Live From Central Park* in 1999?
3. Which *The Bill* character battled alcohol addiction in 1999?
4. Which actress played Mrs Heidelberg in the 1999 film *The Clandestine Marriage*?
5. Which British vocalist released an album of *Songs From the Last Century* in 1999?
6. Which former model presented Channel 5's action-adventure gameshow *Fort Boyard*?
7. Which 1991 film starred Michael J. Fox as an actor researching the role of a tough street cop?
8. Which 1960s series starred Kathleen Harrison as a cockney charwoman who inherits an industrial empire?
9. What was the title of the 1963 number one hit for Billy J. Kramer and the Dakotas?
10. Which 1999 film starred Rik Mayall and Ade Edmondson as the manager and bellboy of a hotel?
11. Which comedian starred as Bren in the BBC 1 series *dinnerladies*?
12. Which UK group had a top five hit with *Question* in 1970?
13. Which 1992 film starred Jack Warden and Bob Hoskins as father and son?
14. Which *Casualty* spin-off starred Michael French as Nick Jordan?
15. Which U.S. vocal group were *Lost in Music* in 1979?
16. In which 1999 film did Susan Sarandon and Natalie Portman appear as mother and daughter?
17. Which short-lived 1960s BBC soap opera was set in an expensive block of flats?
18. Who starred as Catholic priest Father Rivard in the 1979 film *The Runner Stumbles*?
19. Which comedian replaced Rory McGrath as presenter of BBC 1's *Commercial Breakdown*?
20. In 1999, which U.S. rock band released an album of tracks from their *Live Era '87-'93*?

 # General Knowledge

1. Which British explorer is traditionally credited with introducing the potato to Europe?
2. What name is given to the promontory made up of hexagonal basaltic columns on the coast of Antrim in Northern Ireland?
3. Which singer and actress starred in *Funny Girl* and *The Way We Were*?
4. What was the name of the London restaurant launched by supermodels Claudia Schiffer, Naomi Campbell and Elle Macpherson?
5. Which coastal village in Cornwall has the ruins of a castle reputed to be the court of King Arthur?
6. Who wrote *The Children of the New Forest*?
7. Which king was overthrown in the so-called Glorious Revolution?
8. Which Scottish glen was the site of the massacre of the MacDonalds by the Campbells and the English in 1692?
9. What name is given to any memorial to the dead that does not contain a body, of which there is a famous example in Whitehall?
10. Which Irish-American dancer and choreographer came to fame in *Riverdance* and *Lord of the Dance*?
11. On which river does the city of Gloucester stand?
12. From the roots of which tropical American plant is the pudding ingredient tapioca obtained?
13. Which British novelist and screenwriter wrote *The Mask of Dimitrios*?
14. What was the name of the royal dynasty of France from 1328 to 1589?
15. Which Welsh rebel against Henry IV controlled most of Wales by 1404?
16. Between which two South American countries is Lake Titicaca?
17. Which Australian cricketer had a Test match batting average of 99.94 runs?
18. Which small fast warships are used primarily for antisubmarine warfare and convoy work?
19. Which Shakespeare play features the characters Petruchio and Katherine?
20. Which Scottish group recorded the album *The Man Who*?

THE TRIVIA QUIZ BOOK

(?) *General Knowledge*

Your rating: ● 0-5   Join a library   ● 6-10   Keep at it
              ● 11-15 Join a quiz team   ● 16-20 Join Mensa

1. Which Jewish initiation ceremony takes its name from the Hebrew for son of the commandment?
2. What is the small target ball used in bowls called?
3. Which tree provides the staple diet of koalas?
4. Who was the Welsh Secretary who resigned after admitting to an error of judgement in 1998?
5. Which sugar is also known as dextrose or grape sugar?
6. What name is given to the offence of marrying someone while married to someone else?
7. Which atoll in the Pacific Ocean gave its name to a two-piece bathing costume?
8. What was the nickname of the German World War I pilot Manfred von Richthofen?
9. Which former British liner is a tourist attraction in Long Beach, California?
10. Which extinct elephant had imperial and woolly varieties?
11. Which Swedish dramatist wrote *Miss Julie* and *The Ghost Sonata*?
12. Who became King of Scotland after killing Macbeth in battle?
13. What is the largest of the Solomon Islands?
14. What form of direct action takes its name from an English land agent who clashed with the Land League in Ireland?
15. Which Hungarian composer wrote *Psalmus Hungaricus* and *Háry János*?
16. What is a quetzal?
17. Which variety of cabbage has an enlarged turnip-shaped edible stem?
18. What was the name of the short-lived country formed by the Ibo people in eastern Nigeria in 1967?
19. Which former Stone Roses singer was jailed over an incident on a B.A. flight from Paris to Manchester?
20. What is the capital of Mali?

ANSWERS: 1 *Bar Mitzvah.* **2** *The Jack.* **3** *Eucalyptus.* **4** *Ron Davies.* **5** *Glucose.* **6** *Bigamy.* **7** *Bikini.* **8** *The Red Baron.* **9** *The Queen Mary.* **10** *Mammoth.* **11** *August Strindberg.* **12** *Malcolm III.* **13** *Guadalcanal.* **14** *Boycott.* **15** *Zoltán Kodály.* **16** *A bird.* **17** *Kohlrabi.* **18** *Biafra.* **19** *Ian Brown.* **20** *Bamako.*

 # General Knowledge

Your rating:	● 0-5	Join a library	● 6-10	Keep at it
	● 11-15	Join a quiz team	● 16-20	Join Mensa

1. Which system of writing for the blind developed by a French teacher uses characters made up of raised dots?
2. From which European country does Gruyère cheese come?
3. Which unit of speed is equal to one nautical mile per hour?
4. Of which country is Mount Kosciusko the highest mountain?
5. With which sport are the Queensberry Rules associated?
6. What is the capital of South Korea?
7. Which South African leader of the Black Consciousness movement died in police custody in 1977?
8. In which athletics event did Bob Beamon set a world record in 1968?
9. What do the initials Q.C. stand for?
10. Which pop singer starred in the film *The Man Who Fell to Earth*?
11. Which famous diamond became Crown property in 1849 when Britain annexed the Punjab?
12. Who wrote the 15th-century prose romance *Le Morte d'Arthur*?
13. Which author won the 1998 Booker Prize with his novel *Amsterdam*?
14. Who was the first Formula 1 racing driver to win the world title in a car of his own construction?
15. Which dabbling duck is the ancestor of most domestic breeds of duck?
16. What sort of creature is a krait?
17. Which Oscar-winning Italian director made the films *Bicycle Thieves* and *Shoeshine*?
18. Which archipelago in the Pacific Ocean comprises the Ralik and Ratak island chains?
19. In Greek mythology, what was the name of the wild creatures that were half-man and half-horse?
20. Which small marine crustaceans are the principal food of baleen whales?

ANSWERS: 1 *Braille.* 2 *Switzerland.* 3 *Knot.* 4 *Australia.* 5 *Boxing.* 6 *Seoul.* 7 *Steve Biko.* 8 *Long jump.* 9 *Queen's Counsel.* 10 *David Bowie.* 11 *Koh-i-noor.* 12 *Sir Thomas Malory.* 13 *Ian McEwan.* 14 *Jack Brabham.* 15 *Mallard.* 16 *A snake.* 17 *Vittorio De Sica.* 18 *Marshall Islands.* 19 *Centaurs.* 20 *Krill.*

THE TRIVIA QUIZ BOOK

 # *Entertainment*

Your rating: ● **0-5** Buy a TV ● **6-10** Keep at it
● **11-15** Join a quiz team ● **16-20** Enter a quiz show

1. Which comedy actress played Jonathan's sidekick Maddy Magellan in the BBC 1 series *Jonathan Creek*?
2. In which 1999 film did Arnold Schwarzenegger play an alcoholic bodyguard hired to protect a Wall Street banker possessed by the Devil?
3. Who wrote the novel upon which the 1999 BBC 1 dramatisation *Wives and Daughters* was based?
4. What was the title of the album of Hank Williams tracks released in 1999, but recorded in Nashville between 1949 and 1952?
5. Who was the host of the 1970s variety and chat show *Shut That Door!*?
6. Which 1964 film starred Rock Hudson and Gina Lollobrigida as an estranged married couple?
7. Which actor played Fagin in Alan Bleasdale's 1999 ITV adaptation of Dickens' *Oliver Twist*?
8. Which U.S. vocal group had a 1969 top five hit with *I'm Gonna Make You Love Me*?
9. Which actress played *The Muse* in the 1999 film?
10. Which former Radio 1 DJ presented Channel 4's entertainment show *The Priory* alongside Jamie Theakston?
11. Which U.S. group asked *When Will I See You Again?* in 1974?
12. Which actor played H.G. Wells in the 1980 film *Time After Time*?
13. Which GMTV presenter hosted the ITV series *OK!TV*?
14. Which UK group were *Up the Junction* in 1979?
15. Which 1999 film starred Terence Stamp as a cockney career-criminal avenging the death of his daughter in Los Angeles?
16. Which current affairs show ran from 1956-1978 and was replaced by *TV Eye*?
17. Which actor played Mexican folk hero Pancho Villa in the 1968 film *Villa Rides*?
18. What was the title of Rod Stewart's 1983 number one hit?
19. Which BBC 1 game show series offered the final winner a whole year off work?
20. Which Irish boy band pipped Sir Cliff Richard to the 1999 Christmas number one spot?

 *General Knowledge*

Your rating:	● 0-5	Join a library	● 6-10	Keep at it
	● 11-15	Join a quiz team	● 16-20	Join Mensa

1. Which vehicle was invented by English engineer Sir Christopher Cockerell?
2. In which valley in central Yukon was gold discovered in 1896, leading to a famous gold rush?
3. What is the capital of the Federation of Malaysia?
4. What is the largest province of Canada?
5. Which famous bell in the clock tower of the Houses of Parliament is named after Sir Benjamin Hall?
6. With which musical instrument was Fritz Kreisler chiefly associated?
7. Of which European country is Bilbao a port?
8. Which U.S. novelist wrote the *Uncle Remus* stories featuring Brer Rabbit and Brer Fox?
9. How many frames comprise a game of ten-pin bowling?
10. Which American guitarist and singer who died in 1970 had a hit with *Purple Haze*?
11. Which American civil rights leader founded the Organization of Afro-American Unity?
12. In Greek mythology, who was the daughter of King Priam whose prophecies were not believed?
13. Which German composer wrote the operas *Orfeo ed Euridice* and *Alceste*?
14. Which light metallic element has the symbol Ti?
15. Which king of England was the youngest son of William the Conqueror?
16. What sort of creature is a klipspringer?
17. Which American actress was known as the *It Girl*?
18. What is a koto?
19. Who played the sleazy Governor Stanton in the film *Primary Colors*?
20. Which Jane Austen novel features the character Jane Fairfax?

ANSWERS: *1 Hovercraft. 2 Klondike. 3 Kuala Lumpur. 4 Quebec. 5 Big Ben. 6 Violin. 7 Spain. 8 Joel Chandler Harris. 9 Ten. 10 Jimi Hendrix. 11 Malcolm X. 12 Cassandra. 13 Christoph Gluck. 14 Titanium. 15 Henry I. 16 An antelope. 17 Clara Bow. 18 A Japanese musical instrument. 19 John Travolta. 20 Emma.*

 *General Knowledge*

| Your rating: | ● 0-5 Join a library | ● 6-10 Keep at it |
| | ● 11-15 Join a quiz team | ● 16-20 Join Mensa |

1. Which famous Spanish tenor spent much of his youth in Mexico?
2. Who wrote the music for *Show Boat* and the song *Smoke Gets in Your Eyes*?
3. Which word for the citadel of any Russian city was once synonymous with the Soviet government?
4. What is the largest of the Balearic Islands?
5. Which king of Judaea ordered the Massacre of the Innocents?
6. By what first name is pianist and singer Antoine Domino known?
7. Which Roman Catholic order of friars is known as the Black Friars?
8. What nationality was the surrealist painter René Magritte?
9. Of what sort of fish is the dogfish a small variety?
10. Which Asian country was divided at the 38th parallel after World War II?
11. Which British film producer and director was born Sandor Kellner in Hungary in 1893?
12. What is the name of the Winter Olympics event that combines cross-country skiing and shooting?
13. Which large German howitzer used in World War I was named after the wife of Gustav Krupp von Bohlen und Halbach?
14. Who clinched the 1998 Formula 1 Drivers Championship at Suzuka?
15. Which American science-fiction writer wrote *Fahrenheit 451*?
16. Of which small country in the Indian Ocean is Malé the capital?
17. Which English caricaturist illustrated Charles Dickens's *A Christmas Carol*?
18. Which strait separates the South American mainland from Tierra del Fuego?
19. Who was the legendary lover of Hero who swam across the Hellespont each night?
20. Which of Mahler's symphonies is known as the *Symphony of a Thousand*?

ANSWERS: 1 *Placido Domingo*, 2 *Jerome Kern*, 3 *Kremlin*, 4 *Majorca*, 5 *Herod the Great*, 6 *Fats*, 7 *Dominican*, 8 *Belgian*, 9 *Shark*, 10 *Korea*, 11 *Sir Alexander Korda*, 12 *Biathlon*, 13 *Big Bertha*, 14 *Mika Hakkinen*, 15 *Ray Bradbury*, 16 *The Maldives*, 17 *John Leech*, 18 *Strait of Magellan*, 19 *Leander*, 20 *Eighth*.

THE TRIVIA QUIZ BOOK

 *General Knowledge*

Your rating:	● 0-5	Join a library	● 6-10	Keep at it
	● 11-15	Join a quiz team	● 16-20	Join Mensa

1. Which English composer wrote the *Pomp and Circumstance* Marches?
2. For which powerful opiate is diamorphine the technical name?
3. Which computer-generated animated film features the voices of Woody Allen, Sharon Stone and Gene Hackman?
4. What name is given to the roof of the mouth, divided into soft and hard parts?
5. Which East Sussex village was a former site of the Royal Observatory?
6. How many dominoes are there in a normal set?
7. What were the three gifts brought to Jesus by the Magi?
8. In which country did the Boxer Rebellion take place?
9. What is the administrative centre of Kent?
10. By what name is the large American bird *Meleagris gallopavo* better known?
11. Which British clergyman and economist published his famous *Essay on the Principle of Population* in 1798?
12. What is the first name of Agatha Christie's creation Miss Marple?
13. Of which U.S. state is Augusta the capital?
14. Who was cartoonist who created *Batman*?
15. Which famous battle was fought on July 1 1690?
16. Of which Italian range of mountains is Marmolada the highest peak?
17. Which British king began the tradition of the Christmas Day broadcast from the monarch?
18. Which French actor starred in the films *Love Affair* and *Gaslight*?
19. In which city is the Dome of the Rock?
20. Which composer wrote the oratorio *The Messiah*?

ANSWERS: 1 *Sir Edward Elgar, 2 Heroin, 3 Antz, 4 Palate, 5 Herstmonceux, 6 28, 7 Gold, frankincense and myrrh, 8 China, 9 Maidstone, 10 Turkey, 11 Thomas Malthus, 12 June, 13 Maine, 14 Bob Kane, 15 Battle of the Boyne, 16 Dolomites, 17 George V, 18 Charles Boyer, 19 Jerusalem, 20 George Frederick Handel.*

Entertainment

Your rating:
- 0-5 Buy a TV
- 11-15 Join a quiz team
- 6-10 Keep at it
- 16-20 Enter a quiz show

1. Which actor played *Inspector Gadget* in the live action film version of the cartoon?
2. Who asked the questions on TV's *Mastermind*?
3. Which Spice Girl teamed up with Tin Tin Out for the 1999 hit single *What I Am*?
4. Which Shakespearean role was tackled by Mel Gibson in a 1991 Franco Zeffirelli film?
5. Which actor starred as dad Alex Letts in the Channel 4 drama series *Kid in the Corner*?
6. Which UK duo sang about a *Mad World* in 1982?
7. Which *Friends* actress provided the voice of the mother of the boy who befriends *The Iron Giant* in the animated film?
8. Which London landmark's history was documented by the BBC series *Trouble at the Big Top*?
9. What was the title of Sonia's 1989 number one hit?
10. Which star of 1941's *Birth of the Blues* was the mother of actor Larry Hagman?
11. Which late actor played Harry Clancy in the ITV drama *Four Fathers*?
12. Which UK vocalist had a 1984 top five hit with *I Won't Let the Sun Go Down On Me*?
13. Which Oscar-winning actress played Anna in the film reworking of *The King and I*, *Anna and the King*?
14. Which adult version of TV's *TISWAS* featured the talents of Chris Tarrant?
15. Which role was played by Mary Elizabeth Mastrantonio in the 1991 film *Robin Hood: Prince of Thieves*?
16. In which English city was the ITV docu-soap *Shampoo* set?
17. Which soul/rap act had a top five hit with *Re-Rewind the Crowd Say Bo Selecta*?
18. Which boxer was named *Sports Personality of the Century* at the BBC awards in December 1999?
19. Which film starring Emmanuelle Beart, Catherine Deneuve and John Malkovich was an adaptation of Proust's *Remembrance of Things Past*?
20. Which comic actor played TV host Ben Black in the one-off comedy drama *Sex 'n' Death*?

 *General Knowledge*

Your rating: ● 0-5 Join a library ● 6-10 Keep at it
● 11-15 Join a quiz team ● 16-20 Join Mensa

1. Which actor starred in the films *The Graduate*, *Midnight Cowboy* and *Tootsie*?
2. What was the family name of the French emperor Napoleon I?
3. Which Greek mathematician is said to have run naked through the streets of Syracuse after discovering his famous principle?
4. Which singer had number one hits with *Mistletoe and Wine* and *Saviour's Day*?
5. Which French fashion designer was famous for his New Look?
6. What sort of creature is a Camberwell beauty?
7. Who was crowned Holy Roman Emperor by Pope Leo III in the year 800?
8. Which songbird of the thrush family has an orange-red breast, throat and forehead?
9. Who was the first Christian martyr?
10. How many players are there in a hockey team?
11. Which Swedish city and port is on the Sound opposite Copenhagen?
12. What name is given to the study of ancient organisms from fossil remains?
13. Which English poet's works are collected in the 1648 volume *Hesperides*?
14. Which traditional Christmas decoration is a semiparasitic shrub with white berries that grows on the branches of various trees?
15. Which noble gas discovered by William Ramsay and Morris Travers has the symbol Kr?
16. What is the second largest state of Australia?
17. Which town in Turkey was the birthplace of Saint Paul?
18. On which island are the New York City boroughs of Queens and Brooklyn?
19. Which English political philosopher wrote *Leviathan*?
20. Which American name for Father Christmas is a modification of the German for little Christ child?

ANSWERS: *1 Dustin Hoffman. 2 Bonaparte. 3 Archimedes. 4 Cliff Richard. 5 Christian Dior. 6 A butterfly. 7 Charlemagne. 8 Robin. 9 Saint Stephen. 10 Eleven. 11 Malmö. 12 Palaeontology. 13 Robert Herrick. 14 Mistletoe. 15 Krypton. 16 Queensland. 17 Tarsus. 18 Long Island. 19 Thomas Hobbes. 20 Kriss Kringle.*

THE TRIVIA QUIZ BOOK

 *General Knowledge*

Your rating:	● 0-5	Join a library	● 6-10	Keep at it
	● 11-15	Join a quiz team	● 16-20	Join Mensa

1. Which German revolutionary philosopher and economist wrote *Das Kapital* and co-wrote *The Communist Manifesto*?
2. What was the name of the mission fortress in San Antonio, Texas besieged by Mexican troops led by Santa Anna in 1836?
3. Which Australian state was formerly known as Van Dieman's Land?
4. Which fruit is used to make the sauce traditionally served with turkey?
5. Which American film producer and animator created Mickey Mouse?
6. What sort of creature is Bombay duck?
7. Which Australian medical service began in Cloncurry, Queensland in 1928?
8. What name is given to the area around the North Pole enclosed by the parallel of latitude 66° 32' N?
9. What is the nearest star to Earth?
10. Which organisation is represented by the letters P.L.O.?
11. Which French Protestant reformer wrote *Institutes of the Christian Religion*?
12. What name is given to the grounds between the River Cam and certain Cambridge colleges?
13. Which British mountaineer and explorer led the expedition in which Tenzing Norgay and Edmund Hillary reached the summit of Mount Everest?
14. What is the name of the famous ghost ship seen in bad weather off the Cape of Good Hope?
15. Which unit used to measure the power of a lens is equal to the reciprocal of its focal length in metres?
16. How many calories are there in a calorie?
17. Which yellow nonmetallic element has the symbol S?
18. Which Greek dramatist wrote *Electra* and *The Trojan Women*?
19. What name is given to flowers of the genus *Helianthus*?
20. Which singer had a hit in 1975 with *I Believe in Father Christmas*?

ANSWERS: 1 *Karl Marx*. 2 *The Alamo*. 3 *Tasmania*. 4 *Cranberry*. 5 *Walt Disney*. 6 *A fish*. 7 *Flying Doctor Service*. 8 *Arctic Circle*. 9 *The sun*. 10 *Palestine Liberation Organization*. 11 *John Calvin*. 12 *The Backs*. 13 *John Hunt*. 14 *The Flying Dutchman*. 15 *Dioptre*. 16 *One thousand*. 17 *Sulphur*. 18 *Euripides*. 19 *Sunflowers*. 20 *Greg Lake*.

 *General Knowledge*

Your rating: ● 0-5 Join a library   ● 6-10 Keep at it
              ● 11-15 Join a quiz team   ● 16-20 Join Mensa

1. Which family of comic actors starred in the films *Duck Soup* and *A Night at the Opera*?
2. What is the largest state of the United States of America?
3. Which Labour prime minister was defeated by Margaret Thatcher in the 1979 general election?
4. Which much-married actor and former child star was born Joe Yule?
5. What name is given to an agent that kills germs or prevents them from multiplying?
6. Of which South American country is La Paz the administrative capital?
7. Which English noblewoman was said to have ridden naked through the streets of Coventry?
8. What name is given to the art of handwriting?
9. Which Australian-born actor wrote the autobiography *My Wicked, Wicked Ways*?
10. What is the brightest star in the constellation Boötes?
11. Which Russian tsar was the subject of a play by Pushkin and an opera by Mussorgsky?
12. What sort of creature was a tarpan?
13. Which American golfer won the U.S. Masters in 1951, two years after a car accident?
14. What is the second-largest island of Indonesia?
15. Which city in Ohio is the centre of the U.S. rubber industry?
16. Who was the most important of the Muses in Greek mythology?
17. After which Roman god is January named?
18. By what name was the assassinated tyrannical Roman emperor Gaius Caesar known?
19. Which French New Wave director made the films *A bout de souffle* and *Tout va bien*?
20. What was the former name of Ho Chi Minh City?

ANSWERS: 1 *The Marx Brothers,* 2 *Alaska,* 3 *James Callaghan,* 4 *Mickey Rooney,* 5 *Disinfectant,* 6 *Bolivia,* 7 *Lady Godiva,* 8 *Calligraphy,* 9 *Errol Flynn,* 10 *Arcturus,* 11 *Boris Godunov,* 12 *A wild horse,* 13 *Ben Hogan,* 14 *Sumatra,* 15 *Akron,* 16 *Calliope,* 17 *Janus,* 18 *Caligula,* 19 *Jean-Luc Godard,* 20 *Saigon.*

Entertainment

Your rating: ● **0-5** Buy a TV ● **6-10** Keep at it
● **11-15** Join a quiz team ● **16-20** Enter a quiz show

1. Which John Lennon single was re-released to become a top five hit at Christmas 1999?
2. Which late comic actor played the manager of a small building firm in the 1980s sitcom *Cowboys*?
3. Which British pop group's 1999 Christmas single was *Say You'll Be Mine*?
4. Which 1980 film starred Farrah Fawcett and Kirk Douglas as scientists on a space station?
5. Which U.S. singer had a 1989 top five hit with *This Time I Know It's For Real*?
6. What was the title of the 1999 romantic film by Basque director Julio Medem?
7. Which member of TV's *The Bill* married nurse Jenny Delaney in 1999?
8. What was the Troggs' first UK top five hit, in 1966?
9. Who played top Western star of the 1920s Tom Mix in the 1988 film *Sunset*?
10. Who wrote and directed the film *The Loss of Sexual Innocence*?
11. Which comedian, best known as part of a double act, starred as a ruthless property developer in the 1982 drama series *Muck and Brass*?
12. Which group had a 2000 top ten hit with *Steal My Sunshine*?
13. Which actor played the head of the marauding Nordic army in the 1958 film *The Vikings*?
14. Which *Brookside* character accepted a marriage proposal from Nathan?
15. Which producer of Madonna's *Ray of Light* album released his own *Pieces in a Modern Style* in 2000?
16. Which *Casualty* and *Holby City* actor appeared as David Horton's brother Simon in BBC 1's *The Vicar of Dibley*?
17. Which actor played detective Ichabod Crane in the 2000 Tim Burton film *Sleepy Hollow*?
18. Which late 1970s comedy series about a retiree and his friendship with an eccentric vicar starred Arthur Lowe and John Barron?
19. Which former Boomtown Rat starred as rock star Pink in the 1982 film *Pink Floyd The Wall*?
20. Which TV presenter was the host of BBC 1's *National Lottery Stars* show?

THE TRIVIA QUIZ BOOK

(?) *General Knowledge*

Your rating: ● 0-5 Join a library   ● 6-10 Keep at it
● 11-15 Join a quiz team   ● 16-20 Join Mensa

1. Which American actor starred in *Twelve Angry Men* and *On Golden Pond*?
2. By what name was American-born soprano Maria Anna Kalageropoulos known?
3. Which wooded region of Warwickshire is the setting for Shakespeare's *As You Like It*?
4. What name is given to the pack of 78 cards used for fortune-telling?
5. Which famous Russian ballet company was established in Moscow in the late 18th century?
6. Of which southern U.S. state is Montgomery the capital?
7. Which song traditionally sung at New Year's Eve gatherings is associated with Robert Burns?
8. Who was Queen Victoria's husband?
9. Which Conservative prime minister became the 1st Earl of Beaconsfield?
10. What was the name of Ebenezer Scrooge's late business partner in Dickens's *A Christmas Carol*?
11. Which English cricketer who scored 197 centuries was knighted in 1953?
12. What is the indicator that casts a shadow on a sundial called?
13. What measure of the brightness of stars can be either absolute or apparent?
14. Who was the messenger of the gods in Greek mythology?
15. Which American novelist wrote *Tough Guys Don't Dance*?
16. What is the state capital of California?
17. Which legendary Greek hero of the Trojan War was the son of Telamon?
18. Which British composer wrote the opera *New Year*?
19. Which British city contains the ruins of the Roman city of Verulamium?
20. Of which country in the Middle East is Doha the capital?

ANSWERS: 1 *Henry Fonda,* **2** *Maria Callas,* **3** *Forest of Arden,* **4** *Tarot,* **5** *The Bolshoi,* **6** *Alabama,* **7** *Auld Lang Syne,* **8** *Prince Albert,* **9** *Benjamin Disraeli,* **10** *Jacob Marley,* **11** *Jack Hobbs,* **12** *Gnomon,* **13** *Magnitude,* **14** *Hermes,* **15** *Norman Mailer,* **16** *Sacramento,* **17** *Ajax,* **18** *Sir Michael Tippett,* **19** *St Albans,* **20** *Qatar.*

 *General Knowledge*

1. Which title derived from the Latin Caesar was borne by German emperors until 1917?
2. In Greek mythology, what was the name of the winged horse that sprung from the blood of Medusa?
3. Which BBC sitcom swept the board at the 1998 International Emmy Awards?
4. Of which country is Reykjavik the capital?
5. Which former member of The Beatles recorded *Band on the Run* with his band Wings?
6. What is the largest desert in the world?
7. Which Christian festival is celebrated on January 6th?
8. Which extinct big cat was named from its long curved upper canine teeth?
9. What name was given to a Japanese aircraft crashed deliberately by its pilot into its target?
10. Which *E.R.* actor starred opposite Jennifer Lopez in the film *Out of Sight*?
11. Which French novelist gave his name to pleasure derived from causing or observing pain?
12. What is the acronym of the International Association of Poets, Playwrights, Editors, Essayists and Novelists?
13. Which controversial road finally opened on November 17th, 1998?
14. Of which country was Ne Win president from 1974 to 1981?
15. Which British schoolmaster and dramatist wrote *Ralph Roister Doister*?
16. What sort of creature is a flying fox?
17. Which composer's music is used for the carol *Hark, the Herald Angels Sing*?
18. Which U.S. senator was famous for leading an anti-communist witchhunt?
19. In which London theatre did Lilian Baylis establish an opera and ballet company in the 1930s?
20. Which composer wrote *Orpheus in the Underworld* and *The Tales of Hoffmann*?

ANSWERS: 1 *Kaiser*, 2 *Pegasus*, 3 *The Vicar of Dibley*, 4 *Iceland*, 5 *Paul McCartney*, 6 *The Sahara*, 7 *The Epiphany*, 8 *Sabre-toothed tiger*, 9 *Kamikaze*, 10 *George Clooney*, 11 *Marquis de Sade* (sadism), 12 *PEN*, 13 *Newbury bypass*, 14 *Burma*, 15 *Nicholas Udall*, 16 *A fruit bat*, 17 *Felix Mendelssohn*, 18 *Joseph McCarthy*, 19 *Sadler's Wells*, 20 *Jacques Offenbach*.

 *General Knowledge*

1. Which defensive earthwork along the Welsh border is named after a former King of Mercia?
2. By what name is the scapula better known?
3. What was the pen name of author and mathematician Charles Lutwidge Dodgson?
4. What is the smallest state of the United States?
5. Which Austrian racing driver won the world championship in 1975, 1977 and 1984?
6. Of which African country is Kampala the capital?
7. Of which English county is Shrewsbury the administrative centre?
8. What was the name of the British tribe led by Boudicca or Boadicea?
9. Which British-born South African financier had an African country named after him?
10. In which Scottish town was the Royal and Ancient Golf Club founded in 1754?
11. Which Scottish poet was noted for his memorably bad verse collected in *Poetic Gems*?
12. What is the common name for a corposant, the flamelike electrical discharge that sometimes occurs above ships' masts in stormy weather?
13. Which French novelist wrote *Bonjour Tristesse*?
14. Which two cities were the main combatants in the Peloponnesian War?
15. Which British character actor was married to the actress Elsa Lanchester?
16. What is the S.I. unit of electrical resistance?
17. What is the second largest lake in England?
18. Who was the first president of Mozambique?
19. Which Greek mathematician wrote the important geometry work *Elements*?
20. To which British monarch was Caroline of Ansbach queen?

ANSWERS: *1 Offa's Dyke, 2 Shoulder blade, 3 Lewis Carroll, 4 Rhode Island, 5 Niki Lauda, 6 Uganda, 7 Shropshire, 8 Iceni, 9 Cecil Rhodes, 10 St Andrews, 11 William McGonagall, 12 St Elmo's Fire, 13 Françoise Sagan, 14 Athens and Sparta, 15 Charles Laughton, 16 Ohm, 17 Ullswater, 18 Samora Machel, 19 Euclid, 20 George II.*

Sports

| Your rating: | ● 0-5 | Wooden spoon | ● 6-10 | Bronze medal |
| | ● 11-15 | Silver medal | ● 16-20 | Gold medal |

1. In 1999, which British sprinter became the youngest recipient of a World Athletics Championship medal?
2. Which British motor racing driver was Formula 1 world champion in 1969, 1971 and 1973?
3. Which two countries jointly hosted the Euro 2000 football tournament?
4. In golf, what is the opposite of a slice?
5. Which heavyweight boxer was known as the 'Manassa Mauler'?
6. Which rugby league club signed Steve McNamara from Hull?
7. In which year did Spurs sign Tim Sherwood from Blackburn Rovers?
8. For which county cricket team did Donald Kenyon make a record 589 appearances?
9. How many hoops are used in a game of croquet?
10. In 1989, who became the first man to pass 8ft in the high jump?
11. In 1991, which nation won rugby union's World Cup?
12. Which nation beat West Germany on penalties in the final of the 1976 European championships?
13. At the 1988 Olympics, which U.S. swimmer won five gold medals?
14. Which horse did Michael Hills ride to victory in the 1996 Derby?
15. Which city hosted the 1908 Olympic Games?
16. Which nation knocked the Republic of Ireland football team out of the 1990 World Cup?
17. Which snooker player won his third Masters title in 1997?
18. In 1979, who became the youngest U.S. Open women's champion?
19. In which year did France win football's European championships for the first time?
20. Which golfer's was nicknamed 'Boom Boom'?

ANSWERS: 1 Dwain Chambers, 2 Jackie Stewart, 3 Belgium and the Netherlands, 4 A hook, 5 Jack Dempsey, 6 Bradford Bulls, 7 1999, 8 Worcestershire, 9 Six, 10 Javier Sotomayor, 11 Australia, 12 Czechoslovakia, 13 Matt Biondi, 14 Shaunii, 15 London, 16 Italy, 17 Steve Davis, 18 Tracy Austin, 19 1984, 20 Fred Couples.

THE TRIVIA QUIZ BOOK

(?) General Knowledge

Your rating:	● 0-5	Join a library	● 6-10	Keep at it
	● 11-15	Join a quiz team	● 16-20	Join Mensa

1. Which British novelist wrote *A Town Like Alice* and *On The Beach*?
2. By what name are members of the Society of Friends commonly known?
3. Which Tottenham Hotspur player captained England in their friendly against the Czech Republic in 1998?
4. In which English county is the New Forest?
5. Which large breed of working dog, used for mountain rescue, takes its name from a Hospice in the Swiss Alps?
6. What sort of creature is a macaque?
7. By what name was Brazilian footballer Edson Arantes do Nascimento known?
8. Which zodiac sign is also known as the Archer?
9. What name is given to the day before Ash Wednesday, popularly called Pancake Day?
10. What is the Scottish name for New Year's Eve?
11. What name is given to algebraic equations in which the greatest power of a variable is two?
12. The legendary abduction of which women by Roman settlers is a favourite theme in the history of art?
13. Which boxer defeated Simona Lukic in the first women's professional contest under the jurisdiction of the British Boxing Board of Control?
14. Of which Canadian province is St John's the capital?
15. Which British author wrote *Dangerous Ages* and *The Towers of Trebizond*?
16. What is the largest island of the Bismarck Archipelago?
17. Which Italian political theorist wrote *The Prince*?
18. On what date is the feast of Saint Nicholas?
19. Which Charles Dickens novel features the character Thomas Gradgrind?
20. Which American guitarist recorded the album *Hot Rats*?

ANSWERS: 1 *Nevil Shute.* **2** *Quakers.* **3** *Sol Campbell.* **4** *Hampshire.* **5** *St Bernard.* **6** *A monkey.* **7** *Pelé.* **8** *Sagittarius.* **9** *Shrove Tuesday.* **10** *Hogmanay.* **11** *Quadratic equations.* **12** *Sabine women.* **13** *Jane Couch.* **14** *Newfoundland.* **15** *Dame Rose Macaulay.* **16** *New Britain.* **17** *Niccolò Machiavelli.* **18** *December 6th.* **19** *Hard Times.* **20** *Frank Zappa.*

 # General Knowledge

Your rating: ● 0-5   Join a library   ● 6-10   Keep at it
               ● 11-15 Join a quiz team   ● 16-20 Join Mensa

1. Which American tennis player defeated Bjorn Borg in the 1981 men's singles final at Wimbledon?
2. By what name was Arthur Stanley Jefferson known as the comic partner of Oliver Hardy?
3. Which American general was famous for vowing 'I shall return'?
4. By what name is Lady Haden-Guest better known as a Hollywood actress?
5. What nationality was the composer Jean Sibelius?
6. What name is given to the period during which a person or animal suspected of carrying an infectious disease is kept in isolation?
7. Of which U.S. state is Carson City the capital?
8. Which debonair British actor wrote *The Moon's a Balloon* and *Bring on the Empty Horses*?
9. What name is given to the oriental art of paper-folding?
10. In which men's team golf competition do professionals from Europe and the U.S.A. compete every two years?
11. Which diminutive French painter and lithographer led an unconventional life among the music halls and cafes of Montmartre?
12. Who was the Earl of Leicester who summoned a parliament in 1265 and was killed at the Battle of Evesham?
13. Which film was the first to feature the song *White Christmas*?
14. On which Greek island did the poetess Sappho live?
15. Which British dramatist wrote *Rookery Nook*, *Thark* and *The Bed Before Yesterday*?
16. What is the capital of Guyana?
17. Which German composer wrote the cantata *Carmina Burana*?
18. Which British portrait painter was the first president of the Royal Academy of Arts?
19. In ancient Rome, what were thermae?
20. What term was used by Europeans in the Middle Ages to refer to Muslims?

ANSWERS: 1 John McEnroe, 2 Stan Laurel, 3 Douglas MacArthur, 4 Jamie Lee Curtis, 5 Finnish, 6 Quarantine, 7 Nevada, 8 David Niven, 9 Origami, 10 The Ryder Cup, 11 Henri de Toulouse-Lautrec, 12 Simon de Montfort, 13 Holiday Inn, 14 Lesbos, or Lesvos, 15 Ben Travers, 16 Georgetown, 17 Carl Orff, 18 Sir Joshua Reynolds, 19 Public baths, 20 Saracens.

THE TRIVIA QUIZ BOOK

 *General Knowledge*

Your rating: ● 0-5   Join a library   ● 6-10   Keep at it
               ● 11-15   Join a quiz team   ● 16-20   Join Mensa

1. Which gas makes up about 78% of the earth's atmosphere by volume?
2. In which sport do cross-country runners have to find their way using a map and a compass?
3. Which English actress whose films included *Blithe Spirit* and *The VIPs* was famous for playing eccentrics?
4. What was the sequel to the film *Babe* called?
5. Of which European country is Sofia the capital?
6. With which musical instrument was Paul Tortelier associated?
7. Which British political group became the Conservative Party under Robert Peel?
8. What is the largest city in China?
9. What name is given to an instrument used for measuring temperature?
10. In what year did man first land on the moon?
11. Which German physicist originated quantum theory?
12. What was the name of the subject of Petrarch's love sonnets?
13. Which Scottish international striker joined Newcastle United from Everton in 1998?
14. What is the technical name for the muscular tube by which food travels from the mouth to the stomach, also called the gullet?
15. Which French novelist and aviator wrote *The Little Prince*?
16. In which U.S. state is the city of Kalamazoo?
17. By what name is the winter-flowering plant *Helleborus niger* better known?
18. Which Act of 1701 established the Hanoverian succession to the English throne?
19. What sort of creature is a gurnard?
20. Which Thomas Hardy novel features the character Sue Bridehead?

Entertainment

Your rating:	● 0-5	Buy a TV	● 6-10	Keep at it
	● 11-15	Join a quiz team	● 16-20	Enter a quiz show

1. Which song was a hit for both Muriel Smith and Gloria Estefan, over four decades apart?
2. Which 2000 Martin Scorsese film starred Nicolas Cage as Frank, a New York ambulance paramedic?
3. What was the title of Simply Red's first UK number one single?
4. Which 1958 film starred Zsa Zsa Gabor as the rescuer of the officers of a U.S. space ship taken prisoner on Venus?
5. Which U.S. band re-recorded Simon and Garfunkel's 1968 top five hit *Mrs Robinson* in 1992?
6. Who directed the 2000 film *Summer of Sam*?
7. Which British TV comedy writer is normally associated with Ian La Frenais?
8. Which orchestra recorded new adaptations of classical pieces for the 2000 remake of Disney's *Fantasia*?
9. Which 1937 film musical starred Fred Astaire and Ginger Rogers as a ballet dancer and a musical comedy actress who get married?
10. Which comic actor starred as Uriah Heep in the Christmas 1999 BBC 1 adaptation of Dickens's *David Copperfield*?
11. Which Irish singer collaborated with Lonnie Donegan on *Skiffle Sessions*, recorded live in 1998 and released in 2000?
12. Which Oscar-nominated actress played Angela in the 2000 filmic adaptation of the memoir *Angela's Ashes*?
13. In which children's TV show did *The Muppets* originally appear?
14. Which Italian pop trio released the 2000 album *Europop*, featuring their number one hit *Blue (Da Ba Dee)*?
15. Which actress won an Oscar for her portrayal of Blanche DuBois in the 1951 film version of *A Streetcar Named Desire*?
16. Who wrote the story upon which the ITV period drama *The Turn of the Screw* was based?
17. Which song provided a hit for both Robert Palmer and Rod Stewart in the 1980s?
18. In which 2000 thriller did Denzel Washington star as a crippled forensic science expert?
19. Who, along with Michael Parkinson, was the main presenter of BBC 1's 27-hour show *2000 Today*, covering the turn of the millennium?
20. What was the title of the Spice Girls' first number one single?

 *General Knowledge*

Your rating:	● 0-5	Join a library	● 6-10	Keep at it
	● 11-15	Join a quiz team	● 16-20	Join Mensa

1. Which American president resigned as a result of the Watergate scandal?
2. In the Old Testament, which two cities were destroyed by fire and brimstone because of the depravity of their inhabitants?
3. Which art prize was won by Chris Ofili, who uses elephant dung in his work, in 1998?
4. Of which landlocked African country is Kigali the capital?
5. Which Canadian city hosted the 1976 Olympics?
6. What does P.R. stand for in relation to electoral systems?
7. Which plant is Saint Patrick said to have used to explain the Holy Trinity?
8. With which sport were Olga Korbut and Nadia Comaneci associated?
9. What name is given to a self-propelled underwater missile?
10. Who left Manchester United to take over as manager of Blackburn Rovers?
11. Which French Pointillist artist painted *Sunday Afternoon on the Island of the Grande Jatte*?
12. In which South American country does the Orinoco river originate?
13. Which Italian composer wrote the operas *Orfeo* and *The Coronation of Poppea*?
14. By what name was wrestler Martin Ruane better known?
15. Of which island in the Mediterranean Sea is Cagliari the capital?
16. What was the pseudonym of Sir Arthur Thomas Quiller-Couch?
17. Who is the patron saint of sailors?
18. Which ancient Chinese book of divination is also called the *Book of Changes*?
19. What name is given to an integer that is equal to the sum of all its factors except itself?
20. Who was the Conservative leader in the House of Lords who was sacked by William Hague in 1998?

ANSWERS: 1 *Richard Nixon,* **2** *Sodom and Gomorrah,* **3** *Turner Prize,* **4** *Rwanda,* **5** *Montreal,* **6** *Proportional representation,* **7** *Shamrock,* **8** *Gymnastics,* **9** *Torpedo,* **10** *Brian Kidd,* **11** *Georges Seurat,* **12** *Venezuela,* **13** *Claudio Monteverdi,* **14** *Giant Haystacks,* **15** *Sardinia,* **16** *Q,* **17** *Saint Nicholas,* **18** *I Ching,* **19** *Perfect number,* **20** *Viscount Cranborne.*

THE TRIVIA QUIZ BOOK

(?) *General Knowledge*

Your rating:	● 0-5	Join a library	● 6-10	Keep at it
	● 11-15	Join a quiz team	● 16-20	Join Mensa

1. Which British ice-dancers who won gold medals at the 1984 Olympics were famous for their *Barnum* and *Bolero* routines?
2. What was the surname of the French brothers who invented the hot-air balloon?
3. Who wrote *The Two Gentlemen of Verona* and *Love's Labour's Lost*?
4. What activity produces stress levels in men similar to those experienced by fighter pilots in emergency situations according to a study by psychologist Dr David Lewis?
5. Which famous American baseball player was known as the Sultan of Swat?
6. What might be listed in a periodic table?
7. Which famous cycle race was first staged in 1903?
8. What is the largest satellite of the planet Saturn?
9. From which Asian kingdom do Gurkhas come?
10. What is the largest city in Brazil?
11. Which fine French porcelain has been produced in a suburb of Paris since 1756?
12. What name is given to the point in the orbit of the moon at which it is nearest to earth?
13. Which Japanese city hosted the 1972 Winter Olympics?
14. What was the name of Christopher Columbus's flagship?
15. Which American folk singer wrote *This Land is Your Land*?
16. What is the technical term for the windpipe?
17. Who was the guitarist in The Who who wrote the rock opera *Tommy*?
18. What name is given to the hydrated crystalline form of sodium carbonate?
19. Which German printer, traditionally credited with inventing a method of printing with movable metal type, is famous for his 15th-century Bible?
20. Which battle of the Napoleonic Wars took place on 21st October 1805?

ANSWERS: 1 *Jayne Torvill and Christopher Dean*, 2 *Montgolfier*, 3 *William Shakespeare*, 4 *Shopping*, 5 *Babe Ruth*, 6 *Chemical elements*, 7 *Tour de France*, 8 *Titan*, 9 *Nepal*, 10 *São Paulo*, 11 *Sèvres*, 12 *Perigee*, 13 *Sapporo*, 14 *The Santa Maria*, 15 *Woody Guthrie*, 16 *Tracheia*, 17 *Pete Townsend*, 18 *Washing soda*, 19 *Johann Gutenberg*, 20 *Battle of Trafalgar*.

General Knowledge

Your rating: ● 0-5   Join a library   ● 6-10   Keep at it
              ● 11-15   Join a quiz team   ● 16-20   Join Mensa

1.   Which city in Florida is closest to the Walt Disney World complex?
2.   In which country did gymkhanas originate?
3.   What sort of device was patented by Isaac Merrit Singer in 1851?
4.   What was the former name of Zimbabwe?
5.   Which instrument is used in surveying to measure horizontal and vertical angles?
6.   What was the pen name of *Bulldog Drummond* author H. C. McNeile?
7.   Which Ukrainian town was the site of a nuclear reactor explosion in 1986?
8.   In which royal park did the Zoological Society of London open a zoo in the 1820s?
9.   Which Welsh actor buckles his swash in *The Mask of Zorro*?
10. What name is given to vegetarians who will not eat any food of animal origin such as eggs or cheese?
11. Which French singer and actor starred in *Love in the Afternoon* and *Gigi*?
12. Of which European country is Transylvania a part?
13. Which English Restoration dramatist wrote *The Country Wife* and *The Plain Dealer*?
14. Which skin condition is also known as hives and nettle rash?
15. Which British architect laid out Trafalgar Square and St James's Park?
16. What is the brightest star in the constellation Lyra?
17. Which ancient city of Iraq is mentioned in Genesis as Abraham's homeland?
18. What sort of creature is a narwhal?
19. At the foot of which famous mountain is the Swiss ski resort of Zermatt?
20. Which French author wrote the novels *Nana* and *Germinal*?

ANSWERS: 1 Orlando, 2 India, 3 Sewing machine, 4 Rhodesia, 5 Theodolite, 6 Sapper, 7 Chernobyl, 8 Regent's Park, 9 Sir Anthony Hopkins, 10 Vegans, 11 Maurice Chevalier, 12 Romania, 13 William Wycherley, 14 Urticaria, 15 John Nash, 16 Vega, 17 Ur, 2 18 whale, 19 Matterhorn, 20 Emile Zola.

Entertainment

Your rating: ● 0-5   **Buy a TV**   ● 6-10   **Keep at it**
             ● 11-15   **Join a quiz team**   ● 16-20   **Enter a quiz show**

1. Which actress played a model posing as Charles Grodin's wife in the 1979 film *Sunburn*?
2. Which *Brookside* character had a rooftop confrontation with a man she believed drugged and raped her?
3. Which 1963 Searchers number one did C. J. Lewis also have a top five hit with in 1994?
4. Which actor played a former American G.I. trying to find his daughter in Saigon in the 2000 film *Three Seasons*?
5. In the 1970s, which musical quiz was the centrepiece of ITV's *Wednesday Night Out*?
6. Which dance act released an album entitled *The Screen Behind the Mirror* in 2000?
7. Which U.S. general was played by Errol Flynn in the 1941 film *They Died With Their Boots On*?
8. Which *EastEnders* character married Natalie in a 1999 New Year's Eve double wedding ceremony?
9. Who teamed up with fellow TV vet Steve Leonard for the BBC 1 series *Vets in the Wild*?
10. Who was the presenter of ITV's *Better Gardens*?
11. The 2000 album *The Original Labour of Love Collection* contained original tracks which had been covered by which reggae band?
12. In which 2000 film did Robin Williams star as a robot who becomes a human over the course of 200 years?
13. Which comic was the presenter of the short-lived pop music show *Revolver*?
14. Which U.S. soul/hip hop group whose line-up includes producer and multi-instrumentalist Teddy Riley reformed to release a new album in 2000?
15. Which actor played Raymond Chandler's private eye character in the 1969 film *Marlowe*?
16. Which star of former docusoap *The Cruise* hosted BBC 1's *Star for a Night* talent show?
17. In which year did the Beatles hit the number one spot with *Lady Madonna*?
18. Which 2000 film starred Rhys Ifans as a Cockney businessman and Joseph Fiennes as an accountant?
19. Which 2000 Channel 4 series followed the fortunes of a group of people chosen to spend 10 weeks on a desert island?
20. Which U.S. vocalist had a top five hit with *Trapped* in 1985?

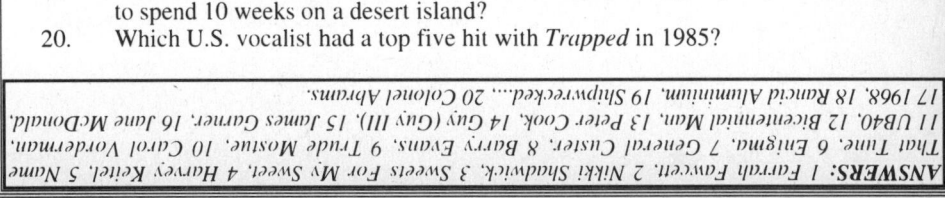

ANSWERS: *1 Farrah Fawcett. 2 Nikki Shadwick. 3 Sweets For My Sweet. 4 Harvey Keitel. 5 Name That Tune. 6 Enigma. 7 General Custer. 8 Barry Evans. 9 Trude Mostue. 10 Carol Vorderman. 11 UB40. 12 Bicentennial Man. 13 Peter Cook. 14 Guy (Guy III). 15 James Garner. 16 June McDonald. 17 1968. 18 Rancid Aluminium. 19 Shipwrecked... 20 Colonel Abrams.*

 # General Knowledge

Your rating:
- 0-5   Join a library
- 11-15   Join a quiz team
- 6-10   Keep at it
- 16-20   Join Mensa

1. Which beautiful youth in Greek mythology fell in love with his own reflection and was turned into a flower?
2. What were the first names of American aviation pioneers the Wright brothers?
3. Which famous story of the French Foreign Legion was written by P. C. Wren?
4. What is the most powerful piece in a game of chess?
5. Which bluish-white metallic element has the symbol Zn?
6. Who was the first Tudor monarch?
7. Which organisation is represented by the initials Y.H.A.?
8. In which country did General Zia ul-Haq lead a military coup in 1977?
9. Which popular musical of the 1930s features *The Lambeth Walk*?
10. What are blood vessels that carry oxygen-depleted blood to the heart called?
11. Which decisive battle of the English Civil War took place on June 14th, 1645?
12. Who wrote *The Day of the Triffids*, *The Kraken Wakes* and *The Midwich Cuckoos*?
13. Which American theatrical impresario was famous for his lavish revues based on the Folies-Bergère?
14. Of which U.S. state is Cheyenne the capital?
15. Which Greek historian and soldier is famous for his *Anabasis*
16. The Vedas are the basic scriptures of which religion?
17. Which grey transition metal has the symbol Zr?
18. Which D H Lawrence novel features the character Tom Brangwen?
19. Which British composer wrote the *Sinfonia Antarctica*, based on his music for the film *Scott of the Antarctic*?
20. Of which mountain range is Mount Narodnaya the highest peak?

ANSWERS: 1 *Narcissus*, 2 *Orville and Wilbur*, 3 *Beau Geste*, 4 *The queen*, 5 *Zinc*, 6 *Henry VII*, 7 *Youth Hostels Association*, 8 *Pakistan*, 9 *Me and My Girl*, 10 *Veins*, 11 *Battle of Naseby*, 12 *John Wyndham*, 13 *Florenz Ziegfeld*, 14 *Wyoming*, 15 *Xenophon*, 16 *Hinduism*, 17 *Zirconium*, 18 *The Rainbow*, 19 *Ralph Vaughan Williams*, 20 *The Urals*.

THE TRIVIA QUIZ BOOK

(?) *General Knowledge*

Your rating:	● 0-5	Join a library	● 6-10	Keep at it
	● 11-15	Join a quiz team	● 16-20	Join Mensa

1. Which essayist and critic collaborated with his sister Mary on *Tales from Shakespeare*?
2. Who was the supreme deity of Greek mythology?
3. For what do the initials NASA stand?
4. Who was the first Australian to win the women's singles at Wimbledon?
5. Which London cathedral contains the epitaph '*Si monumentum requiris, circumspice*,' referring to Sir Christopher Wren?
6. What is the capital of Russia?
7. Which well-known children's story was written by Swiss author Johann Weiss?
8. What do we call the small variety of marrow known as zucchini in America?
9. Who created the fictional barrister Horace Rumpole?
10. Which region of Cumbria was made a national park in 1951?
11. Which American novelist won a Pulitzer Prize for his novel *Rabbit is Rich*?
12. What was the South Dakota site of the last major battle between American Indians and U.S. troops in 1890?
13. What does ... —- ... stand for in morse code?
14. Of which country was Todor Zhivkov head of state?
15. Which English city has the Latin name Eboracum?
16. What sort of creature is a lammergeier?
17. In which U.S. state is Yosemite National Park?
18. Which European country did King Zog flee in 1939?
19. Which animated film features the voices of Val Kilmer, Ralph Fiennes and Sandra Bullock?
20. Which Charles Dickens novel features the character Arthur Clennam?

ANSWERS: 1 *Charles Lamb*, 2 *Zeus*, 3 *National Aeronautics and Space Administration*, 4 *Margaret Court*, 5 *St Paul's*, 6 *Moscow*, 7 *The Swiss Family Robinson*, 8 *Courgette*, 9 *John Mortimer*, 10 *The Lake District*, 11 *John Updike*, 12 *Wounded Knee*, 13 *S.O.S.*, 14 *Bulgaria*, 15 *York*, 16 *A vulture*, 17 *California*, 18 *Albania*, 19 *The Prince of Egypt*, 20 *Little Dorrit*.

 # General Knowledge

Your rating:	● 0-5	Join a library	● 6-10	Keep at it
	● 11-15	Join a quiz team	● 16-20	Join Mensa

1. Which bridge across the River Thames has a central portion which lifts to allow large ships to pass through it into the Pool of London?
2. Who wrote *The Vortex, Hay Fever* and *Blithe Spirit*?
3. What does the abbreviation C.I.A. stand for?
4. Of which Caribbean country was Welsh buccaneer Sir Henry Morgan appointed lieutenant governor in 1674?
5. Which English art gallery houses the Velazquez painting *The Rokeby Venus*?
6. What do the initials Y.M.C.A. stand for?
7. Which officer of the Crown conducts inquests in England and Wales?
8. Which Danish author wrote *The Snow Queen, The Ugly Duckling* and *The Little Mermaid*?
9. What is the highest British decoration for civilian bravery?
10. In which novel by George Du Maurier did the sinister hypnotist Svengali appear?
11. Which French post-impressionist painter was a schoolfriend of author Emile Zola?
12. What is the state capital of Louisiana?
13. What is the largest city in Switzerland?
14. What was the name of the three-headed dog in Greek mythology who guarded the entrance to the underworld?
15. Which Irish dramatist wrote *The Recruiting Officer* and *The Beaux' Stratagem*?
16. In which European country is the city of Uppsala?
17. Which American architect designed the Guggenheim Museum in New York?
18. What relation was Napoleon III to Napoleon I?
19. In which country is the town of Ypres, scene of three major battles of World War I?
20. Which Welsh town is the burial place of Yale University founder Elihu Yale?

ANSWERS: *1 Tower Bridge. 2 Sir Noel Coward. 3 Central Intelligence Agency. 4 Jamaica. 5 The National Gallery. 6 Young Men's Christian Association. 7 Coroner. 8 Hans Christian Andersen. 9 George Cross. 10 Trilby. 11 Paul Cezanne. 12 Baton Rouge. 13 Zurich. 14 Cerberus. 15 George Farquhar. 16 Sweden. 17 Frank Lloyd Wright. 18 Nephew. 19 Belgium. 20 Wrexham.*

Entertainment

Your rating: ● **0-5** Buy a TV ● **6-10** Keep at it
● **11-15** Join a quiz team ● **16-20** Enter a quiz show

1. Which 1948 musical film featured Judy Garland and Gene Kelly and a score by Cole Porter?
2. Which Spice Girl became a celebrity interviewer for a one-off Channel 4 show in 2000?
3. What type of creatures were Zig and Zag, who had a top five hit in 1994 with *Them Girls Them Girls*?
4. Which actress starred as a hairdresser who begins to suffer the tortures of Christ on the cross in the 2000 film *Stigmata*?
5. Which 1970s police drama depicted the tensions caused when Scotland Yard officers are invited to join a northern force as undercover men?
6. Which band released an album in 2000 entitled *In Concert With the London Symphony Orchestra*, recorded at the Royal Albert Hall?
7. Who played Will Scarlett in the 1991 film *Robin Hood - Prince of Thieves*?
8. What was the title of the BBC 1 sitcom set in a vet's surgery by the writer of *Men Behaving Badly*, Simon Nye?
9. What was the title of Primal Scream's sixth album release?
10. Which ITV comedy series starred Brian Conley as P.E. teacher Mr Digby?
11. Which actor played middle-aged rebel Lester Burnham in the 2000 film *American Beauty*?
12. In which 2000 BBC 1 crime thriller did Clive Owen star as a police detective chief inspector battling with both a rare eye virus and a murder case?
13. Which producer and instrumentalist released an album entitled *Metamorphosis* in 2000?
14. Which early 1970s sitcom starred Diana Dors with a northern accent?
15. In which 1980 film did Walter Matthau play a C.I.A. agent who writes a revealing book?
16. Which actress starred as Mrs Bradley in BBC 1's *The Mrs Bradley Mysteries*?
17. What was the title of Russ Abbot's 1984 top ten hit?
18. Which 2000 film, set in Kentucky, featured Nick Nolte, Albert Finney and Sharon Stone?
19. Which BBC 2 drama series featuring the ancient family of Groan was adapted from the gothic novels of Mervyn Peake?
20. Which hirsute U.S. group had a 1984 top ten hit with *Gimme All Your Lovin'*?

ANSWERS: 1 *The Pirate.* 2 *Victoria Beckham (Victoria's Secrets).* 3 *Puppet aliens.* 4 *Patricia Arquette.* 5 *Strangers.* 6 *Deep Purple.* 7 *Christian Slater.* 8 *Beast.* 9 *Exterminator.* 10 *The Grimleys.* 11 *Kevin Spacey.* 12 *Second Sight.* 13 *Jean Michel Jarre.* 14 *Queenie's Castle.* 15 *Hopscotch.* 16 *Diana Rigg.* 17 *Atmosphere.* 18 *Simpatico.* 19 *Gormenghast.* 20 *ZZ Top.*

General Knowledge

Your rating:
- **0-5** Join a library
- **11-15** Join a quiz team
- **6-10** Keep at it
- **16-20** Join Mensa

1. Which German city is the capital of Bavaria?
2. What name is given to an official count of the population that takes place every ten years in the UK?
3. Which five-a-side court game was invented in the United States by James Naismith?
4. Who replaced Barry Norman as the presenter of BBC 1's film review programme?
5. Which British zoologist wrote *The Naked Ape* and *Manwatching*?
6. In which U.S. state is the city of Anchorage?
7. Which district of Wandsworth is famous for its dogs' home and former power station?
8. What name is given to animals such as the gazelle, eland and gnu?
9. Which East Sussex town was the scene of the Battle of Hastings?
10. Of which African country is N'djamena the capital?
11. Which British designer and leader of the Arts and Crafts movement founded the Kelmscott Press in 1890?
12. What name is given to flying mammals of the order *Chiroptera*?
13. Which Portuguese saint is often invoked as a finder of lost property?
14. What does the symbol of a circle with an X across it mean when found on a clothing label?
15. Which two South American countries fought the Chaco War between 1932 and 1935?
16. Bauxite is the principal ore of which metal?
17. Which English poet and dramatist wrote *All For Love* and *Marriage à la Mode*?
18. What name is given to the central point of a heraldic shield?
19. Which former K.G.B. chief was president of the Soviet Union from 1983 to 1984?
20. Which Labour politician was home secretary from 1940 to 1945?

ANSWERS: 1 *Munich.* 2 *Census.* 3 *Basketball.* 4 *Jonathan Ross.* 5 *Desmond Morris.* 6 *Alaska.* 7 *Battersea.* 8 *Antelopes.* 9 *Battle.* 10 *Chad.* 11 *William Morris.* 12 *Bats.* 13 *Saint Anthony of Padua.* 14 *Do not dry clean.* 15 *Bolivia and Paraguay.* 16 *Aluminium.* 17 *John Dryden.* 18 *Fess point.* 19 *Yuri Andropov.* 20 *Herbert Morrison.*

 # General Knowledge

| Your rating: | ● 0-5 | Join a library | ● 6-10 | Keep at it |
| | ● 11-15 | Join a quiz team | ● 16-20 | Join Mensa |

1. Which mountain system in South America extends from Tierra del Fuego to Panama?
2. What name is given to suffocation due to fluid in the air passages?
3. Which Czech tennis player failed a drugs test at Wimbledon in 1998?
4. What was the name of *Don Quixote*'s squire in the novel by Cervantes?
5. Which Paris fortress was stormed on July 14 1789 at the beginning of the French Revolution?
6. Foil, épée and sabre are disciplines in which sport?
7. Fine Gael and Fianna Fáil are the two main political parties in which country?
8. In which novel did H. E. Bates create the Larkin family?
9. Who killed Duncan I, King of the Scots from 1034 to 1040?
10. What is the capital of Turkey?
11. Which German film-maker directed *The Bitter Tears of Petra von Kant*?
12. What name is given to a swelling in the wall of an artery, caused by a weakness?
13. Which French poet wrote *Les Fleurs du Mal*?
14. Which minister borrowed £373,000 from Geoffrey Robinson to purchase a home in Notting Hill?
15. Madame Du Barry was the last mistress of which French king?
16. With which country is the batik technique of dyeing fabrics associated?
17. What sort of creature is a bateleur?
18. Of which country was Fulgencio Batista y Zaldivar dictator?
19. Of which English king was Anne of Bohemia queen?
20. Which channel separates the mainland of Australia from Tasmania?

 *General Knowledge*

Your rating:
- 0-5   Join a library
- 11-15   Join a quiz team
- 6-10   Keep at it
- 16-20   Join Mensa

1. Which former vaudeville comedian and juggler starred in *The Bank Dick* and *My Little Chickadee*?
2. What name is given to the cleansing of fabrics or garments using a solvent other than water?
3. Which English city is famous for its Georgian architecture such as the Royal Crescent?
4. Which British novelist and dramatist wrote *Joseph Andrews* and *Tom Jones*?
5. In which English county are the Clee Hills?
6. Who succeeded Leopold III as King of the Belgians in 1951?
7. Which British racing driver won the world championship in 1976?
8. What name is given to a stone fruit such as a cherry, plum or almond?
9. Which 11th-century embroidered linen strip depicts the Norman conquest of Britain?
10. Which Hollywood actor narrated the 1981 series *Big Jim and the Figaro Club*?
11. What name is given to the legally enforceable right to receive daylight into a building if it has been unobstructed for twenty years?
12. Of which woodwind instrument is the basset horn an example?
13. Which French composer wrote *The Sorcerer's Apprentice*?
14. In which European country is the village of Fatima, a centre of Roman Catholic pilgrimage?
15. Which Indian novelist wrote *Swami and Friends* and *The Man-Eater of Malgudi*?
16. Of which country is Antananarivo the capital?
17. Which noble gas has the symbol Xe?
18. Which Thomas Hardy novel features the character Clem Yeobright?
19. What is Sharon's surname in *Birds of a Feather*?
20. What sort of creature is a ringlet?

ANSWERS: 1 W. C. Fields. 2 Dry cleaning. 3 Bath. 4 Henry Fielding. 5 Shropshire. 6 Baudouin. 7 James Hunt. 8 Drupe. 9 Bayeux Tapestry. 10 Bob Hoskins. 11 Ancient lights. 12 Clarinet. 13 Paul Dukas. 14 Portugal. 15 R. K. Narayan. 16 Madagascar. 17 Xenon. 18 The Return of the Native. 19 Theodopolopodous. 20 A butterfly.

THE TRIVIA QUIZ BOOK

Entertainment

Your rating:
● 0-5   **Buy a TV**   ● 6-10   **Keep at it**
● 11-15   **Join a quiz team**   ● 16-20   **Enter a quiz show**

1. Which actress played Gary Cooper's wife in the 1961 film *The Naked Edge*?
2. Which BBC 1 series aimed to follow the fortunes of a group of volunteers chosen to spend a year on an isolated Hebridean island?
3. What was Elvis Presley's only 1958 U.K. number one hit?
4. Which 2000 film starred Tommy Lee Jones as a parole supervisor?
5. What sort of creature was Hanna-Barbera's *Snagglepuss*?
6. The 2000 album *Tales From New York City* was a compilation of 40 tracks recorded by which U.S. duo?
7. Which actor played the *Thief* in the 1981 film of the same name?
8. Which actress played Euro-Lottery winner Alison Braithwaite in the ITV series *At Home With the Braithwaites*?
9. What was the title of Blondie's live greatest hits collection, released in 2000?
10. Which actor played holiday company boss David Janus in BBC 1's *Sunburn*?
11. Which *Frasier* actor provided the voice of Stinky Pete the Prospector in the 2000 sequel *Toy Story 2*?
12. Which BBC 1 drama series set in a textile factory featured John Simm, Christopher Eccleston and Sarah Lancashire?
13. Which Swedish singer had a 2000 top five hit with *Glorious*?
14. Which *EastEnders* actor formerly made appearances in *Pennies From Heaven*, *The Sweeney* and *The Professionals*?
15. Which 1966 film was directed by John Mills, starred his daughter Hayley, and was co-written by his wife Mary?
16. Which 2000 ITV drama, about the hunt for a serial killer, starred Alun Armstrong as real-life Assistant Chief Constable George Oldfield?
17. Which U.S. rap group had a 1991 hit with *Can I Kick It*?
18. Which Oscar-winning actor played an eccentric millionaire in the 2000 film remake *The House on Haunted Hill*?
19. Which newsreader joined Nick Ross in 2000 as co-presenter of BBC 1's *Crimewatch*?
20. What was the title of U.S. group Deep Blue Something's 1996 number one hit?

ANSWERS: 1 *Deborah Kerr*, 2 *Castaway 2000*, 3 *Jailhouse Rock*, 4 *Double Jeopardy*, 5 *Lion*, 6 *Simon & Garfunkel*, 7 *James Caan*, 8 *Amanda Redman*, 9 *Livid*, 10 *Paul Nicholas*, 11 *Kelsey Grammer*, 12 *Clocking Off*, 13 *Andreas Johnson*, 14 *Tony Caunter* (*Roy Evans*), 15 *Sky West and Crooked*, 16 *This is Personal - The Hunt for the Yorkshire Ripper*, 17 *A Tribe Called Quest*, 18 *Geoffrey Rush*, 19 *Fiona Bruce*, 20 *Breakfast at Tiffany's*.

 *General Knowledge*

Your rating: ● 0-5 Join a library ● 6-10 Keep at it
● 11-15 Join a quiz team ● 16-20 Join Mensa

1. Which American composer wrote the marches *The Stars and Stripes Forever* and *Liberty Bell*?
2. In which famous battle of 1314 did Robert the Bruce defeat the English under Edward II?
3. Which Russian tennis player won the men's singles at the 1999 Australian Open?
4. In which European country are the Cantabrian Mountains?
5. According to legend, which Danish king of England proved his inability to induce the waves to recede?
6. In which novel do the characters William Dobbin and Rawdon Crawley appear?
7. Which English admiral was captain of *HMS Bounty* when its crew mutinied in 1789?
8. Of which island state of the West Indies is Bridgetown the capital?
9. Which star in the constellation Carina is the second brightest in the sky?
10. Which actor won the Cecil B. DeMille Award at the 1966 Golden Globe Awards?
11. Which play by Pedro de Alarcón was the basis of a ballet by Manuel de Falla?
12. What sort of portrait is named after an 18th century French finance minister?
13. Which river rises in Spain and flows to the Atlantic Ocean at Lisbon?
14. Which London-born artist's forenames were Joseph Mallord William?
15. Which Austrian psychiatrist wrote *Totem and Taboo* and *Beyond the Pleasure Principle*?
16. What was the nickname of English king Edmund II?
17. Who played *The Candidate* in the 1972 film?
18. What was the assumed name of French tightrope walker Jean-François Gravelet?
19. Which South African headland was formerly known as the Cape of Storms?
20. What sort of creature is a sitatunga?

ANSWERS: *1 John Philip Sousa, 2 Bannockburn, 3 Yevgeny Kafelnikov, 4 Spain, 5 Canute, or Cnut, 6 Vanity Fair, 7 William Bligh, 8 Barbados, 9 Canopus, 10 Charlton Heston, 11 The Three-Cornered Hat, 12 Silhouette, 13 River Tagus, 14 Turner, 15 Sigmund Freud, 16 Ironside, 17 Robert Redford, 18 Charles Blondin, 19 Cape of Good Hope, 20 An antelope.*

 *General Knowledge*

Your rating:	● 0-5	Join a library	● 6-10	Keep at it
	● 11-15	Join a quiz team	● 16-20	Join Mensa

1. Which silent film comedian starred in *The Navigator*, *The General* and *The Cameraman*?
2. What name is given to a blade that can be attached to the muzzle of a firearm?
3. In which English county is the Forest of Dean?
4. What was the name of the family in the sitcom *Bless This House*?
5. Which channel separates the island of Anglesey from the Welsh mainland?
6. What sort of creature is a shrike?
7. Which men's athletics competition consists of ten events over two days?
8. With which German composer is the Bavarian town of Bayreuth associated?
9. Who wrote *The Spy Who Came in from the Cold* and *A Perfect Spy*?
10. Mount Kosciusko is the highest peak of which continent?
11. Which popular children's book was written by German author Erich Kastner?
12. Against which disease did Edward Jenner develop the first effective vaccine?
13. Which British novelist wrote *The Cloister and the Hearth*?
14. December 10, 1938, was the first day of shooting of which epic film?
15. Which British poet wrote *Queen Mab* and *Prometheus Unbound*?
16. Who was the first Archbishop of Canterbury?
17. Which American science-fiction writer founded the Church of Scientology?
18. Which village in West Yorkshire is the home of the Brontë sisters?
19. Which former prime minister was made a Companion of Honour in the 1999 New Year Honours list?
20. Who choreographed the dances for *The King and I*, *West Side Story* and *Fiddler on the Roof*?

ANSWERS: 1 *Buster Keaton*, 2 *Bayonet*, 3 *Gloucestershire*, 4 *The Abbotts*, 5 *Menai Strait*, 6 *A bird*, 7 *Decathlon*, 8 *Richard Wagner*, 9 *John Le Carré*, 10 *Australia*, 11 *Emil and the Detectives*, 12 *Smallpox*, 13 *Charles Reade*, 14 *Gone with the Wind*, 15 *Percy Bysshe Shelley*, 16 *St Augustine*, 17 *L Ron Hubbard*, 18 *Haworth*, 19 *John Major*, 20 *Jerome Robbins*.

 *General Knowledge*

Your rating: ● 0-5   Join a library   ● 6-10   Keep at it
              ● 11-15 Join a quiz team   ● 16-20 Join Mensa

1. Which of the knights of the Round Table had an adulterous affair with Guinevere?
2. What is the largest island in the Mediterranean Sea?
3. In which city in Texas was John F Kennedy assassinated?
4. About whom is the 1998 film *The General*?
5. Which American novelist wrote *Moby Dick* and *Billy Budd*?
6. In which country are the Snowy Mountains?
7. Which British ornithologist and wildlife painter was the son of a famous explorer?
8. Of which American state is Memphis the largest city?
9. In which year did artist Henri Matisse die?
10. Which unit used to express sound intensity is one tenth of a bel?
11. Which Russian composer wrote the operas *The Snow Maiden* and *The Golden Cockerel*?
12. What name is given to the courts held by Judge Jeffreys following Monmouth's Rebellion?
13. Which British poet wrote *On First Looking into Chapman's Homer*?
14. Who starred as Peter Mayle in the TV drama *A Year In Provence*?
15. Agate, jasper and onyx are varieties of what form of quartz?
16. Who wrote *The Wonderful Wizard of Oz*?
17. Which rocket launcher takes its name from a musical instrument played by American comedian Bob Burns?
18. In what year did Princess Anne marry Lieutenant Mark Phillips?
19. On which bay is the Spanish seaside resort of Santander?
20. Which Austrian composer wrote the lieder *Death and the Maiden* and *The Trout*?

ANSWERS: *1 Sir Lancelot, 2 Sicily, 3 Dallas, 4 Martin Cahill, 5 Herman Melville, 6 Australia, 7 Sir Peter Scott, 8 Tennessee, 9 1954, 10 Decibel, 11 Nikolai Rimsky-Korsakov, 12 Bloody Assizes, 13 John Keats, 14 John Thaw, 15 Chalcedony, 16 L Frank Baum, 17 Bazooka, 18 1973, 19 Bay of Biscay, 20 Franz Schubert.*

Entertainment

Your rating: ● 0-5   **Buy a TV**   ● 6-10   **Keep at it**
               ● 11-15   **Join a quiz team**   ● 16-20   **Enter a quiz show**

1. Which Hollywood duo starred in the title roles of the 1939 film *The Story of Vernon and Irene Castle*?
2. Which *Coronation Street* character became Mrs Kevin Webster in 2000?
3. What was the title of Celine Dion's first U.K. number one hit, in 1994?
4. Which 2000 British comedy film, by *Twin Town* director Kevin Allen, is about a Glaswegian hairdresser struggling to enter an international competition?
5. Which actress is known for her roles as Doris Luke in *Crossroads*, Mrs Blewett in *Open All Hours* and Nora Batty in *The Last of the Summer Wine*?
6. Which 1971 John Lennon album was re-packaged and re-released in 2000?
7. Which 1990 film scripted by Harold Pinter starred Rupert Everett and Natasha Richardson as a couple trying to rekindle their romance in Venice?
8. Which 2000 ITV drama was adapted from Catherine Cookson's only thriller novel?
9. Which British soul singer had a 2000 number one hit with *Rise*?
10. Which BBC 1 series featured the work of Trude Mostue and Joe and Emma Inglis?
11. Which 2000 film starred Leonardo DiCaprio as Richard, an American tourist in Thailand?
12. Which Channel 4 medical drama featured Doctors Greene, Corday, Carter and Benton?
13. Which band released their 13th studio album, *Bloodflowers*, in 2000?
14. Which *Coronation Street* character, played by Eileen Derbyshire, has been a regular since 1961?
15. Which actor played Ted Danson's *Dad* in the 1989 film of the same name?
16. Which ex-Spice Girl enjoyed a *World Walkabout* on BBC 1 in 2000?
17. What was the title of Dire Straits' 1985 top five hit?
18. Which English actor played novelist Maurice Bendrix in the 2000 film *The End of the Affair*?
19. Which former *Coronation Street* actress played bank secretary Barbara in the BBC 1 comedy series *The Peter Principle*?
20. With whom did Aretha Franklin duet on the 1987 number one hit *I Knew You Were Waiting (For Me)*?

ANSWERS: 1 *Fred Astaire and Ginger Rogers*, **2** *Alison*, **3** *I Think Twice*, **4** *The Big Tease*, **5** *Kathy Staff*, **6** *Imagine*, **7** *The Comfort of Strangers*, **8** *Catherine Cookson's The Secret*, **9** *Gabrielle*, **10** *Vets in Practice*, **11** *The Beach*, **12** *ER*, **13** *The Cure*, **14** *Emily*, **15** *Jack Lemmon*, **16** *Geri Halliwell*, **17** *Money for Nothing*, **18** *Ralph Fiennes*, **19** *Beverley Callard*, **20** *George Michael*.

General Knowledge

1. Which famous British actor and director was married to Vivien Leigh and Joan Plowright?
2. In the Old Testament, which city was captured by Joshua when its walls fell at the blast of the Israelites' trumpets?
3. Which flamboyant world featherweight boxing champion became an MBE in 1999?
4. What animal was *Ed* in the 1996 film starring Matt LeBlanc?
5. Which British novelist wrote the *Raj Quartet*, which includes *The Jewel in the Crown*?
6. Of which English county is Reading the administrative centre?
7. Which famous battle is known as Custer's last stand?
8. How many pieces does each player have in a game of draughts?
9. What name is given to the temperature at which the solid form of a substance becomes a liquid?
10. What are the names of Shakespeare's *Two Gentlemen of Verona*?
11. Which French composer and member of Les Six wrote the music for the film *The Lavender Hill Mob*?
12. What nationality was the mural painter Diego Rivera?
13. Which battle of the Napoleonic Wars took place on December 2 1805?
14. What is the title of the ninth *Star Trek* film, the third to feature the cast of *The Next Generation*?
15. What nationality was the painter Ando Hiroshige?
16. What were the first names of the first Siamese twins?
17. Which British clergyman, after whom an Oxford college is named, preached a famous sermon which effectively began the Oxford Movement?
18. Who was the third president of the United States and chief author of the Declaration of Independence?
19. Which British dramatist wrote *French Without Tears*?
20. In which ocean is the volcanic Lord Howe Island?

 *General Knowledge*

Your rating: ● 0-5   Join a library   ● 6-10   Keep at it
              ● 11-15 Join a quiz team   ● 16-20   Join Mensa

1. Which British actress and mistress of the future Edward VII was known as the *Jersey Lily*?
2. Which strait separates Chile and Tierra del Fuego?
3. Who wrote *War and Peace*?
4. What is the largest coral reef in the world?
5. Which natural phenomena does a vulcanologist study?
6. Of which U.S. state is Honolulu the capital?
7. Which comic actor starred in the films *I'm All Right, Jack* and *Dr Strangelove*?
8. The Monument in London was designed by Sir Christopher Wren to commemorate which event of 1666?
9. Who played Clark Gable in 1976 film *Gable and Lombard*?
10. In which English county is the resort of Skegness?
11. Which former Nottinghamshire and England fast bowler was at the centre of the bodyline controversy in the 1932-33 Ashes series?
12. What was the name of the state council of ancient Rome?
13. Which 1998 film featured Jane Horrocks, Michael Caine and Ewan McGregor?
14. Sandbach is a market town in which English county?
15. Which British novelist wrote *Strangers and Brothers*?
16. Of which planet is the Great Red Spot a feature?
17. In which imaginary country is Anthony Hope's novel *The Prisoner of Zenda* set?
18. Which Verdi opera was premiered in Florence in May, 1847?
19. What is the SI unit of work or energy?
20. Who was the first Roman emperor?

 *General Knowledge*

Your rating: ● 0-5   Join a library   ● 6-10   Keep at it
              ● 11-15   Join a quiz team   ● 16-20   Join Mensa

1. Which Verdi opera is based on Alexandre Dumas's *La Dame aux Camélias*?
2. What is the title of the spiritual ruler of Tibet?
3. Which Shakespeare play features the characters Regan, Goneril and Cordelia?
4. Who does Liza Minnellli play in 1972 film *Cabaret*?
5. Which famous singer is married to jazz composer and musician Johnny Dankworth?
6. How many red balls are on the table at the start of a game of snooker?
7. Which star of *The Full Monty* became an OBE in 1999?
8. To which drink did the city of Jerez de la Frontera give its name?
9. What was the stage name of Australian soprano Helen Porter Mitchell, after whom a sauce and a type of toast are named?
10. In which year was *Abba - the Movie* released?
11. What was the name of the principal legislative assembly of Russia from 1906 to 1917?
12. Which Cuban runner won the 400m and 800m at the 1976 Olympics?
13. In which country of the Americas is the state of Tabasco?
14. With which German school of design was Walter Gropius associated?
15. Which Indian film director made *Pather Panchali* and *The Chess Players*?
16. For which historic region of Europe is Vlaanderen the Flemish name?
17. Which Cuban bay was invaded by exiles backed by the United States in 1961?
18. Who was Poet Laureate from 1968-72?
19. Which former Master of the King's Musick wrote *The Garden of Fand* and *Tintagel*?
20. Who was the Muse of tragedy in Greek mythology?

Entertainment

Your rating: ● 0-5   **Buy a TV**   ● 6-10   **Keep at it**
● 11-15   **Join a quiz team**   ● 16-20   **Enter a quiz show**

1. In which 1990 film did Nick Nolte play a racist corrupt New York cop?
2. Which *EastEnders* character returned to the show in 2000 to exact his revenge on Steve Owen, played by Martin Kemp?
3. What was the title of Johnny Kidd and the Pirates' 1960 number one hit?
4. Which 2000 film adaptation of a Chekhov play starred Alan Bates and Charlotte Rampling as brother and sister?
5. Which children's programme did Stu Francis become the presenter of in 1980?
6. What was the title of Tracy Chapman's fifth album, released in 2000?
7. Who played *Rasputin the Mad Monk* in the 1966 film?
8. Which BBC 1 drama series featured women's football team the Castlefield Blues?
9. Which Canadian singer released an album of love songs entitled *Both Sides Now* in 2000?
10. Which ex-*Casualty* star played Paul in the ITV drama series *Reach for the Moon*?
11. Which 2000 film by Mike Leigh is an account of a crisis in the careers of light opera partnership Gilbert and Sullivan?
12. Which BBC 1 series scrutinised the work of Bristol's bouncers and doormen?
13. Which 1985 film starred Ethan Hawke and River Phoenix as two young boys who build a spacecraft?
14. Who played Robin of Loxley in the Eighties series *Robin of Sherwood*?
15. What was the title of Cliff Richard's second number one hit, in 1959?
16. In *EastEnders*, what was the name of Beppe Di Marco's estranged wife, who returned in 2000 to see her son?
17. Which U.S. vocal group had a 1978 top ten hit with *More Than a Woman*?
18. Which Channel 5 series about life in modern Britain featured, amongst others, a documentary about a probation officer turned glamour model?
19. Which comic actor played the chairman of a factory's union works committee in the 1959 film *I'm All Right, Jack*?
20. Which BBC 2 series featured the advice of ex-Wall Street financial expert Alvin Hall?

ANSWERS: 1 *Q&A*, **2** *Matthew Rose*, **3** *Shakin' All Over*, **4** *The Cherry Orchard*, **5** *Crackerjack*, **6** *Telling Stories*, **7** *Christopher Lee*, **8** *Playing the Field*, **9** *Joni Mitchell*, **10** *Jonathan Kerrigan*, **11** *Topsy-Turvy*, **12** *Muscle*, **13** *Explorers*, **14** *Michael Praed*, **15** *Travellin' Light*, **16** *Sandra*, **17** *Tavares*, **18** *Family Confidential*, **19** *Peter Sellers*, **20** *Your Money or Your Life*.

 # General Knowledge

Your rating:
- 0-5 Join a library
- 11-15 Join a quiz team
- 6-10 Keep at it
- 16-20 Join Mensa

1. By what name was Russian revolutionary Lev Bronstein known?
2. What type of Spanish music and dance was developed by Andalusian gypsies?
3. Who played Tommy Devon in the 1974 series *The Zoo Gang*?
4. What is the base number of the decimal system?
5. Which British dramatist wrote *Equus* and *Amadeus*?
6. What sort of creature is a jerboa?
7. Which Chicago Bulls basketball star announced his retirement in 1999?
8. In which English county is the village of Tolpuddle, famous for its trade union martyrs?
9. Who composed the music for the ballet *Romeo and Juliet* which was first performed in 1938?
10. Who wrote *The Hobbit* and *The Lord of the Rings*?
11. In Norse mythology, what was the name of the rainbow bridge that linked Asgard with earth, or Midgard?
12. What is the largest city of the Canary Islands?
13. Which English poet is famous for his *Elegy Written in a Country Churchyard*?
14. Drammen is a seaport in which European country?
15. Which purified wax obtained from sheep's wool is used as a base for skin creams and soaps?
16. Which marooned Scottish sailor's adventures inspired Daniel Defoe's novel *Robinson Crusoe*?
17. What is the third highest mountain in the world?
18. Which English-born boxer was world heavyweight champion from 1897-1899?
19. Whose fables include *Asleep with one eye open* and *Crying wolf too often*?
20. Who was the first Astronomer Royal?

ANSWERS: 1 *Leon Trotsky*, 2 *Flamenco*, 3 *John Mills*, 4 *Ten*, 5 *Peter Shaffer*, 6 *A rodent*, 7 *Michael Jordan*, 8 *Dorset*, 9 *Prokofiev*, 10 *J R R Tolkien*, 11 *Bifrost*, 12 *Las Palmas*, 13 *Thomas Gray*, 14 *Norway*, 15 *Lanolin*, 16 *Alexander Selkirk*, 17 *Mount Kangchenjunga*, 18 *Bob Fitzsimmons*, 19 *Aesop*, 20 *John Flamsteed*.

 # General Knowledge

Your rating: ● 0-5 Join a library ● 6-10 Keep at it
● 11-15 Join a quiz team ● 16-20 Join Mensa

1. Which red supergiant is the second largest star in Orion?
2. What is the name of the principal chapel of the Vatican, famous for its ceiling decorated by Michelangelo?
3. Who was television's *The Gaffer*?
4. What is the collective name for Lakes Superior, Michigan, Huron, Erie and Ontario?
5. With which musical instrument was Andrés Segovia associated?
6. What natural phenomena does a seismologist study?
7. Which former Take That star received a record number of nominations for the 1999 Brit Awards?
8. Who played *The Cable Guy* in a 1996 film?
9. Which Italian composer wrote *The Four Seasons*?
10. What is the capital of El Salvador?
11. Which British politician helped to form NATO, as foreign secretary in the postwar Labour government?
12. In which country is the Great Bear Lake?
13. Which American president was defeated in the 1932 election by Franklin D Roosevelt?
14. Painter James Tissot's London house was near which cricket ground?
15. Of which U.S. state is Topeka the capital?
16. What nationality was the operatic soprano Kirsten Flagstad?
17. Which Irish author wrote the novellas *First Love* and *The Expelled*?
18. To what rank in the Royal Navy was The Duke of York promoted in 1999?
19. Which court painter to Henry VIII designed the woodcut series *The Dance of Death*?
20. Of which country is Graz the second largest city?

ANSWERS: 1 *Betelgeuse*. 2 *Sistine Chapel*. 3 *Bill Maynard*. 4 *The Great Lakes*. 5 *Guitar*. 6 *Earthquakes*. 7 *Robbie Williams*. 8 *Jim Carrey*. 9 *Antonio Vivaldi*. 10 *San Salvador*. 11 *Ernest Bevin*. 12 *Canada*. 13 *Herbert Hoover*. 14 *Lord's*. 15 *Kansas*. 16 *Norwegian*. 17 *Samuel Beckett*. 18 *Commander*. 19 *Hans Holbein the Younger*. 20 *Austria*.

General Knowledge

Your rating:	● 0-5	Join a library	● 6-10	Keep at it
	● 11-15	Join a quiz team	● 16-20	Join Mensa

1. In Greek mythology, what was the name of the king whose touch turned everything into gold?
2. Who wrote *The Great Gatsby* and *Tender is the Night*?
3. Which event planned by Prince Albert took place in the Crystal Palace in 1851?
4. Which U.S. author's children's books include *Superfudge*?
5. Which French river flows through Paris to the English channel?
6. What is the capital of the Canadian province of Ontario?
7. Which American president issued the Emancipation Proclamation that freed slaves in the rebellious southern states of the U.S.?
8. What name is given to a long narrow sea inlet lying between steep mountain slopes, especially in Norway?
9. Who originally hosted the TV game show *You Bet!*?
10. Who wrote the novel *Vanity Fair*?
11. Which German philosopher wrote a *Critique of Pure Reason* and a *Critique of Practical Reason*?
12. What was the former name for the nuclear power station, Sellafield?
13. Who painted 1859's *Absinthe Drinker*?
14. The viral disease Lassa fever is named after a village in which African country?
15. Which French novelist wrote *Madame Bovary*?
16. What was jazz composer and pianist Duke Ellington's first name?
17. What name was given to the nationwide campaign to promote economic and industrial growth in China that began in 1958?
18. Which British poet and Jesuit priest wrote *The Wreck of the Deutschland*?
19. What nationality was Halldór Laxness, the 1955 winner of the Nobel prize for literature?
20. Who played *The Abominable Doctor Phibes*?

ANSWERS: 1 *Midas*, **2** *F Scott Fitzgerald*, **3** *The Great Exhibition*, **4** *Judy Blume*, **5** *River Seine*, **6** *Toronto*, **7** *Abraham Lincoln*, **8** *Fjord, or fiord*, **9** *Bruce Forsyth*, **10** *William Makepeace Thackeray*, **11** *Immanuel Kant*, **12** *Windscale*, **13** *Manet*, **14** *Nigeria*, **15** *Gustave Flaubert*, **16** *Edward*, **17** *The Great Leap Forward*, **18** *Gerard Manley Hopkins*, **19** *Icelandic*, **20** *Vincent Price*.

Entertainment

Your rating:	● 0-5	Buy a TV	● 6-10	Keep at it
	● 11-15	Join a quiz team	● 16-20	Enter a quiz show

1. What nationality were the duo Modern Talking, who had a 1986 top five hit with *Brother Louie*?
2. Which comic actor played Vyvyan in the TV comedy series *The Young Ones*?
3. Which Clannad singer released an album in 2000 entitled *Whisper to the Wild Water*?
4. Which *Gone With the Wind* star played an American divorcee in the 1965 film *Ship of Fools*?
5. Which former *Doctor Who* appeared as David in the ITV series *At Home With the Braithwaites*?
6. What was the title of the album released by Oasis in 2000?
7. Which Geordie duo presented the BBC 1 game show *Friends Like These*?
8. Which actor played Tom Ripley in the 2000 film *The Talented Mr Ripley*?
9. Which BBC 1 soap celebrated its 15th birthday in 2000?
10. Which U.S. singer's 2000 debut single was *Caught Out There*, featuring the line "I hate you so much right now!"?
11. What was Margo and Jerry's surname in the comedy series *The Good Life*?
12. In which 1968 film did David Niven and Deborah Kerr star as husband and wife?
13. Which TV presenter and steeplejack conducted a BBC 2 tour of his *Magnificent Monuments*?
14. In which year did Elton John have a number one hit with *Sacrifice*?
15. In which 2000 film did Tom Hanks play a prison warder in charge of Death Row?
16. Which TV doctor was the presenter of BBC 2's *Trust Me, I'm a Doctor*?
17. Which U.S. group had a number one hit in 1964 with *Baby Love*?
18. Which swimming actress starred in the 1955 film *Jupiter's Darling*?
19. In which city's gay community was the Channel 4 sequel *Queer as Folk 2* set?
20. What was the title of Sweet Sensation's only number one hit?

ANSWERS: *1* German, *2* Adrian Edmondson, *3* Maire Brennan, *4* Vivien Leigh, *5* Peter Davison, *6* Standing on the Shoulders of Giants, *7* Ant and Dec, *8* Matt Damon, *9* EastEnders, *10* Kells, *11* Leadbetter, *12* Eye of the Devil, *13* Fred Dibnah, *14* 1990, *15* The Green Mile, *16* Dr Phil Hammond, *17* The Supremes, *18* Esther Williams, *19* Manchester, *20* Sad Sweet Dreamer.

 # General Knowledge

1. Which British novelist wrote *Barchester Towers* and *The Eustace Diamonds*?
2. Who was the mother of Liza Minnelli?
3. Off which English county do the Manacle Rocks, a dangerous reef, lie?
4. What is the lightest gas?
5. Which Scottish hero was proclaimed warden of Scotland in 1297?
6. What is the administrative centre of Suffolk?
7. What is the brightest star in the sky?
8. Who directed the 1976 film *Gator*?
9. Which district of Devon was created by the union of Torquay, Paignton and Brixham?
10. In which town near Jerusalem was Jesus born?
11. Which daughter of Lord Redesdale wrote *Love in a Cold Climate*?
12. What was the stage name of the music hall male impersonator Matilda Alice Powles?
13. Which Russian chess player held the world championship from 1975 to 1985?
14. Who composed the opera *Cosi Fan Tutte*?
15. Which chemical element has the symbol Se?
16. What nationality was the Nobel prize-winning writer Pär Lagerkvist?
17. Which Cambodian communist movement was led by Pol Pot?
18. What was the controversial 1991 book by Bret Easton Ellis recently made into a film?
19. Which Irish prime minister signed the Anglo-Irish Agreement in 1985?
20. What is the capital of Indonesia?

ANSWERS: 1 *Anthony Trollope,* 2 *Judy Garland,* 3 *Cornwall,* 4 *Hydrogen,* 5 *William Wallace,* 6 *Ipswich,* 7 *Sirius, or the Dog Star,* 8 *Burt Reynolds,* 9 *Torbay,* 10 *Bethlehem,* 11 *Nancy Mitford,* 12 *Vesta Tilley,* 13 *Anatoly Karpov,* 14 *Mozart,* 15 *Selenium,* 16 *Swedish,* 17 *Khmer Rouge,* 18 *American Psycho,* 19 *Garret Fitzgerald,* 20 *Jakarta.*

 *General Knowledge*

Your rating: ● 0-5   Join a library   ● 6-10   Keep at it
                ● 11-15 Join a quiz team ● 16-20   Join Mensa

1. Which former electrician in a Polish shipyard was awarded the 1983 Nobel Peace Prize?
2. With which World War II fighter plane is Reginald Mitchell associated?
3. Which British film director made the films *Psycho*, *Notorious* and *The Birds*?
4. Who was the king's jester in the play *Hamlet*?
5. Which English river flows through Newcastle, Gateshead and Jarrow?
6. Of which U.S. state is Jefferson City the capital?
7. Which Greek physician gave his name to an oath taken by medical students?
8. In which country is the city of Tijuana?
9. Who played the title role in the film *Meet Joe Black*?
10. What is the term for a sculpture or painting showing the Virgin Mary supporting the dead Christ on her lap?
11. Which Swiss psychiatrist originated the concept of introvert and extrovert personalities?
12. In what year was the United Nations established?
13. On which river is the motor car manufacturing town of Pontiac?
14. Who wrote *The Autobiography of Alice B Toklas*?
15. Which Queen of the Netherlands abdicated in 1980?
16. What name is given to the French-speaking inhabitants of Belgium?
17. Which American jazz pianist and composer had the nickname Fatha?
18. In radio broadcasting, what does FM stand for?
19. Who was voted Best Actor at the 1954 Golden Globe Awards?
20. Between which two lakes is the Swiss resort of Interlaken?

ANSWERS: 1 *Lech Walesa*, 2 *Spitfire*, 3 *Sir Alfred Hitchcock*, 4 *Yorick*, 5 *River Tyne*, 6 *Missouri*, 7 *Hippocrates*, 8 *Mexico*, 9 *Brad Pitt*, 10 *Pietà*, 11 *Carl Gustav Jung*, 12 *1945*, 13 *Clinton River*, 14 *Gertrude Stein*, 15 *Juliana*, 16 *Walloons*, 17 *Earl Hines*, 18 *Frequency modulation*, 19 *Marlon Brando*, 20 *Thun and Brienz*.

 **General Knowledge**

Your rating: ● 0-5   Join a library   ● 6-10   Keep at it
               ● 11-15 Join a quiz team   ● 16-20   Join Mensa

1. Which French author wrote *Around the World in Eighty Days* and *Journey to the Centre of the Earth*?
2. Which Italian city lies at the foot of Mount Vesuvius opposite ancient Pompeii?
3. Which cricket team gave the West Indies their first ever 5-0 Test series defeat in 1999?
4. What is the largest planet in our solar system?
5. According to Muslims, who was the last of the prophets?
6. In which country was Adolf Hitler born?
7. What is the second largest of the Balearic islands?
8. Which singer plays the Goblin King in the 1986 film *Labyrinth*?
9. What name is given to a wind reaching force 12 on the Beaufort Scale?
10. Which port did Abuja replace as the capital of Nigeria?
11. Which West Indian island is politically divided between the Dominican Republic and Haiti?
12. What is the world's longest railway?
13. What nationality is the conductor Karl Rickenbacher?
14. Jugendstil was the German form of which art movement?
15. Which unit of length is equal to the mean distance between the earth and the sun?
16. What is the second largest city in Pakistan?
17. Who wrote *The Prisoner of Zenda*?
18. Which Australian tennis player won the men's singles at Wimbledon in 1956 and 1957?
19. Who was the first woman MP to sit in the House of Commons?
20. By what name was horror film star William Pratt better known?

ANSWERS: *1 Jules Verne, 2 Naples, 3 South Africa, 4 Jupiter, 5 Mohammed, 6 Austria, 7 Minorca, 8 David Bowie, 9 Hurricane, 10 Lagos, 11 Hispaniola, 12 The Trans-Siberian Railway, 13 Swiss, 14 Art Nouveau, 15 Astronomical unit, 16 Lahore, 17 Anthony Hope, 18 Lew Hoad, 19 Lady Astor, 20 Boris Karloff.*

THE TRIVIA QUIZ BOOK

Entertainment

Your rating:	● 0-5	Buy a TV	● 6-10	Keep at it
	● 11-15	Join a quiz team	● 16-20	Enter a quiz show

1. In which sitcom did Tony Britton and Nigel Havers play father and son doctors Toby and Tom Latimer?
2. Which Scandinavian quartet's second album was entitled *Aquarius*?
3. Which 1950 film featured Humphrey Bogart as an innocent murder suspect?
4. Which 2000 BBC 2 drama followed the fortunes of 17-year-old foster child David in his search for his father?
5. What nationality is Lene Marlin, who had a 2000 top ten hit with *Sitting Down Here*?
6. Who presented the BBC 1 series *The Crime Squad*?
7. Which former *E.R.* star played Major Archie Gates in the 2000 film *Three Kings*?
8. Which comedian, creator of Dennis Pennis, starred as amoral marketing man Bob Slay in the BBC 2 sitcom *Perfect World*?
9. Which U.S. singer had a number one hit in 2000 with a revamped version of Don McLean's *American Pie*?
10. Which *Carry On* star played George opposite Peggy Mount's Gabrielle Dragon in the Sixties sitcom *George and the Dragon*?
11. Which Western star played an Irish big-game catcher in 1962's *Hatari!*?
12. Which comedian replaced Jack Dee as a team captain on the BBC 1 celebrity panel game show *It's Only TV But I Like It*?
13. Which UK group had a 1986 top ten hit with *Calling All the Heroes*?
14. For her performance in which 2000 film did British actress Janet McTeer win a Best Actress Oscar nomination?
15. Which singer had top ten hits in the Sixties with *Hold Me Tight* and *Cupid*?
16. Which 1981 film set in Libya featured Rod Steiger as Mussolini?
17. Which Asian sketch show returned for its third series on BBC 2 in 2000?
18. Which song was a number one hit for Gerry and the Pacemakers in 1963 and, as part of a triple-A side, for Robson and Jerome in 1996?
19. Which U.S. former rapper produced, directed, wrote and acted in the 2000 film sequel *Next Friday*?
20. Which former U.S. TV legal drama featured the law firm McKenzie, Brackman, Chaney and Kuzak?

ANSWERS: 1 *Don't Wait Up*, 2 Aqua, 3 *In a Lonely Place*, 4 *Nature Boy*, 5 Norwegian, 6 Sue Lawley, 7 George Clooney, 8 Paul Kaye, 9 Madonna, 10 Sid James, 11 John Wayne, 12 Phill Jupitus, 13 *It Bites*, 14 *Tumbleweeds*, 15 Johnny Nash, 16 *Lion of the Desert*, 17 *Goodness Gracious Me*, 18 *You'll Never Walk Alone*, 19 Ice Cube, 20 *LA Law*.

 **General Knowledge**

Your rating: ● 0-5   Join a library   ● 6-10   Keep at it
              ● 11-15   Join a quiz team   ● 16-20   Join Mensa

1. On which Manhattan street is the New York Stock Exchange situated?
2. In Greek mythology, which Cretan monster was killed by Theseus?
3. Which Olympic sport was developed from jujitsu by Jigoro Kano?
4. A record-breaking exhibition of paintings by which French Impressionist opened at the Royal Academy in 1999?
5. Which English city is at the mouth of the River Wear?
6. Who succeeded Jeremy Thorpe as leader of the Liberal Party?
7. The Mosquito Coast is an area of which Central American country?
8. Which famous battle in June 1815 ended the Napoleonic Wars?
9. What is the highest number on a British bingo card?
10. Which comedian played Kevin Turvey in the sketch series *A Kick Up the Eighties*?
11. Which British engineer invented the bouncing bombs used to destroy the Ruhr dams in World War II?
12. What name is given to the offspring of a female donkey and a male horse?
13. Which novel by Pierre Choderlos de Laclos features the seducer Valmont?
14. Who played Blott in the 1985 TV comedy serial *Blott on the Landscape*?
15. Which Wiltshire village is the site of Europe's largest stone circle?
16. Of which sea is the Sea of Azov an arm?
17. Which Italian scholar was the author of the Vulgate Bible?
18. Which writer of nonsense verse began as a zoological draughtsman?
19. Which Roman goddess is identified with the Greek Athena?
20. What sort of creature is a tinamou?

ANSWERS: 1 Wall Street. 2 The Minotaur. 3 Judo. 4 Claude Monet. 5 Sunderland. 6 David Steel. 7 Nicaragua. 8 Battle of Waterloo. 9 90. 10 Rik Mayall. 11 Sir Barnes Wallis. 12 Hinny. 13 Les Liaisons dangereuses. 14 David Suchet. 15 Avebury. 16 Black Sea. 17 Saint Jerome. 18 Edward Lear. 19 Minerva. 20 A bird.

THE TRIVIA QUIZ BOOK

 *General Knowledge*

Your rating: ● 0-5   Join a library   ● 6-10   Keep at it
● 11-15 Join a quiz team   ● 16-20 Join Mensa

1. Which Japanese city was largely destroyed by the first atomic bomb used in warfare?
2. After which king is the Authorised Version of the English Bible that appeared in 1611 named?
3. Who directed 1997 film *L.A. Confidential*?
4. Who wrote the Pulitzer Prize-winning novel *Gone with the Wind*?
5. Which British composer is famous for his operatic collaborations with W.S. Gilbert?
6. Of which country was Mohammed Reza Pahlavi shah until 1979?
7. Which metallic element has the chemical symbol Sn?
8. What are the forenames of art duo Proesch and Passmore?
9. Which official of the House of Lords summons MPs to hear the Queen's Speech?
10. In which sport are there styles known as snatch and clean and jerk?
11. Which Austrian conductor was principal conductor of the Berlin Philharmonic from 1955 to 1989?
12. What was the name of the third and favourite wife of Mohammed?
13. Which American author created the detective Mike Hammer?
14. In which island group is Ibiza?
15. What is a sphygmomanometer used to measure?
16. In which U.S. state is Death Valley?
17. Of which country was Achmed Sukarno the first president?
18. Which author's thrillers include *Hornet's Nest* and *Unnatural Exposure*?
19. Which mountain range includes K2, the world's second highest mountain?
20. What name is given to a solution in water of the gas hydrogen chloride?

THE TRIVIA QUIZ BOOK

 *General Knowledge*

| Your rating: | ● 0-5 | Join a library | ● 6-10 | Keep at it |
| | ● 11-15 | Join a quiz team | ● 16-20 | Join Mensa |

1. Which Nahuatl-speaking people ruled an empire in Mexico before their defeat by Hernán Cortés in the 16th century?
2. Which strait connects the Sea of Marmara with the Aegean Sea?
3. Which two actresses play sisters in the film *Practical Magic*?
4. What name was given to the military alliance between the Soviet Union and other East European states signed in 1955?
5. Which British poet, painter and engraver wrote *Jerusalem* and *Songs of Innocence*?
6. By what name is the striped big cat *Panthera tigris* known?
7. On which river does the city of Cologne stand?
8. What was the subtitle of 1995's *Ace Ventura* film?
9. Which British novelist wrote *The Woman in White* and *The Moonstone*?
10. Who stood down as leader of the Liberal Democrats in 1999?
11. Which British philosopher wrote *Language, Truth and Logic* and *The Problem of Knowledge*?
12. What name is given to a solution in water of magnesium hydroxide?
13. Which British actor starred in the films *Lost Horizon* and *Random Harvest*?
14. Which book opens "My desert-island, all-time, top five most memorable split-ups..."?
15. Which British artist was noted for his religious paintings set in his native village of Cookham?
16. What is the capital of Liechtenstein?
17. What was Angus Deayton's character name in the sketch show *KYTV*?
18. Which mythological creature represented by a famous sculpture at Giza had a lion's body and a human head?
19. In Hinduism, what name is given to the sum of one's actions, carried forward from one life to the next?
20. Which 1998 film starred Joseph Fiennes and Gwyneth Paltrow?

ANSWERS: *1 Aztecs, 2 Dardanelles, 3 Sandra Bullock and Nicole Kidman, 4 Warsaw Pact, 5 William Blake, 6 Tiger, 7 River Rhine, 8 When Nature Calls, 9 Wilkie Collins, 10 Paddy Ashdown, 11 A J Ayer, 12 Milk of magnesia, 13 Ronald Colman, 14 High Fidelity by Nick Hornby, 15 Sir Stanley Spencer, 16 Vaduz, 17 Mike Channel, 18 Sphinx, 19 Karma, 20 Shakespeare in Love.*

THE TRIVIA QUIZ BOOK

Entertainment

Your rating: ● 0-5   **Buy a TV**   ● 6-10   **Keep at it**
● 11-15   **Join a quiz team**   ● 16-20   **Enter a quiz show**

1. Which actress from BBC 1's *Casualty* released an album in 2000 entitled *Time Stands Still*?
2. Which 1979 Bond film starring Roger Moore was set in outer space?
3. Which scientist and Labour peer presented *Child of Our Time* in 2000, the first instalment of a BBC project following a group of children over the next 20 years?
4. What was the title of All Saints' 2000 number one hit, taken from the film *The Beach*?
5. Which English actor played Hector MacDonald, Laird of Glenbogle, in the BBC 1 series *Monarch of the Glen*?
6. In which 2000 film did Al Pacino star as TV producer Lowell Bergman?
7. In which Channel 4 comedy series did Sarah Jessica Parker star as New York columnist Carrie Bradshaw?
8. What was the title of U.S. boy band 98°'s second album?
9. Which ex-*EastEnders* star played Danny Kane in the former BBC 1 drama series *The Paradise Club*?
10. In which 1961 film did Ann-Margret play Bette Davis' daughter?
11. Which interior designer featured alongside garden expert Diarmuid Gavin in the BBC 2 home makeover series *Home Front: Inside Out*?
12. Which singer's first hit was *My Coo-Ca-Choo*, which reached number two in 1973?
13. Which actress played *Joan of Arc* in the 2000 Luc Besson film of the same name?
14. Who was the host of BBC 1's *Celebrity Ready, Steady, Cook*?
15. What was the Prodigy's 1991 top five hit?
16. Who played Maggie Smith's lecherous husband in the 1981 film *Quartet*?
17. Which *Coronation Street* teenager discovered she was pregnant in 2000?
18. Which UK group asked *Can You Feel the Force?* in 1979?
19. Which British actor played Harold Smith in the 2000 film *Whatever Happened to Harold Smith??*
20. What were the names of the middle-aged couple played by Julia McKenzie and Anton Rodgers in the sitcoms *Fresh Fields* and *French Fields*?

ANSWERS: 1 *Rebecca Wheatley*, **2** *Moonraker*, **3** *Professor Robert Winston*, **4** *Pure Shores*, **5** *Richard Briers*, **6** *The Insider*, **7** *Sex and the City*, **8** *98°* and *Rising*, **9** *Leslie Grantham*, **10** *Pocketful of Miracles*, **11** *Laurence Llewelyn-Bowen*, **12** *Alvin Stardust*, **13** *Milla Jovovich*, **14** *Fern Britton*, **15** *Charly*, **16** *Alan Bates*, **17** *Sarah Louise Platt*, **18** *Real Thing*, **19** *Tom Courtenay*, **20** *Hester and William Fields*.

 # General Knowledge

1. Which of the Apostles refused to believe in the resurrection until he had seen and touched Christ?
2. What was the popular name for Mussolini's Fasci di Combattimento?
3. Monta Rosa, the highest mountain in the Pennine Alps, is on the border between which two countries?
4. Of which Irish boy band is Ronan Keating lead singer?
5. Which American dancer, singer and actor was born Frederick Austerlitz?
6. Who was the first president of the United States?
7. Which German town is famous for its castle which was used as a high-security POW camp in World War II?
8. Which comedian wrote the 1997 novel *The Detainees*?
9. Which building in Washington D.C. gave its name to the scandal that led to the resignation of President Nixon?
10. By what name is the clavicle usually known?
11. Which British philosopher coined the phrase 'survival of the fittest'?
12. Who was the Egyptian god of learning, portrayed as a scribe with the head of an ibis?
13. Which film was based on Ted Lewis' novel *Jack's Return Home*?
14. Who defeated Anatoly Karpov in 1985 to become world chess champion?
15. Which daughter of Lord Redesdale wrote *The American Way of Death*?
16. What was Fats Waller's real first name?
17. Which tragic cellist is played by Emily Watson in the controversial film *Hilary and Jackie*?
18. With which visual art movement is American Roy Lichtenstein associated?
19. Of which African country is Blantyre-Limbe the largest city?
20. Which American composer wrote two operas with libretti by Gertrude Stein?

 # General Knowledge

| Your rating: | ● 0-5 | Join a library | ● 6-10 | Keep at it |
| | ● 11-15 | Join a quiz team | ● 16-20 | Join Mensa |

1. Which British missionary was played by Ingrid Bergman in the film *The Inn of the Sixth Happiness*?
2. Who wrote the historical novel *Lorna Doone*?
3. What is the longest river in Scotland?
4. From what sort of tree do conkers come?
5. Which venomous spider gets its name from its habit of killing and eating the male after mating?
6. What sort of creature is an avocet?
7. What is the SI unit of power, equal to one joule per second?
8. Who authored the thriller novel *Birds of Prey*?
9. What was the stage name of American magician and escapologist Erich Weiss?
10. Which monolith in Northern Territory, Australia is the largest in the world?
11. Which leading member of Sinn Fein was killed by republicans in 1922, after taking part in negotiations that led to the formation of the Irish Free State?
12. What name is given to the region of the body between the diaphragm and the neck in mammals?
13. Which English architect designed Castle Howard and wrote the plays *The Relapse* and *The Provok'd Wife*?
14. In which county of the Republic of Ireland is Arklow?
15. Which famous English poet died in the Greek town of Missolonghi?
16. What type of moss is also known as bog or peat moss?
17. In which Spanish city did Christopher Columbus die?
18. Who directed the 1994 film *Ladybird Ladybird*?
19. Who was the eighth president of the United States?
20. Who won a Best Actress Oscar for her performance in *Hud*?

 *General Knowledge*

Your rating: ● 0-5 Join a library ● 6-10 Keep at it
● 11-15 Join a quiz team ● 16-20 Join Mensa

1. Which Irish village is famous for its castle which contains a stone that is kissed to give the power of persuasive speech?
2. Who directed the films *Jaws* and *Close Encounters of the Third Kind*?
3. Which former Poet Laureate posthumously became the first person to win the Whitbread Book of the Year award twice?
4. What name was given to the small cell in which over 100 British soldiers were allegedly confined overnight in 1756?
5. Who directed the 1990 film *Ghost*?
6. To which European country do the Azores belong?
7. Which Irish port is famous for its lead crystal glass?
8. Which British dramatist wrote *Absurd Person Singular* and *The Norman Conquests*?
9. Who composed the opera *Gianni Schicchi*?
10. What is the capital of the United States?
11. Which English soldier and statesman, who changed sides during the Wars of the Roses, was known as The Kingmaker?
12. What nationality was the Nobel prize-winning poet Gabriela Mistral?
13. Which English poet wrote *The Faerie Queene*?
14. What in the world of art is a polyptych?
15. Which savage Scandinavian warriors' name means bear shirts?
16. Blackwater fever is a serious complication of which infectious disease?
17. Which horror writer penned *The Green Mile*?
18. Which prehistoric mound near Avebury is the largest man-made hill in Europe?
19. Who succeeded Theodore Roosevelt as U.S. president and split the Republican Party, leading to his defeat in the 1912 election?
20. Which Rugby Union team defeated Colomiers of France to win the 1999 European Cup?

ANSWERS: 1 *Blarney.* 2 *Steven Spielberg.* 3 *Ted Hughes.* 4 *Black Hole of Calcutta.* 5 *Jerry Zucker.* 6 *Portugal.* 7 *Waterford.* 8 *Alan Ayckbourn.* 9 *Puccini.* 10 *Washington D.C.* 11 *Richard Neville, Earl of Warwick.* 12 *Chilean.* 13 *Edmund Spenser.* 14 *A picture consisting of four or more leaves or panels.* 15 *Berserkers or berserkers.* 16 *Malaria.* 17 *Stephen King.* 18 *Silbury Hill.* 19 *William Howard Taft.* 20 *Ulster.*

Entertainment

Your rating:
- 0-5 **Buy a TV**
- 11-15 **Join a quiz team**
- 6-10 **Keep at it**
- 16-20 **Enter a quiz show**

1. Which Dutch-based pop act had a top five hit in 2000 with *Shalala Lala*?
2. Which 1973 film starred Gene Hackman as a paroled criminal and Al Pacino as his fellow traveller?
3. Who was the main presenter of BBC 2's *Crufts 2000* coverage?
4. Who hosted The Brit Awards 2000?
5. Which 2000 BBC 1 documentary series examined the issue of young people and their use of narcotics?
6. Which actor featured as John Malkovich's best friend in the 2000 film *Being John Malkovich*?
7. Which surrealist television comedy show of the Fifties, inspired by the *Goons*, featured sketches written by Spike Milligan?
8. Which Yorkshire band released their second album in 2000, entitled *Drawn From Memory*?
9. Which 1978 film starred Burt Reynolds as the self-proclaimed greatest stuntman in the world?
10. Which TV presenter made a public commitment to give up smoking in 2000, tying in with the BBC's *Kick the Habit* season?
11. What was the title of Technotronic's 1989 top five hit?
12. Which 2000 film by *Boogie Nights* director Paul Thomas Anderson featured Jason Robards and Tom Cruise as father and son?
13. Which BBC 1 home improvement series was presented by Lowri Turner and Nick Knowles?
14. With which former Michael Jackson hit did Marti Webb have a top five single in 1985?
15. Which actor was *The Man Without a Star* in the 1955 western?
16. Who was the *Troubleshooter - Back in Business* of the BBC 2 series?
17. In which year did Elvis Presley hit the UK number one spot with *Return to Sender* and *Good Luck Charm*?
18. For his performance as Dr Larch in which 2000 film did Michael Caine win a Best Supporting Actor Oscar?
19. Who presented the inter-continental Eighties quiz show *Top of the World*?
20. Which London rock, reggae and bhangra outfit released their third album, *Community Music*, in 2000?

ANSWERS: 1 *Vengaboys, 2 Scarecrow, 3 Gaby Roslin, 4 Davina McCall, 5 Children of Drugs, 6 Charlie Sheen, 7 A Show Called Fred, 8 Embrace, 9 Hooper, 10 Dale Winton, 11 Pump Up the Jam, 12 Magnolia, 13 DIY SOS, 14 Ben, 15 Kirk Douglas, 16 John Harvey-Jones, 17 1962, 18 The Cider House Rules, 19 Eamonn Andrews, 20 Asian Dub Foundation.*

 *General Knowledge*

| Your rating: | ● 0-5 | Join a library | ● 6-10 | Keep at it |
| | ● 11-15 | Join a quiz team | ● 16-20 | Join Mensa |

1. Which 4,000 mile long trade route connected China with the Mediterranean?
2. "1801 - I have just returned from a visit to my landlord" are the opening lines of which book?
3. Which Swiss tennis player won the women's singles at the 1999 Australian Open?
4. In Gaelic folklore, which wailing female spirit announces someone's imminent death?
5. Which senior Anglican churchman is called the Primate of All England?
6. In which field was English physicist William Henry Fox Talbot a pioneer?
7. What is the largest of the Society Islands?
8. Who was sacked as England coach by the Football Association after an 'error of judgement' in a newspaper interview?
9. What was the name of Andy Warhol's art studio?
10. Which Thomas Hardy novel features the character Gabriel Oak?
11. Which American dramatist wrote *Who's Afraid of Virginia Woolf*?
12. In Greek mythology, which legendary king of Corinth was condemned to roll a boulder to the top of a hill?
13. Which team did the Denver Broncos beat to win the 1999 Super Bowl?
14. Who directed the 1995 film *Get Shorty*?
15. Which group of related African languages includes Swahili, Xhosa and Zulu?
16. What is the administrative centre and main port of the Orkneys?
17. What is the second most abundant element in the earth's crust after oxygen?
18. What was the subtitle of Mahler's Symphony No. 2 in C minor?
19. Which American novelist wrote *The Jungle* and the 11-volume *Lanny Budd* series of novels?
20. What measure of the explosive power of a nuclear weapon is equal to an explosion of 1000 tons of TNT?

ANSWERS: 1 Silk Road. 2 Wuthering Heights. 3 Martina Hingis. 4 Banshee. 5 The Archbishop of Canterbury. 6 Photography. 7 Tahiti. 8 Glenn Hoddle. 9 The Factory. 10 Far from the Madding Crowd. 11 Edward Albee. 12 Sisyphus. 13 Atlanta Falcons. 14 Barry Sonnenfeld. 15 Bantu. 16 Kirkwall. 17 Silicon. 18 Resurrection Symphony. 19 Upton Sinclair. 20 Kiloton.

 *General Knowledge*

Your rating: • 0-5   Join a library   • 6-10   Keep at it
             • 11-15 Join a quiz team   • 16-20 Join Mensa

1. What name is given to members of a Protestant church which baptises only those considered old enough to accept the Christian faith?
2. Who was the consort of Queen Victoria?
3. Which confederation of North American Plains Indian tribes was also known as the Dakota?
4. Which film won Best Motion Picture (Drama) accolade at the 1972 Golden Globe Awards?
5. Which African animal's name means 'river horse'?
6. What is the fourth largest continent?
7. Which Indian religion was founded by Guru Nanak?
8. What name is given to the aquatic larvae of frogs and toads?
9. Whose novels include *Nostromo*?
10. Of which U.S. state is Columbia the capital?
11. Which French city, known as Aquae Sextiae by the Romans, was the birthplace of artist Paul Cézanne?
12. What name is given to the four containers in which the ancient Egyptians preserved the viscera of an embalmed body?
13. In which museum and art gallery is the statue Venus de Milo housed?
14. Who was the Spanish founder of the Jesuits?
15. Which Pulitzer Prize-winning American composer is best known for his *Adagio for Strings*?
16. Of which Canadian province is Edmonton the capital?
17. Which hot wind blows from the deserts of north Africa across the Mediterranean to south Italy?
18. Who composed the 1937 cantata *In Honour of the City of London*?
19. Of which south-east Asian republic did Prince Souphanouvong become president in 1975?
20. Which Spanish composer and pianist wrote the piano series *Iberia*?

 *General Knowledge*

Your rating: ● 0-5   Join a library   ● 6-10   Keep at it
              ● 11-15 Join a quiz team   ● 16-20   Join Mensa

1. Which English king married Eleanor of Castile and erected a series of crosses, such as Charing Cross, on her funeral route?
2. The shooting of which seabird leads to a curse on the Ancient Mariner in Coleridge's famous poem?
3. In the Christian church, what name is given to the process of conferring the status of saint on a dead person?
4. Who played Ronnie Barker's son Raymond in the sitcom *Going Straight*?
5. Which unit of pressure is equal to 100,000 newtons per square metre?
6. Of which Baltic republic of the former U.S.S.R. is Tallinn the capital?
7. What sort of creature is a barbel?
8. In which century did Rembrandt live?
9. Which famous white marble mausoleum in India was built by Shah Jahan for his favourite wife?
10. Which Shakespeare play features the characters Beatrice and Benedick?
11. Which French Impressionist artist of English parentage painted a series of pictures of the floods at Port-Marly?
12. What name is given to the ability of an electrical component to store charge?
13. Who directed the 1997 film *G.I. Jane*?
14. What is the majority ethnic group in Sri Lanka?
15. Which road runs from Dawson Creek in Canada to Fairbanks in the United States?
16. What is the capital of French Guiana?
17. In which book does Mr. Worldly Wiseman appear?
18. What nationality was former world chess champion José Raúl Capablanca?
19. Which decisive battle in the Hundred Years' War took place on the 25th October 1415?
20. What is the highest peak in Washington state?

ANSWERS: *1 Edward I. 2 Albatross. 3 Canonisation. 4 Nicholas Lyndhurst. 5 Bar. 6 Estonia. 7 A fish. 8 17th. 9 Taj Mahal. 10 Much Ado About Nothing. 11 Alfred Sisley. 12 Capacitance. 13 Ridley Scott. 14 Sinhalese. 15 Alaska Highway. 16 Cayenne. 17 Great Expectations. 18 Cuban. 19 Battle of Agincourt. 20 Mount Rainier.*

Entertainment

Your rating: ● 0-5   Buy a TV   ● 6-10   Keep at it
● 11-15   Join a quiz team   ● 16-20   Enter a quiz show

1. Which actress starred as *Nadine* in the 1987 film?
2. Who took over from Liza Tarbuck as presenter of Channel 4's *She's Gotta Have It*?
3. Which Canadian rocker had a number one hit in 2000 with *Don't Give It Up*, a collaboration with dance act Chicane?
4. Which former *Drop the Dead Donkey* actor starred as private detective Leo Beckett in the BBC 1 drama series *Dirty Work*?
5. Which Oscar-nominated actor played middleweight boxing champion Rubin Carter in the 2000 film *The Hurricane*?
6. What was the name of *The Lookalikes Agency* featured in the ITV documentary series?
7. Which German West End singing star released an album entitled *Punishing Kiss* in 2000?
8. What was the name of Herman Munster's wife in the TV sitcom *The Munsters*?
9. In which 1950 film did Clark Gable play the mayor of a northern California city?
10. Which newsreader presented the ITV show *What Will They Think of Next*?
11. Which UK group had a top five hit in 1978 with *Lay Your Love on Me*?
12. For her performance in which 2000 film did Angelina Jolie win a Best Supporting Actress Oscar?
13. What was the title of Paul Simon's 1986 top five hit?
14. Which British film-maker directed the 1988 film *High Hopes*?
15. Which Channel 4 series, presented by Mike Brewer and Richard Sutton, offered tips on buying second-hand cars?
16. Who had a 1987 top five hit with *(Something Inside) So Strong*?
17. Which 2000 film, created mainly on desktop computer equipment, followed the grisly tale of 'The Jersey Devil'?
18. Which comedy actor played Ashley to Janet Dibley's Elaine in the former sitcom *The Two of Us*?
19. Which former American punk singer released a 2000 album entitled *Gung Ho*?
20. Which 1949 Esther Williams film featured the Oscar-winning song *Baby It's Cold Outside*?

ANSWERS: 1 *Kim Basinger,* 2 *Jayne Middlemiss,* 3 *Bryan Adams,* 4 *Neil Pearson,* 5 *Denzel Washington,* 6 *Derrick's Doubles,* 7 *Ute Lemper,* 8 *Lily,* 9 *Key to the City,* 10 *Kirsty Young,* 11 *Racey,* 12 *Girl, Interrupted,* 13 *You Can Call Me Al,* 14 *Mike Leigh,* 15 *Deals on Wheels,* 16 *Labi Siffre,* 17 *The Last Broadcast,* 18 *Nicholas Lyndhurst,* 19 *Patti Smith,* 20 *Neptune's Daughter.*

 *General Knowledge*

| Your rating: | ● 0-5 | Join a library | ● 6-10 | Keep at it |
| | ● 11-15 | Join a quiz team | ● 16-20 | Join Mensa |

1. Which British dramatist wrote *Look Back in Anger* and *The Entertainer*?
2. By what name is the 16th century French physician and astrologer Michel de Notredame better known?
3. Who composed the symphonic fairy-tale *Peter and the Wolf*?
4. In which Shakespeare play does the fairy Puck appear?
5. What is the second largest continent?
6. Of which European country is Tirana the capital?
7. Of what sort of bird is the capercaillie the largest European variety?
8. Which French aviator was the first man to fly across the English Channel?
9. Who played the inventor in the 1940 film *Edison, the Man*?
10. What is the largest breed of terrier, originally bred in Yorkshire?
11. Which Anglo-Saxon kingdom was formed by the union of Bernicia and Deira?
12. What was the capital of the Philippines from 1948 to 1976?
13. Which Indian leg spinner was the second player in history to take all ten wickets in a Test innings?
14. By what name is the flowering plant *Saintpaulia ionantha* better known?
15. Which British novelist wrote *A High Wind in Jamaica*?
16. In which European city is the Prado museum of art?
17. What is the third largest state in the United States?
18. Rock crystal is a transparent colourless form of which mineral?
19. Which Paris-born artist lived in Tahiti from 1891?
20. By what name is Mainland in the Orkneys also known?

 # General Knowledge

Your rating: ● 0-5   Join a library   ● 6-10   Keep at it
● 11-15   Join a quiz team   ● 16-20   Join Mensa

1. Which American aviator, film producer and entrepreneur became a recluse from 1950 until his death in 1976?
2. What is the second highest mountain in the world?
3. Who played Ron Glum in the 1978 sitcom *The Glums*?
4. Of which country was Archbishop Makarios president?
5. Which deep Scottish loch is associated with sightings of a monster?
6. What is the capital of Norway?
7. *Gimme Shelter* is a 1970 documentary film about which pop group?
8. In what part of the body are the humerus, radius and ulna found?
9. What name for a traitor is derived from a Norwegian army officer who collaborated with the Nazis?
10. Which widely cultivated cereal grass is also called Indian corn?
11. Which hard reddish wood comes from tropical trees of the genus *Swietenia*?
12. The Nore is a sandbank at the mouth of which British river?
13. Which French painter worked with the Paris Customs Office from 1871-93?
14. What name was given to the members of the French Protestant Church who faced persecution in the 16th and 17th centuries?
15. Which Byzantine emperor ordered the codification of Roman law in the Corpus Juris Civilis?
16. What is the capital of Puerto Rico?
17. Who created Winnie-the-Pooh?
18. Which Norwegian dramatist wrote *An Enemy of the People* and *The Master Builder*?
19. Which Greek tragic dramatist wrote the *Oresteia* trilogy and *Seven Against Thebes*?
20. What name is given to the geological period of the Mesozoic era between the Triassic and Cretaceous periods?

ANSWERS: 1 *Howard Hughes*, 2 *K2*, 3 *Ian Lavender*, 4 *Cyprus*, 5 *Loch Ness*, 6 *Oslo*, 7 *The Rolling Stones*, 8 *The arm*, 9 *Quisling*, 10 *Maize*, 11 *Mahogany*, 12 *River Thames*, 13 *Henri Rousseau*, 14 *Huguenots*, 15 *Justinian I*, 16 *San Juan*, 17 *A.A. Milne*, 18 *Henrik Ibsen*, 19 *Aeschylus*, 20 *Jurassic period*.

 *General Knowledge*

Your rating:
- 0-5 Join a library
- 11-15 Join a quiz team
- 6-10 Keep at it
- 16-20 Join Mensa

1. Which American awards are given annually in the fields of journalism, literature and musical composition?
2. With what syncopated form of jazz was Scott Joplin associated?
3. Who became the first monk to hold the office of Archbishop of Westminster in 1976?
4. What was the title of the second film collaboration between Walt Disney and Pixar, the makers of *Toy Story*?
5. What is the name of the brown pigment made from the ink of cuttlefish?
6. What is the most southerly point of South America?
7. Which creatures does an ornithologist study?
8. Which city is the administrative centre of Norfolk?
9. How many humps does a Bactrian camel have?
10. The painting *Do Not Go Gentle Into That Good Night* by Ceri Richards was inspired by a poem by whom?
11. Which American journalist, screenwriter and author wrote the novel *A Death in the Family*?
12. By what name was the actress Beatrice Stella Tanner, the original Eliza in Shaw's *Pygmalion*, known?
13. Who composed the 1982 opera *The Photographer*?
14. Of which country is Yaounde the capital?
15. Which Scottish philosopher and historian wrote *A Treatise of Human Nature*?
16. What is the state capital of North Carolina?
17. What did the initials of the rail company LNER stand for?
18. Which constellation includes Sirius, the brightest star in the sky?
19. What sort of creature is a guenon?
20. Which comic actor played Mr. Kent in the 1982 sitcom *Goodbye Mr. Kent*?

Entertainment

Your rating: ● 0-5   **Buy a TV**   ● 6-10   **Keep at it**
                ● 11-15   **Join a quiz team**   ● 16-20   **Enter a quiz show**

1. Which actor narrated the ITV documentary series *Savage Planet*?
2. What was the title of Elastica's second album, released in 2000?
3. Who presented the technological BBC 2 series *Techno Games 2000*?
4. Which Shakespeare comedy was adapted into a 2000 romantic musical directed by Kenneth Branagh?
5. Which 2000 Channel 4 series explored the effect the internet has had on our lives?
6. Which U.S. country singer released an album in 2000 entitled *Real Live Woman*?
7. Which 1990s drama series starred Russ Abbot and Michael Williams as friends Ted Fenwick and Billy Balsam?
8. Which actor starred as the title character in the 1972 film *The Life and Times of Judge Roy Bean*?
9. Which *Emmerdale* character died in 2000 after being injured in a major road accident?
10. Which U.S. female singer had a 1964 top five hit with *As Usual*?
11. Who directed the 2000 film *Any Given Sunday*, starring Al Pacino?
12. Which comedian embarked upon his own ITV chat and entertainment show in 2000?
13. What was the title of Robert Palmer's 1988 top ten hit?
14. In which Devon zoo was the BBC 1 docusoap *Zoo Keepers* set?
15. Which U.S. group claimed that *Na Na is the Saddest Word* in 1975?
16. Which British actress played a young Australian woman who joins an Indian cult in the 2000 film *Holy Smoke*?
17. Which 1980s science-fiction series featured the man/gorilla hybrid, Gor?
18. Which singer/songwriter released *Ecstasy* in 2000, his first studio album for four years?
19. In which 1984 film did Elliott Gould star as Alby Sherman, a Brooklyn restaurant owner?
20. In which *Airport* was the BBC 1 docusoap of the same name based?

ANSWERS: 1 *Ian Holm*, 2 *The Menace*, 3 *Ulrika Jonsson*, 4 *Love's Labour's Lost*, 5 *Living in the e-world*, 6 *Trisha Yearwood*, 7 *September Song*, 8 *Paul Newman*, 9 *Butch Dingle*, 10 *Brenda Lee*, 11 *Oliver Stone*, 12 *Brian Conley* (*The Brian Conley Show*), 13 *She Makes My Day*, 14 *Paignton Zoo*, 15 *Stylistics*, 16 *Kate Winslet*, 17 *First Born*, 18 *Lou Reed*, 19 *Over the Brooklyn Bridge*, 20 *Heathrow*.

 *General Knowledge*

| Your rating: | ● 0-5 | Join a library | ● 6-10 | Keep at it |
| | ● 11-15 | Join a quiz team | ● 16-20 | Join Mensa |

1. In South African politics, what does the abbreviation ANC stand for?
2. What name is given to the section of the Atlantic Ocean between the British Isles and the continent north of the Strait of Dover?
3. Who did Diana Ross portray in 1972 film *Lady Sings the Blues*?
4. What was the legendary capital of King Arthur's kingdom?
5. Which French novelist wrote *Les Misérables* and *Notre-Dame de Paris*, which was filmed as *The Hunchback of Notre Dame*?
6. In which country did the game of mahjong originate?
7. How many people usually sit on a jury?
8. Which artist won the 1989 Turner Prize?
9. Which actor played Alf Roberts for many years in *Coronation Street*?
10. In which English county is Maiden Castle?
11. Which Russian pianist, composer and conductor wrote a famous *Rhapsody on a Theme of Paganini*?
12. What is the best-known novel by Thomas Hughes?
13. Which British engineer set the land-speed record nine times and the water-speed record three times?
14. On a story by whom was the 1998 film *The Gingerbread Man* based?
15. Which region of Canada comprises the districts of Mackenzie, Keewatin and Franklin?
16. What name is given to an abscess in the tissue surrounding a tonsil?
17. Which radioactive gas has the symbol Rn?
18. What was E.M. Forster's first novel?
19. Which Greek hero of the Trojan wars was murdered by his wife Clytemnestra and her lover Aegisthus?
20. What name is given to the study of the behaviour and flow of air around objects?

 **General Knowledge**

Your rating:	● 0-5	Join a library	● 6-10	Keep at it
	● 11-15	Join a quiz team	● 16-20	Join Mensa

1. Which annual literary prize for novels written in English was established in 1968?
2. What name is given to the condition of having an abnormally low body temperature, often associated with the elderly?
3. In which town in Kent would you find the promenade 'The Pantiles'?
4. What name is given to the rubber disc used in ice hockey?
5. Which French composer wrote the orchestral work *La Mer*?
6. In which country did kabuki theatre originate?
7. In which year did the Tate gallery open in Millbank, London?
8. Which film starred Michael Keaton as a father who comes back to life as a snowman?
9. What name is given to the proportion of water vapour in the atmosphere?
10. Which light volcanic rock derived from acidic lava is used as an abrasive?
11. Which English mathematician gave his name to a form of algebra also called symbolic logic?
12. What name is given to the minimum mass of fissile material capable of sustaining a chain reaction?
13. Which Japanese director made the films *Seven Samurai* and *Ran*?
14. Which comedienne started by billing herself 'The Sea Monster'?
15. Which Italian motorcyclist won a record 15 world championship titles?
16. What is the capital of Croatia?
17. Who played Marsha Stubbs in the TV drama *Soldier, Soldier*?
18. Who was minister of aircraft production 1942-45 and chancellor of the Exchequer 1947-50?
19. Which American pioneer led the first settlement in Kentucky?
20. What form of sugar is also known as milk sugar?

ANSWERS: 1 *Booker Prize*, 2 *Hypothermia*, 3 *(Royal) Tunbridge Wells*, 4 *Puck*, 5 *Claude Debussy*, 6 *Japan*, 7 *1897*, 8 *Jack Frost*, 9 *Humidity*, 10 *Pumice*, 11 *George Boole*, 12 *Critical mass*, 13 *Akira Kurosawa*, 14 *Jo Brand*, 15 *Giacomo Agostini*, 16 *Zagreb*, 17 *Denise Welch*, 18 *Sir Stafford Cripps*, 19 *Daniel Boone*, 20 *Lactose*.

 *General Knowledge*

Your rating: ● 0-5 Join a library ● 6-10 Keep at it
● 11-15 Join a quiz team ● 16-20 Join Mensa

1. Which small guitar associated with George Formby was patented in Hawaii in 1917?
2. What were the works of painters Michael Andrews, Ron Kitaj, Frank Auerbach, Lucien Freud, Francis Bacon and Leon Kossoff collectively exhibited as in 1987?
3. Which European peninsula is occupied by Spain and Portugal?
4. Who accepted the job of England football coach in 1999?
5. To what sort of crops is the boll weevil a major pest?
6. What is the capital of Afghanistan?
7. What is the name of the curved wooden missile used by Australian aborigines?
8. Which classic won Best Film accolade at the 1957 British Academy Awards?
9. Which extinct snow-topped Tanzanian volcano is the highest mountain in Africa?
10. What name is given to the art of producing miniature trees by selective pruning?
11. Which group of French artists whose name was Hebrew for prophets included Pierre Bonnard, Edouard Vuillard and Maurice Denis?
12. In Greek mythology, who was the youngest of the Titans and the Father of Zeus?
13. What crop accounts for 75% of Cuba's exports?
14. What was the maiden name of tennis player Billie Jean King?
15. Which keyboard instrument was invented by Bartolommeo Cristofori?
16. What is the name of the quarter day that falls on March 25th?
17. What was the title of Irvine Welsh's 1998 novel about a corrupt policeman?
18. Which SI unit of mass is based on the platinum-iridium prototype kept at the International Museum of Weights and Measures in France?
19. In cricket, is extra cover on the on or the off side?
20. Which Kurdish guerrilla leader's arrest led to worldwide protests in 1999?

ANSWERS: 1 *Ukulele.* **2** *School of London.* **3** *Iberian Peninsula.* **4** *Kevin Keegan.* **5** *Cotton.* **6** *Kabul.* **7** *Boomerang.* **8** *The Bridge on the River Kwai.* **9** *Mount Kilimanjaro.* **10** *Bonsai.* **11** *Les Nabis.* **12** *Cronus.* **13** *Sugar.* **14** *Moffitt.* **15** *Piano.* **16** *Lady Day.* **17** *Filth.* **18** *Kilogram.* **19** *Off.* **20** *Abdullah Ocalan.*

Sports

Your rating: ● **0-5**   **Wooden spoon**   ● **6-10**   **Bronze medal**
● **11-15**   **Silver medal**   ● **16-20**   **Gold medal**

1. Which U.S. female sprinter won three gold medals at the 1988 Olympic Games?
2. Who scored the opening goal of Euro 96?
3. Which city hosted the 1964 Winter Olympics?
4. Which British athlete broke the men's triple jump world record in 1995?
5. Which golfer won the U.S. Open in 1992?
6. Which rugby union club signed Dean Ryan from Wasps?
7. Who topped Scotland's group (Group 9) in the Euro 2000 qualifiers?
8. Which West Indies batsman was the first to reach 8000 runs in Test cricket?
9. After which U.S. tennis player is the main stadium at Flushing Meadows named?
10. Which nation knocked Germany out of the World Cup in 1994 ?
11. At the 1996 Olympics, who became men's singles tennis champion?
12. Which French motor racing driver was Formula One world champion three times during the 1980s?
13. Who was the first footballer to be sent off in a Wembley F.A. Cup final?
14. Which Scottish snooker player was the 1994 Masters champion?
15. Which boxer won bantamweight gold at the 1978 Commonwealth Games?
16. Which sport is played by Batley Bulldogs?
17. Which golfer won the 1995 Masters?
18. At which racecourse is the 2000 Guineas run?
19. In which German city was the 1988 European championship final held?
20. Which city was the first to host the Olympic Games twice?

THE TRIVIA QUIZ BOOK

 *General Knowledge*

Your rating:	● 0-5	Join a library	● 6-10	Keep at it
	● 11-15	Join a quiz team	● 16-20	Join Mensa

1. Which American actor starred in the films *Casablanca*, *The Big Sleep* and *The African Queen*?
2. What was the capital of West Germany from 1949 to 1990?
3. In which novel does Hannibal Lecter appear prior to *The Silence of the Lambs*?
4. What is the traditional costume of Japan, still used by women for formal wear?
5. Which well-known radio and TV series was based on the medical stories of A.J. Cronin?
6. What sort of creature is an ibex?
7. Who played the lead in the 1954 film *The Glenn Miller Story*?
8. What did the country of Upper Volta become in 1984?
9. Which black American civil rights campaigner was assassinated in Memphis in 1968?
10. On what date is Independence Day celebrated in the United States?
11. Which British composer and conductor was musical director of Sadler's Wells from 1928 to 1947?
12. In Greek mythology, who commanded the Myrmidons in the Trojan War?
13. Who wrote *Captain Corelli's Mandolin*?
14. What relation was the emperor Caligula to the Roman general Agrippa?
15. Which British preacher founded the Salvation Army?
16. What nationality was the famous murderer Dr Crippen?
17. In which year was current affairs presenter Peter Snow born?
18. What is the county town of County Kildare?
19. Which wading bird was revered by the ancient Egyptians as a symbol of the god Thoth?
20. What is the state capital of Idaho?

ANSWERS: 1 *Humphrey Bogart, 2 Bonn, 3 Red Dragon, 4 Kimono, 5 Dr Finlay's Casebook, 6 A wild goat, 7 James Stewart, 8 Burkina Faso, 9 Martin Luther King Jr, 10 July 4, 11 Constant Lambert, 12 Achilles, 13 Louis de Bernières, 14 Grandson, 15 William Booth, 16 American, 17 1938, 18 Naas, 19 Sacred ibis, 20 Boise.*

 # General Knowledge

1. Which American actor starred in the films *East of Eden*, *Rebel without a Cause* and *Giant*?
2. In Greek mythology, who was the son of Daedalus who plunged to his death when he flew too near to the sun?
3. The Painted Desert lies in which U.S. state?
4. What name is given to a phase in the economic cycle characterised by high output, falling unemployment and rising prices and profits?
5. Which large intelligent black-and-white predator is a member of the dolphin family?
6. Who was the second wife of Henry VIII?
7. Which historical theatre of war is known as Krym in Russian?
8. What is the art technique of serigraphy better known as?
9. Which former *Neighbours* actress picked up two awards at the 1999 Brits?
10. What is the capital of Ukraine?
11. Which town on the West Bank of the River Jordan stands on the site of the biblical town of Shechem?
12. In Freudian psychology, what name is given to the part of the unconscious mind governed by instinctive forces?
13. Who plays Foggy Dewhurst in the BBC 1 comedy series *Last of the Summer Wine*?
14. What nationality was the philosopher Soren Kierkegaard?
15. Which British sociologist and pioneer of pensions wrote *Life and Labour of the People in London*?
16. What sort of creature is a bongo?
17. Who was the last king of Lydia, famous for his wealth?
18. Which Oscar-winning actor directed the 1978 film *Goin' South*?
19. Which American consumer campaigner wrote *Unsafe at Any Speed*?
20. In what style of jazz or blues piano does the left hand establish a driving repetitive rhythm while the right provides a variety of syncopation?

ANSWERS: 1 James Dean, 2 Icarus, 3 Arizona, 4 Boom, 5 Killer whale, 6 Anne Boleyn, 7 The Crimea, 8 Silk-screen printing, 9 Natalie Imbruglia, 10 Kiev, 11 Nablus, 12 The id, 13 Brian Wilde, 14 Danish, 15 Charles Booth, 16 An antelope, 17 Croesus, 18 Jack Nicholson, 19 Ralph Nader, 20 Boogie-woogie.

THE TRIVIA QUIZ BOOK

(?) *General Knowledge*

Your rating:	● 0-5	Join a library	● 6-10	Keep at it
	● 11-15	Join a quiz team	● 16-20	Join Mensa

1. Which English novelist wrote *Little Lord Fauntleroy* and *The Secret Garden*?
2. What name is given to a well sunk into an aquifer in which water rises under its own pressure?
3. Who played *The Elusive Pimpernel* in the 1950 film?
4. What is the capital of Wales?
5. Which Roman general abandoned his wife Octavia to live with Cleopatra in Egypt?
6. What sort of creature is an auk?
7. Whose autobiography was *Goodbye to All That*?
8. Which mallet-and-ball game is played on a lawn with six hoops and a peg?
9. What is the name of the collection of ancient Egyptian manuscripts buried with mummies as a guide to the afterlife?
10. Which Irish band was voted Best International Group at the 1999 Brit Awards?
11. Which king of England was married to Margaret of Anjou?
12. Of which London cathedral was poet John Donne appointed Dean in 1621?
13. Which Berkshire village was made famous by the paintings of Sir Stanley Spencer?
14. Of what art movement is Gino Severini's painting *Dancer-Helix-Sea* an example?
15. Which Russian city was known as Molotov between 1940 and 1957?
16. At which Kent resort is local Quaker Benjamin Beale said to have invented the bathing machine?
17. Which comedian was born Eddie McGinnis in 1942?
18. What does AI stand for in computer science?
19. Which county in the Irish Republic has Lifford as its county town?
20. On which river does the Wiltshire town of Marlborough stand?

ANSWERS: *1 Frances Hodgson Burnett, 2 Artesian well, 3 David Niven, 4 Cardiff, 5 Mark Antony, 6 A seabird, 7 Robert Graves, 8 Croquet, 9 Book of the Dead, 10 The Corrs, 11 Henry VI, 12 St Paul's, 13 Cookham-on-Thames, 14 Futurism, 15 Perm, 16 Margate, 17 Eddie Large, 18 Artificial intelligence, 19 Donegal, 20 River Kennet.*

Entertainment

Your rating: ● 0-5 Buy a TV ● 6-10 Keep at it
● 11-15 Join a quiz team ● 16-20 Enter a quiz show

1. Which Beatle starred alongside Peter Sellers in the 1969 film *The Magic Christian*?
2. Which comic duo starred as *Randall & Hopkirk (Deceased)* in the BBC 1 remake series?
3. What was the title of No Doubt's 2000 album, a follow-up to 1997's *Tragic Kingdom*?
4. Which actress starred as *Erin Brockovich* in the 2000 film of the same name?
5. Which actor played the sophisticated independent spy in the TV series *Danger Man*?
6. Which British R&B artist had a number one hit in 2000 with *Fill Me In*?
7. In which 1951 film did Alec Guinness star as a research scientist who invents a cloth that is everlasting and dirt resisting?
8. In which World War II drama series did John Thaw appear as a French Catholic priest?
9. Which female vocalist had a number one hit in 1968 with *Those Were the Days*?
10. Which 2000 film featured British stars including Ray Winstone, Jonny Lee Miller, Jude Law and Denise Van Outen?
11. Which UK group had a 1981 top ten hit with *One in Ten*?
12. Which actor played Floyd, proprietor of the Blue Water Grill, in the 1988 film *Full Moon in Blue Water*?
13. Which actor played A&E boss Robert Kingsford in the ITV drama series *Always and Everyone*?
14. What was the title of Buddy Holly's only UK number one single?
15. Who won a Best Actress Oscar for her performance in the 2000 film *Boys Don't Cry*?
16. Which BBC weekend football programme has been broadcast since 1964?
17. Which TLC member collaborated with Melanie C on the 2000 number one hit *Never Be the Same Again*?
18. Which 1959 film starring Peter Sellers featured the fictional Grand Duchy of Grand Fenwick, the world's smallest country?
19. Which star of *The 11 O'Clock Show* acquired his own Channel 4 comedy series in 2000?
20. What was the title of Paul Weller's 2000 album release - the fifth of his solo career?

ANSWERS: *1 Ringo Starr. 2 Vic Reeves & Bob Mortimer. 3 Return of Saturn. 4 Julia Roberts. 5 Patrick McGoohan. 6 Craig David. 7 The Man in the White Suit. 8 Monsignor Renard. 9 Mary Hopkin. 10 Love, Honour & Obey. 11 UB40. 12 Gene Hackman. 13 Martin Shaw. 14 It Doesn't Matter Anymore. 15 Hilary Swank. 16 Match of the Day. 17 Lisa 'Left Eye' Lopes. 18 The Mouse That Roared. 19 Ali G (Da Ali G Show). 20 Heliocentric.*

THE TRIVIA QUIZ BOOK

 *General Knowledge*

Your rating: ● 0-5   Join a library   ● 6-10   Keep at it
                ● 11-15   Join a quiz team   ● 16-20   Join Mensa

1. Which member of the Royal Family abandoned plans to marry Group Captain Peter Townsend in 1955?
2. In the Old Testament, who was given the Ten Commandments?
3. Who plays gangster John Smith in the 1996 film *Last Man Standing*?
4. With which art form is Donatello associated?
5. Which Scottish poet wrote *Tam o'Shanter* and *Holy Willie's Prayer*?
6. Of which Australian state is Sydney the capital?
7. Which duo co-scripted and starred in the 1997 film *Good Will Hunting*?
8. What does the abbreviation CID stand for?
9. Which park to the west of Paris contains Longchamp racecourse?
10. Which former president of the Philippines fled into exile in 1986?
11. Which Italian electrical engineer succeeded in transmitting a radio signal across the Atlantic in 1901?
12. What name is given to the membrane lining the abdominal cavity?
13. The Crimea Peninsula is part of which European country?
14. Who was the wife of Louis XVI of France?
15. Which Italian composer wrote the opera *Lucia di Lammermoor*?
16. What sort of creature is a markhor?
17. Who became archduchess of Austria and queen of Hungary in 1740?
18. On which Scottish island are the Cuillin Hills?
19. Which English writer and friend of Dr Johnson wrote the novel *Evelina*?
20. Who was President of the United States from 1881-1885?

ANSWERS: *1 Princess Margaret, 2 Moses, 3 Bruce Willis, 4 Sculpture, 5 Robert Burns, 6 New South Wales, 7 Ben Affleck and Matt Damon, 8 Criminal Investigation Department, 9 Bois de Boulogne, 10 Ferdinand Marcos, 11 Guglielmo Marconi, 12 Peritoneum, 13 Ukraine, 14 Marie Antoinette, 15 Gaetano Donizetti, 16 A wild goat, 17 Maria Theresa, 18 Skye, 19 Fanny Burney, 20 Chester A Arthur.*

THE TRIVIA QUIZ BOOK

 General Knowledge

Your rating:	● 0-5	Join a library	● 6-10	Keep at it
	● 11-15	Join a quiz team	● 16-20	Join Mensa

1. Which racing driver was runner-up in the world championships from 1955-58?
2. Who was the last British tennis player to win the men's singles at Wimbledon?
3. In which English county is the picturesque village of Clovelly?
4. What is the most famous novel by James Fenimore Cooper?
5. Which jazz saxophonist was known as Bird or Yardbird?
6. By what name was American boxer Rocco Francis Marchegiano known?
7. What is the chief island of the Society Islands in French Polynesia?
8. Which British novelist wrote *Pride and Prejudice* and *Sense and Sensibility*?
9. By what name was the British ballerina born Lilian Alicia Marks better known?
10. Which nonmetallic element is a constituent of all organic substances?
11. Which American novelist wrote *The Ginger Man* and *The Onion Eaters*?
12. Who was president of Argentina from 1946-55 and 1973-74?
13. Who composed the 1883 opera *Henry VIII*?
14. What is the highest mountain in New Zealand?
15. Which town in West Sussex has a castle that is the seat of the Duke of Norfolk?
16. What name is given to an agent that causes cancer?
17. How much, in dollars, was Dustin Hoffman paid for the film *The Graduate*?
18. In which South American country is the resort of Mar del Plata?
19. Which famous British historical novelist had the middle name Doddridge?
20. What sort of creature is a margay?

ANSWERS: 1 *Stirling Moss*, 2 *Fred Perry*, 3 *Devon*, 4 *The Last of the Mohicans*, 5 *Charlie Parker*, 6 *Rocky Marciano*, 7 *Tahiti*, 8 *Jane Austen*, 9 *Dame Alicia Markova*, 10 *Carbon*, 11 *J P Donleavy*, 12 *Juan Perón*, 13 *Saint-Saëns*, 14 *Mount Cook*, 15 *Arundel*, 16 *Carcinogen*, 17 *$17,000*, 18 *Argentina*, 19 *R D Blackmore*, 20 *A cat*.

THE TRIVIA QUIZ BOOK

 *General Knowledge*

| Your rating: | ● 0-5 | Join a library | ● 6-10 | Keep at it |
| | ● 11-15 | Join a quiz team | ● 16-20 | Join Mensa |

1. Which American silversmith was famous for his night ride to warn the people of Massachusetts of the approach of British troops?
2. What item of clothing is named after the officer who led the Charge of the Light Brigade in the Crimean War?
3. Who directed the 1996 film *The English Patient*?
4. Of which country is Margrethe II the reigning queen?
5. Which prophetic book is the last in the New Testament?
6. What is the capital of France?
7. Whose catchphrase is 'I wanna tell you a story'?
8. Which French mime artiste was best known for his white-faced character Bip?
9. Who was the last shah of Iran?
10. Which reedlike plant was used by the ancient Egyptians to make paper?
11. Which English dramatist and poet was killed in a tavern in Deptford in 1593?
12. What name is given to the transfer of heat within a fluid by means of motion of the fluid?
13. Vienna and Belgrade lie on the banks of which river?
14. Who was the supreme god in Babylonian mythology?
15. Which French poet is best known for his collection of fairy tales *Contes de ma mère l'oye*?
16. What is the administrative centre of Dorset?
17. Which silvery-white transition metal has the symbol Re?
18. Of which female political figure was Joyce Grenfell the niece?
19. Which 'effect' is responsible for the apparent change in pitch of a siren as a vehicle approaches and then recedes?
20. Who is the patron saint of Venice?

ANSWERS: 1 *Paul Revere.* 2 *Cardigan.* 3 *Anthony Minghella.* 4 *Denmark.* 5 *Book of Revelation.* 6 *Paris.* 7 *Max Bygraves.* 8 *Marcel Marceau.* 9 *Muhammad Reza Pahlavi.* 10 *Papyrus.* 11 *Christopher Marlowe.* 12 *Convection.* 13 *River Danube.* 14 *Marduk.* 15 *Charles Perrault.* 16 *Dorchester.* 17 *Rhenium.* 18 *Nancy Astor.* 19 *Doppler effect.* 20 *Saint Mark.*

Entertainment

Your rating:
● 0-5   **Buy a TV**   ● 6-10   **Keep at it**
● 11-15   **Join a quiz team**   ● 16-20   **Enter a quiz show**

1. Which actor played professional fencer Steve McTear in the 2000 ITV drama *The Last Musketeer*?
2. Which British actress played Mary Panton in the 2000 filmic adaptation of Somerset Maugham's short novel *Up at the Villa*?
3. Who played TV gameshow host *Bob Martin* in the ITV comedy drama of the same name?
4. What was the title of the number one hit by dance act Fragma that topped the charts in April 2000?
5. In which BBC 1 drama did Francesca Annis star as Ellen Richmond, whose husband Harry goes missing at sea?
6. Which actor played Lucky Luciano in the 1991 film *Mobsters*?
7. Which actress played *Coronation Street*'s Elsie Tanner?
8. In which year did Harry Enfield have a top five hit with *Loadsamoney (Doin' Up the House)*?
9. Whose *All Stars* appeared alongside the midweek Lottery draw?
10. Which of Winnie the Pooh's friends became the star of his own film in 2000?
11. Which former *Emmerdale* star played prison officer Karen Betts in the ITV drama series *Bad Girls*?
12. Which U.S. group had a top ten hit in 1996 with *Peaches*?
13. Which actor's first directing venture was the 1991 film *Nothing But Trouble*?
14. Which *Emmerdale* vicar revealed his love for Woolpack landlady Bernice Blackstock in 2000?
15. Which UK group claimed that *Even the Bad Times Are Good* in the top five in 1967?
16. Which 2000 animated film was a spin-off from a series of Nintendo games?
17. Which soap opera did Noele Gordon star in until 1981?
18. Which U.S. teen singer, who hit the charts with *I Wanna Love You Forever*, released her debut album, *Sweet Kisses*, in 2000?
19. Which 1965 film starred George Peppard as an amnesiac?
20. Which former *Beverly Hills 90210* actress starred in Channel 5's U.S. drama series *Charmed*?

ANSWERS: 1 *Robson Green*. 2 *Kristin Scott Thomas*. 3 *Michael Barrymore*. 4 *Toca's Miracle*. 5 *Deceit*. 6 *Christian Slater*. 7 *Pat Phoenix*. 8 *1988*. 9 *Dale Winton's*. 10 *Tigger (The Tigger Movie)*. 11 *Claire King*. 12 *Presidents of the United States of America*. 13 *Dan Aykroyd's*. 14 *Rev. Ashley Thomas*. 15 *Tremeloes*. 16 *Pokemon - The First Movie*. 17 *Crossroads*. 18 *Jessica Simpson*. 19 *The Third Day*. 20 *Shannen Doherty*.

 *General Knowledge*

Your rating: ● 0-5   Join a library   ● 6-10   Keep at it
                   ● 11-15 Join a quiz team   ● 16-20 Join Mensa

1. The hull of which Tudor warship was raised and placed in dry dock in Portsmouth in 1982?
2. What are the four fundamental operations of arithmetic?
3. On which of the Channel Islands did Gerald Durrell found a zoo in 1959?
4. Which artist painted 1913's *Violin and Guitar*?
5. Which Greek philosopher was tutor to Alexander the Great?
6. In which principality is the resort of Monte Carlo?
7. 'It is a truth universally acknowledged that a single man in possession of a good fortune, must be in want of a wife'. The opening lines of which novel?
8. How many parts of oxygen are there to one part of carbon in carbon dioxide?
9. Which British heavyweight boxer knocked down Muhammad Ali in a fight at Wembley in the 1960s?
10. In which county is the horse racing town of Newmarket?
11. Which Scottish historian and essayist wrote *Sartor Resartus* and *The French Revolution*?
12. To which genus of shrubs and trees does the butterfly bush belong?
13. Who starred as Felix Cramer in the 1990 BBC TV drama series *A Sense of Guilt*?
14. What was the first synthetic transuranic element?
15. Which hormone is also called epinephrine?
16. In which country are the Plains of Abraham?
17. Who directed the 1986 film *Aliens*?
18. Who was the father of the Duke of Monmouth, who led a rebellion against James II?
19. Which semiprecious stone is the birthstone for October?
20. What is the capital of the Netherlands Antilles?

ANSWERS: 1 *Mary Rose*, 2 Addition, subtraction, multiplication and division, 3 Jersey, 4 Picasso, 5 Aristotle, 6 Monaco, 7 *Pride and Prejudice, by Jane Austen*, 8 Two, 9 Henry Cooper, 10 Suffolk, 11 *Thomas Carlyle*, 12 Buddleia, 13 *Trevor Eve*, 14 Neptunium, 15 Adrenaline, 16 Canada, 17 James Cameron, 18 Charles II, 19 Opal, 20 Willemstad.

 # General Knowledge

Your rating:	● 0-5	Join a library	● 6-10	Keep at it
	● 11-15	Join a quiz team	● 16-20	Join Mensa

1. In which 1805 battle was Admiral Nelson mortally wounded?
2. What name is given to the group of chalk rocks off the west coast of the Isle of Wight?
3. Which British singer died in 1999 on the day she was due to go to Buckingham Palace to receive her OBE?
4. Who were the parents of Cain and Abel?
5. Who wrote *The Tenant of Wildfell Hall*?
6. What is the capital of Argentina?
7. In Greek mythology, which handsome youth was allowed to return from the underworld to be with Aphrodite?
8. Which TV programme was set in the imaginary village of Crinkly Bottom?
9. What is the name given to the bottom layer of a painting, such as the canvas?
10. In which English county is Newton Abbot?
11. Which Nobel prize-winning novelist wrote *The Three Daughters of Madame Liang*?
12. What is the full name of AMPAS, the organisation responsible for the Oscars?
13. Which former Master of the Rolls died in 1999 at the age of 100?
14. Who painted 1642's *The Night Watch*?
15. Which American tennis player was the first man to achieve the Grand Slam, in 1938?
16. What is the capital of the Central African Republic?
17. With which musical instrument is Gerald Moore associated?
18. Who starred as *Carrie* in the 1976 film?
19. Which American harmonica player had pieces composed for him by Vaughan Williams and Milhaud?
20. Of which Austrian state is Klagenfurt the capital?

ANSWERS: *1 Battle of Trafalgar. 2 The Needles. 3 Dusty Springfield. 4 Adam and Eve. 5 Anne Brontë. 6 Buenos Aires. 7 Adonis. 8 Noel's House Party. 9 Support. 10 Devon. 11 Pearl S Buck. 12 Academy of Motion Picture Arts and Sciences. 13 Lord Denning. 14 Rembrandt. 15 Don Budge. 16 Bangui. 17 Piano. 18 Sissy Spacek. 19 Larry Adler. 20 Carinthia.*

 # General Knowledge

Your rating: ● 0-5 Join a library   ● 6-10 Keep at it
● 11-15 Join a quiz team   ● 16-20 Join Mensa

1. Of which English county is Lewes the administrative centre?
2. What name is given to the arm of the Mediterranean Sea between Italy and the Balkan peninsula?
3. Which porcine puppet pairing were created by Jan and Vlasta Dalibor?
4. What are the first names of David and Victoria Beckham's son?
5. Who invented the jet engine?
6. Of which African country is Addis Ababa the capital?
7. Which event in the life of Christ does Maundy Thursday commemorate?
8. Which novel by H.G. Wells is partly set in the year 802701?
9. What is the London residence of the British monarch?
10. Of which organisation was Trygve Lie the first secretary-general?
11. Which Scottish-born American industrialist and philanthropist founded the Keystone Bridge Company in 1865?
12. Who was the first vice-president and second president of The United States?
13. What is the name of the garden suburb south-west of Birmingham founded by George Cadbury in 1897?
14. In which castle near Newport on the Isle of Wight was Charles I imprisoned?
15. In Greek mythology, what was the name of the daughter of King Minos abandoned by Theseus on the island of Naxos?
16. What sort of creature is an addax?
17. Which Indian city is the capital of Karnataka state?
18. Which comedian's real name is Thomas Derbyshire?
19. Which Brazilian tennis player won the women's singles at Wimbledon in 1959, 1960 and 1964?
20. How many books are there in the New Testament?

ANSWERS: 1 East Sussex, 2 Adriatic Sea, 3 Pinky & Perky, 4 Brooklyn Joseph, 5 Sir Frank Whittle, 6 Ethiopia, 7 The Last Supper, 8 The Time Machine, 9 Buckingham Palace, 10 United Nations, 11 Andrew Carnegie, 12 John Adams, 13 Bourneville, 14 Carisbrooke, 15 Ariadne, 16 Antelope, 17 Bangalore, 18 Tommy Cannon, 19 Maria Bueno, 20 27.

Entertainment

Your rating: ● 0-5   Buy a TV   ● 6-10   Keep at it
               ● 11-15 Join a quiz team   ● 16-20 Enter a quiz show

1. Which BBC 1 panel quiz show featured team captains Suggs and Noddy Holder?
2. Which comedian had his own *Happy Hour* on BBC 1?
3. Which singer/songwriter released an album of love songs in 2000 entitled *Silver and Gold*?
4. Which British actor played Patrick Bateman in the 2000 filmic adaptation of Bret Easton Ellis' *American Psycho*?
5. Which Eighties sitcom starred Tracey Ullman, Dawn French, Jennifer Saunders and Ruby Wax?
6. Which former member of Another Level had a 2000 top ten hit with his collaboration with the True Steppers, *Buggin' Me*?
7. Which actress played Irma in the 1963 film *Irma La Douce*?
8. Who was the presenter of BBC 1's *Whatever You Want*?
9. Which UK group had a 1964 number one single with *Little Children*?
10. Which actor wrote and directed the 2000 film *Cradle Will Rock*?
11. Which 2000 BBC 2 adaptation of a Gustave Flaubert novel starred Australian actress Frances O'Connor in the title role?
12. Which UK band's first number one single was *Some Might Say*, which hit the charts in 1995?
13. What was the name of the mermaid princess in the 1989 Disney animation *The Little Mermaid*?
14. Which Channel 4 comedy sketch show featured Doon MacKichan, Fiona Allen and Sally Philips?
15. In which year did Pulp first have a top ten hit with *Disco 2000*?
16. Which 2000 Rob Reiner film starred Bruce Willis and Michelle Pfeiffer as suburban couple Ben and Katie?
17. Which comic actor starred alongside Prunella Scales as George Starling in the Sixties sitcom *The Marriage Lines*?
18. Which U.S. singer had a 2000 top ten hit with *He Wasn't Man Enough*?
19. Which comic presenter became a regular panelist in David Gower's team on BBC 1's sports quiz *They Think It's All Over* in 1999?
20. Which *Friends* star appeared in the 1987 film *Masters of the Universe*?

ANSWERS: *1 A Question of Pop, 2 Jack Dee, 3 Neil Young, 4 Christian Bale, 5 Girls on Top, 6 Dane Bowers, 7 Shirley MacLaine, 8 Gaby Roslin, 9 Billy J Kramer & the Dakotas, 10 Tim Robbins, 11 Madame Bovary, 12 Oasis', 13 Ariel, 14 Smack the Pony, 15 1995, 16 The Story of Us, 17 Richard Briers, 18 Toni Braxton, 19 Jonathan Ross, 20 Courteney Cox.*

 # General Knowledge

Your rating:	● 0-5 Join a library	● 6-10 Keep at it
	● 11-15 Join a quiz team	● 16-20 Join Mensa

1. Which Greek shipping magnate married Jacqueline Kennedy in 1968?
2. The Fastnet race is part of which sailing competition?
3. Which talk show host plays Sethe in Jonathan Demme's film version of Toni Morrison's novel *Beloved*?
4. In which religion is the aim to break the chain of karma by achieving nirvana?
5. Who was the Greek god of war, identified with the Roman Mars?
6. In which 1932 comic novel does Great Aunt Ada Doom appear?
7. Which Asiatic people were united in the early 13th century by Genghis Khan?
8. What name is given to an organism living in or on another organism of a different species?
9. Which sign of the zodiac is represented by a ram?
10. What are comedians Paul and Barry Elliot better known as?
11. Which German author wrote the novels *Steppenwolf* and *The Glass Bead Game*?
12. What is the second largest city in Mexico?
13. Which type of pasta is named after the Italian phrase 'small tongues'?
14. In Roman mythology, what was the name of the goddess of the dawn?
15. Which French artist painted *Impression, Sunrise* from which the Impressionists took their name?
16. What sort of creature is an oribi?
17. Who composed the 1746 oratorio *Judas Maccabaeus*?
18. In which garden near Jerusalem was Jesus betrayed by Judas Iscariot?
19. Of which U.S. state is Helena the capital?
20. How many stations of the cross are there on the walls of churches?

ANSWERS: 1 *Aristotle Onassis*, 2 *Admiral's Cup*, 3 *Oprah Winfrey*, 4 *Buddhism*, 5 *Ares*, 6 *Cold Comfort Farm*, 7 *Mongols*, 8 *Parasite*, 9 *Aries*, 10 *The Chuckle Brothers*, 11 *Hermann Hesse*, 12 *Guadalajara*, 13 *Linguini*, 14 *Aurora*, 15 *Claude Monet*, 16 *An antelope*, 17 *Handel*, 18 *Gethsemane*, 19 *Montana*, 20 *14*.

 # General Knowledge

Your rating:	● 0-5	Join a library	● 6-10	Keep at it
	● 11-15	Join a quiz team	● 16-20	Join Mensa

1. Which London cemetery contains the graves of Karl Marx and George Eliot?
2. What name is given to the great plague that swept through Europe in the mid-14th century?
3. In which U.S. state is the city of Omaha?
4. In which 1991 film did Gerard Depardieu star alongside Andie MacDowell?
5. With which sporting event is Baron Pierre de Coubertin associated?
6. What is the capital of the Republic of Ireland?
7. In the New Testament, who was the first person to see Jesus after the resurrection?
8. Who had a No1 hit with *Hit Me Baby One More Time*?
9. What name is shared by a city in North Wales and a resort in Northern Ireland?
10. In Greek mythology, what name was given to the crew of Jason's ship on the quest for the Golden Fleece?
11. Which Greek comic dramatist wrote *The Wasps*, *The Birds* and *The Frogs*?
12. What area of Germany is known as the Schwarzwald in German?
13. Which London street was associated with writers of little talent in the 18th century?
14. What job did Ian Lavender do in the sitcom *Have I Got You...Where You Want Me?*?
15. Who wrote *Down and Out in Paris and London* and *The Road to Wigan Pier*?
16. What is the capital of Laos?
17. What is the face value of the specially minted coins distributed by the Queen as Maundy money?
18. In chess, what does the symbol KBP stand for?
19. Which British pianist initiated daily lunchtime concerts at the National Gallery during World War II?
20. What name is given to a disturbance of the normal rhythm of the heart?

ANSWERS: 1 Highgate. **2** Black Death. **3** Nebraska. **4** Green Card. **5** Olympic Games. **6** Dublin. **7** St Mary Magdalene. **8** Britney Spears. **9** Bangor. **10** Argonauts. **11** Aristophanes. **12** The Black Forest. **13** Grub Street. **14** Dentist. **15** George Orwell. **16** Vientiane. **17** Four old pence. **18** King's Bishop's Pawn. **19** Dame Myra Hess. **20** Arrhythmia.

 **General Knowledge**

Your rating:
- 0-5   Join a library
- 11-15   Join a quiz team
- 6-10   Keep at it
- 16-20   Join Mensa

1. Which Russian-born American science-fiction author wrote the *Foundation* trilogy?
2. By what nickname was snooker player Alex Higgins known?
3. Lanzarote and Tenerife belong to which island group?
4. What is the highest British military decoration for bravery?
5. Which large flightless African bird can reach speeds of up to 40 miles per hour when running?
6. How many Muses are there in Greek mythology?
7. What was Dorothy's surname in the film *The Wizard of Oz*?
8. What name is given to a group of lions?
9. Which British novelist wrote *Watership Down*?
10. Which style of design took its name from the 1925 Exposition Internationale des Arts Décoratifs in Paris?
11. Which famous U.S. pioneer and lawman was shot dead from behind while playing poker in 1876?
12. In the Old Testament, what was the name of the chest in which the Israelites kept the Tablets of the Law?
13. Which American author and critic wrote the novels *Burr* and *Myra Breckinridge*?
14. In which European country is the village of Blenheim, scene of a 1704 battle?
15. Which brittle metallic element has the symbol Bi?
16. In Greek mythology, who was the twin sister of Apollo?
17. Who was the Roman procurator of Judaea from 26 to 36 AD?
18. Who presents the British improvisation show *Whose Line Is It Anyway*?
19. Which of Gustav Mahler's symphonies is known as the *Resurrection Symphony*?
20. On what date does the grouse-shooting season end in Britain?

ANSWERS: 1 *Isaac Asimov*, 2 *Hurricane*, 3 *The Canary Islands*, 4 *Victoria Cross*, 5 *Ostrich*, 6 *Nine*, 7 *Gale*, 8 *Pride*, 9 *Richard Adams*, 10 *Art Deco*, 11 *Wild Bill Hickok*, 12 *Ark of the Covenant*, 13 *Gore Vidal*, 14 *Germany*, 15 *Bismuth*, 16 *Artemis*, 17 *Pontius Pilate*, 18 *Clive Anderson*, 19 *The Second*, 20 *December 10*.

Entertainment

Your rating: ● **0-5** Buy a TV   ● **6-10** Keep at it
● **11-15** Join a quiz team   ● **16-20** Enter a quiz show

1. Who was David Wicks' mum in TV's *EastEnders*?
2. Which U.S. group had hits in the Seventies with *Easy* and *Three Times a Lady*?
3. Who directed and starred in the 1941 film *Citizen Kane*?
4. In which hospital was BBC 1's *Casualty* set?
5. Who had a huge hit in 1990 with *Nothing Compares 2 U*?
6. Which of the Attenborough brothers starred in the 1963 film *The Great Escape*?
7. Who played *Columbo* on TV?
8. Who was *Now and Forever* in the charts in 1994?
9. What is the pub called in *Coronation Street*?
10. Which Motown star released an album entitled *One Woman - The Ultimate Collection*?
11. Which former *Roseanne* star played *King Ralph* in the 1991 film?
12. Which *TFI Friday* host originally co-presented *The Big Breakfast* with Gaby Roslin?
13. What job did Sinbad originally do in Channel 4's *Brookside*?
14. Which *Saturday Night Fever* star appeared in the 1989 film *Look Who's Talking*?
15. Which member of the Ewings was famously mysteriously shot in *Dallas*?
16. What type of car was *Herbie* in the series of Disney films?
17. Which fruity band had a hit with *Linger* in 1994?
18. On whose novel was the 1990 film *Misery* based?
19. With which instrument did Liberace find fame?
20. Where did *EastEnders*' Melanie and Natalie's joint hen night take place in 1999?

ANSWERS: 1 *Pat*, 2 *The Commodores*, 3 *Orson Welles*, 4 *Holby City Hospital*, 5 *Sinead O'Connor*, 6 *Richard Attenborough*, 7 *Peter Falk*, 8 *Richard Marx*, 9 *The Rover's Return*, 10 *Diana Ross*, 11 *John Goodman*, 12 *Chris Evans*, 13 *A window cleaner*, 14 *John Travolta*, 15 *JR*, 16 *A Volkswagen beetle*, 17 *Cranberries*, 18 *Stephen King's*, 19 *The piano*, 20 *Amsterdam*.

General Knowledge

1. Which American car manufacturer introduced the assembly line for producing the famous Model T?
2. Who was arrested for the assassination of President Kennedy in 1963?
3. Who wrote the thriller *The Partner*?
4. What name is given to the act of maliciously setting fire to something?
5. Which North American river is the chief tributary of the Mississippi?
6. What was the former name of the New York town of Ossining, famous for its prison?
7. If something were falcate, what would it be shaped like?
8. What is the most distant of the giant planets?
9. Which legendary creature has the form of a woman above the waist and a fish below?
10. What is the capital of Austria?
11. What name is given to a goatskin pouch worn with a kilt in Highland dress?
12. Who asked for the body of Jesus after the crucifixion and arranged for its burial?
13. Which actress is the elder sister of Warren Beatty?
14. Of what type of tree are the pecan and the shagbark examples?
15. Which river is formed by the confluence of the Rivers Goyt and Tame at Stockport?
16. Which German author wrote *Death in Venice* and *The Magic Mountain*?
17. What name was given to the agreement reached by Britain and France in 1904?
18. Which English poet wrote *Poems Descriptive of Rural Life and Scenery* and *The Shepherd's Calendar*?
19. Who played *Edward Scissorhands*?
20. Which English king married Philippa of Hainault in 1328?

ANSWERS: 1 *Henry Ford.* 2 *Lee Harvey Oswald.* 3 *John Grisham.* 4 *Arson.* 5 *Missouri River.* 6 *Sing Sing.* 7 *A sickle.* 8 *Neptune.* 9 *Mermaid.* 10 *Vienna.* 11 *Sporran.* 12 *Joseph of Arimathea.* 13 *Shirley MacLaine.* 14 *Hickory.* 15 *River Mersey.* 16 *Thomas Mann.* 17 *Entente Cordiale.* 18 *John Clare.* 19 *Johnny Depp.* 20 *Edward III.*

 # General Knowledge

Your rating:
- 0-5 Join a library
- 11-15 Join a quiz team
- 6-10 Keep at it
- 16-20 Join Mensa

1. Which Nazi politician was arrested when he made a secret trip to Scotland in 1941 to negotiate peace?
2. By what name was American film director Sean O'Feeney, whose films included *Stagecoach* and *The Grapes of Wrath*, better known?
3. What is the U.S. term for autumn?
4. What is the chief river of Australia?
5. Which Chilean island famous for its giant stone sculptures is also called Rapa Nui?
6. Of which Middle Eastern sultanate is Muscat the capital?
7. Which extremely poisonous element has the symbol As?
8. Who played the killer in the 1954 film *Rear Window*?
9. Which fictional British naval officer of the Napoleonic Wars was created by C.S. Forester?
10. What is the name of the equatorial belt, noted for its calms and squalls, where the trade winds converge?
11. Which London theatre was the home of the National Theatre from 1963 to 1976?
12. What was the name of the ceremony at which people found guilty by the Spanish Inquisition were sentenced?
13. Which English poet and critic wrote *Dover Beach* and *Sohrab and Rustum*?
14. What is the minimum number of tennis strokes a player needs to make to win a set?
15. Which novel inspired Jean Rhys's *Wide Sargasso Sea*?
16. What is the largest of the Mariana Islands in the West Pacific Ocean?
17. Which American inventor developed the first safety lift?
18. Which German director made the films *Aguirre, Wrath of God* and *Fitzcarraldo*?
19. In which country is the seaport of Aden?
20. What name was given to the religious dramas performed throughout medieval Europe on Good Friday?

ANSWERS: 1 *Rudolf Hess*, 2 *John Ford*, 3 *Fall*, 4 *Murray River*, 5 *Easter Island*, 6 *Oman*, 7 *Arsenic*, 8 *Raymond Burr*, 9 *Horatio Hornblower*, 10 *The doldrums*, 11 *The Old Vic*, 12 *Auto-da-fé*, 13 *Matthew Arnold*, 14 *Twelve*, 15 *Jane Eyre*, 16 *Guam*, 17 *Elisha Graves Otis*, 18 *Werner Herzog*, 19 *Yemen*, 20 *Passion plays*.

 *General Knowledge*

Your rating: ● 0-5   Join a library   ● 6-10   Keep at it
                    ● 11-15 Join a quiz team   ● 16-20   Join Mensa

1. Which English poet wrote *Paradise Lost* and *Paradise Regained*?
2. What name is given to an explosive mixture of saltpetre, charcoal and sulphur, used in fireworks?
3. Split is a seaport on which European sea?
4. By what name is the crane fly commonly known?
5. Which Australian city was the venue for the 1956 Olympics?
6. What sort of creature is a guppy?
7. Which brothers played *The Fabulous Baker Boys* on film?
8. What is the capital of the Philippines?
9. Which rare Indonesian monitor lizard is the largest living lizard?
10. Who wrote *The House at Pooh Corner* and *When We Were Very Young*?
11. Which German composer wrote the operas *Cardillac* and *Mathis der Maler*?
12. What was the name of the celebration organised in 1951 to commemorate the Great Exhibition of 1851?
13. Which war began in 1861 and ended in 1865?
14. Which artist worked from 1795 until his death on drawings concerning the comparative anatomy of *Man, Tiger, and Fowl*?
15. Which actress became Greek minister of culture and science in 1981?
16. What was the title of the chief magistrate of Venice from 697 to 1797?
17. Of which island country of the West Indies is Roseau the capital?
18. Parts of which animal were formerly cooked and eaten in a humble pie?
19. Which British composer and organist wrote the 1887 oratorio *The Crucifixion*?
20. Which Charles Dickens novel features the character John Jarndyce?

Entertainment

Your rating: ● 0-5   **Buy a TV**   ● 6-10   **Keep at it**
                ● 11-15   **Join a quiz team**   ● 16-20   **Enter a quiz show**

1. Which U.S. soul singer released an album entitled *Music Box*?
2. What was Wayne's best friend called in the Nineties films *Wayne's World* and *Wayne's World 2*?
3. Who played Captain Kirk in TV's *Star Trek*?
4. Who were destined to *Stay Together* in the top five in 1994?
5. Who played adventurous young detective *Anna Lee* in the TV series of the same name?
6. Which *Top Gun* star played Joseph, an Irish tenant farmer in the 1992 film *Far and Away*?
7. Which BBC1 current affairs show was co-presented by Tom Mangold?
8. Which group originally recorded *Light My Fire*?
9. Who presented the TV series *Life On Earth*?
10. Who directed the controversial 1989 film *Do the Right Thing*?
11. On which channel did the late-night cookery series *Get Stuffed* appear?
12. Which Icelandic singer released an album entitled *Debut*?
13. Which morning programme was formerly presented by Anne Diamond and Nick Owen?
14. What is the West End's longest-running play?
15. In which children's cartoon was Baron Greenback the baddie?
16. Which flautist had a 1978 top five hit with his recording of *Annie's Song*?
17. About which sport was the 1977 film *Pumping Iron*?
18. Which Dutch dance act had a 1994 top ten hit with *Let the Beat Control Your Body*?
19. Which member of the royal family introduced the art series *The Royal Collection*?
20. Which pop singer starred in the 1985 film *Desperately Seeking Susan*?

ANSWERS: *1 Mariah Carey, 2 Garth, 3 William Shatner, 4 Suede, 5 Imogen Stubbs, 6 Tom Cruise, 7 Here and Now, 8 The Doors, 9 David Attenborough, 10 Spike Lee, 11 ITV, 12 Bjork, 13 Good Morning, 14 The Mousetrap, 15 Dangermouse, 16 James Galway, 17 Body Building, 18 2 Unlimited, 19 Prince Charles, 20 Madonna.*

 # General Knowledge

Your rating: ● 0-5   Join a library   ● 6-10   Keep at it
● 11-15   Join a quiz team   ● 16-20   Join Mensa

1. Which British actor has actress daughters called Hayley and Juliet?
2. From where did London's fruit and vegetable market move to Nine Elms in 1973?
3. Which western hero did Kevin Costner play in a 1994 Lawrence Kasdan film?
4. In which country is a wild dog known as a dingo found?
5. What was the name of the raft used by Thor Heyerdahl on his 1947 expedition?
6. What is the French name for the English Channel?
7. Who wrote the novel *Westward Ho!*?
8. Which Russian goldsmith and jeweller was famous for his jewelled Easter eggs?
9. Which country was created in 1947 as a separate state for the Muslim minority in India?
10. Diplodocus, Iguanodon and Triceratops are examples of what sort of creature?
11. Which Saudi Arabian city is believed to contain the tomb of Muhammad?
12. To which university does the Courtauld Institute of Art belong?
13. Which entertainer was famous for his Emu's attacks on Michael Parkinson?
14. What does DMA stand for in computer technology?
15. Which British poet wrote *Fighting Terms*, *My Sad Captains* and *Jack Straw's Castle*?
16. What part of the body is affected by Ménière's disease?
17. At which Ugandan airport were Israeli hostages rescued from a hijacked plane in 1976?
18. What is the Hebrew name for Calvary?
19. Lake Titicaca is on the border of which two South American countries?
20. Which Jane Austen novel features the character Fanny Price?

 *General Knowledge*

Your rating: ● 0-5 Join a library   ● 6-10 Keep at it
 ● 11-15 Join a quiz team   ● 16-20 Join Mensa

1. Which group of islands in the Aegean Sea includes Rhodes, Kos and Patmos?
2. What name is given to a court convened to try a member of the services?
3. Which trombonist and bandleader is associated with *Moonlight Serenade* and *In the Mood*?
4. How many strokes under par is a birdie on a golf hole?
5. Which famous singer won an Oscar for his nonsinging role in the film *From Here To Eternity*?
6. What is the world's highest mountain system?
7. Which sculptor's only equestrian statue, *General Lynch*, was destroyed by a revolution in Chile?
8. What is the young of an eel called?
9. Which Leicestershire market town is famous for its pork pies?
10. In the arts world, what does the abbreviation ENO stand for?
11. Which division of Oceania in the south-west Pacific includes the Bismarck Archipelago, the Solomon Islands, New Caledonia and Fiji?
12. In which U.S. state is the city of Minneapolis?
13. Which Hungarian pianist and composer is best known for his *Variations on a Nursery Theme*?
14. What does the Latin phrase 'mea culpa' mean?
15. Which legendary king of Sparta was the husband of Helen of Troy?
16. Who wrote the novels *Tropic of Cancer* and *Tropic of Capricorn*?
17. Which Scottish football teams plays at Easter Road?
18. Who played *The District Nurse* in a BBC television series?
19. Which Labour politician who helped to draft the UN charter won the Nobel peace prize in 1959?
20. What is the second largest island of the Philippines?

ANSWERS: 1 *Dodecanese.* **2** *Court-martial.* **3** *Glenn Miller.* **4** *One.* **5** *Frank Sinatra.* **6** *The Himalayas.* **7** *Rodin.* **8** *An elver.* **9** *Melton Mowbray.* **10** *English National Opera.* **11** *Melanesia.* **12** *Minnesota.* **13** *Ernö (or Ernst von) Dohnanyi.* **14** *My fault.* **15** *Menelaus.* **16** *Henry Miller.* **17** *Hibernian.* **18** *Nerys Hughes.* **19** *Philip John Noel-Baker.* **20** *Mindanao.*

 *General Knowledge*

Your rating: ● 0-5 Join a library ● 6-10 Keep at it
● 11-15 Join a quiz team ● 16-20 Join Mensa

1. Which uncompromising and outspoken minister of the Free Presbyterian Church of Ulster became a Democratic Unionist MP in 1974?
2. What was the title of the heir to the French throne from 1350 to 1830?
3. In which European country is the region of Transylvania?
4. Which Scottish motor racing driver was world champion in 1963 and 1965?
5. What name is given to the band of light crossing the night sky composed of innumerable stars that are too faint to be seen individually?
6. Of which Italian island is Palermo the capital?
7. Which Australian bird is also known as a laughing jackass?
8. Who is wife and assistant of magician Paul Daniels?
9. Which village near Balmoral is famous for its Gathering, the most celebrated of the Highland Games?
10. Who wrote *Lord Jim*, *Heart of Darkness* and *Nostromo*?
11. Which composer wrote *The Prince of Denmark's March*, the basis of the *Trumpet Voluntary* wrongly attributed to Purcell?
12. What name is given to aquatic vertebrates of the classes Chondrichthyes and Osteichthyes?
13. Which two British politicians were members of the European Commission that resigned en masse in 1999?
14. Who played Sonny in the 1972 film *The Godfather*?
15. Which Scottish historian and philosopher wrote a *History of India* and *Elements of Political Economy*?
16. What is the county town of County Clare?
17. Which statesman, who was dominated by George III, was prime minister from 1770 to 1782?
18. What sort of creature is a sidewinder?
19. Who painted *The Raft of the Medusa*?
20. Which dancer was originally to have played the Fred Astaire role in the film *Easter Parade*?

Entertainment

Your rating:	● 0-5	Buy a TV	● 6-10	Keep at it
	● 11-15	Join a quiz team	● 16-20	Enter a quiz show

1. Which legendary cricketing all-rounder was formerly a team captain opposite Bill Beaumont on TV's *A Question of Sport*?

2. Which group had a 1964 number one hit with *You Really Got Me*?

3. Which ITV Australian soap was set in Summer Bay?

4. Who was the bald leader of the *Magnificent Seven* in the 1960 film?

5. Which TV mini-series featured the Arnett family?

6. Who was *Without You* but with a number one hit in 1994?

7. Which comedian played the mummy's boy in the TV sitcom *Sorry*?

8. Upon whose novel was the 1986 film *The Mosquito Coast* based?

9. Which soul diva released an album and a single entitled *So Close*?

10. Who played the cross-dressing *Mrs Doubtfire* in the 1993 comedy film?

11. How many members did the Scandinavian pop group ABBA have?

12. Who played Gordon Brittas in the comedy series *The Brittas Empire*?

13. Which group harmonised on the 1964 top ten hit *I Get Around*?

14. Who presented the variety-cum game show *Talking Telephone Numbers* alongside Emma Forbes?

15. Which Swedish band had a top five hit with *The Sign* in 1994?

16. Which sitcom writer was behind the comedy series *Luv*?

17. Which singer and chat show host collaborated with Roger Whittaker on the 1986 top ten hit *The Skye Boat Song*?

18. What was the title of Robert De Niro's 1993 directorial debut?

19. Which all-female U.S. band were *Downtown* in the charts in 1994?

20. Who played Scrooge in the 1988 film *Scrooged*?

ANSWERS: 1 Ian Botham. 2 The Kinks. 3 Home and Away. 4 Yul Brynner. 5 Laurel Avenue. 6 Mariah Carey. 7 Ronnie Corbett. 8 Paul Theroux's. 9 Dina Carroll. 10 Robin Williams. 11 Four. 12 Chris Barrie. 13 The Beach Boys. 14 Phillip Schofield. 15 Ace of Base. 16 Carla Lane. 17 Des O'Connor. 18 A Bronx Tale. 19 SWV. 20 Bill Murray.

THE TRIVIA QUIZ BOOK

 *General Knowledge*

Your rating:	● 0-5	Join a library	● 6-10	Keep at it
	● 11-15	Join a quiz team	● 16-20	Join Mensa

1. Which British bacteriologist has been credited with the discovery of the antibiotic penicillin?
2. Who directed the films *A Bridge Too Far*, *Gandhi* and *A Chorus Line*?
3. What in printing do the letters u.c. stand for?
4. In which U.S. state is Atlantic City on which the original monopoly board game was based?
5. Which eye infection is sometimes called pinkeye?
6. On which river is the Aswan High Dam?
7. Which actress tearfully received the Best Actress Oscar for her role in *Shakespeare in Love*?
8. In which sport might you use a suplex?
9. Which former member of the Beatles followed John Lennon into the *Rock 'n' Roll Hall of Fame*?
10. Who was director of the FBI from 1924 to 1972?
11. Which French composer wrote the operas *Romeo and Juliet* and *Faust*?
12. What is the longest river in Scandinavia?
13. Which two balloonists were the first to circumnavigate the globe?
14. Who was the second wife of Napoleon Bonaparte?
15. Which comedy impresionist's real name is Robert Nankerville?
16. What is the capital of the Yugoslav republic of Macedonia?
17. Which dry or liquid measure is equal to eight gallons or four pecks in the UK?
18. What nationality was Gustave Flaubert, author of *Madame Bovary*?
19. Which 17th-century English sect that flourished under the Commonwealth was led by Gerrard Winstanley?
20. What sort of creature is a coypu?

ANSWERS: *1 Sir Alexander Fleming, 2 Sir Richard Attenborough, 3 Upper case, 4 New Jersey, 5 Conjunctivitis, 6 River Nile, 7 Gwyneth Paltrow, 8 Wrestling - it is a hold, 9 Paul McCartney, 10 J Edgar Hoover, 11 Charles Gounod, 12 River Glomma, 13 Bertrand Piccard and Brian Jones, 14 Marie Louise, 15 Bobby Davro, 16 Skopje, 17 Bushel, 18 French, 19 The Diggers, 20 An aquatic rodent.*

 *General Knowledge*

Your rating: ● 0-5 Join a library   ● 6-10   Keep at it
              ● 11-15 Join a quiz team ● 16-20 Join Mensa

1. Which recent U.S. president was a former director of the CIA?
2. What name is given to an auction in which the auctioneer gradually reduces the bidding price?
3. Which island of the Inner Hebrides houses Fingal's Cave?
4. What name is given to the chief law officer of the crown and head of the English Bar?
5. Which British novelist created James Bond?
6. From which poisonous plant is the drug atropine derived?
7. Which comic actor's catch-phrase is 'I'm Free'?
8. What name is given to the skeleton of the head of a vertebrate animal?
9. Which mountain system of north-west Africa stretches from the Atlantic coast of Morocco to Tunisia?
10. How many days after the Resurrection is Christ said to have ascended into heaven?
11. Which British poet wrote *Façade*, for which Sir William Walton wrote a musical accompaniment?
12. Who was Chancellor of West Germany 1969-74 and winner of the 1971 Nobel Peace Prize?
13. Which Russian author wrote the novel *Oblomov*?
14. Who did Terence Alexander play in *Bergerac*?
15. Which Chinese dynasty lasted from 1368 to 1644?
16. What is the largest city in New Zealand?
17. What has been the official residence of French presidents since the 1870s?
18. In which year was t.v. cook Keith Floyd born?
19. Who founded a garden village at Bournville near Birmingham in 1894?
20. Which George Eliot novel features the character Tom Tulliver?

 *General Knowledge*

Your rating:
- 0-5   Join a library
- 11-15   Join a quiz team
- 6-10   Keep at it
- 16-20   Join Mensa

1. Which American tennis player won the men's singles at Wimbledon in 1974 and 1982?
2. In which London street did the Great Fire of London break out in a baker's shop in 1666?
3. Which Labour politician was deputy prime minister in the wartime coalition and prime minister from 1945 to 1951?
4. For which film did Steven Spielberg win the Oscar for Best Director at the 1999 Academy Awards?
5. What in medical terms is HRT?
6. From what fruit is cider made?
7. Which unit used to express depths of water is equal to six feet?
8. Which vegetable is known as an eggplant in the United States?
9. In which English county is the River Lyn, scene of severe flooding in 1952?
10. What name is given to the rich fruit cake traditionally eaten in Lent or at Easter?
11. Which British statesman delivered the Tamworth manifesto, which was the foundation of the Conservative Party?
12. What is the name of the preserved Neolithic village on Mainland in the Orkney Islands?
13. Which British satirical poet wrote *Hudibras*?
14. Who played Harry in the film *When Harry Met Sally*?
15. Which French town on the Scarpe River gave its name to a type of tapestry?
16. Who was the Roman goddess of flowers and spring?
17. Gussie Fink-Nottle and Aunt Agatha are whose comic creations?
18. Which British commander in World War II was nicknamed the Auk?
19. Of which French island in the West Indies is Fort-de-France the capital?
20. For which English county did the cricketer W.G. Grace play?

ANSWERS: 1 Jimmy Connors, 2 Pudding Lane, 3 Clement Attlee, 4 Saving Private Ryan, 5 Hormone replacement therapy, 6 Apples, 7 Fathom, 8 Aubergine, 9 Devon, 10 Simnel cake, 11 Sir Robert Peel, 12 Skara Brae, 13 Samuel Butler, 14 Billy Crystal, 15 Arras, 16 Flora, 17 P.G. Wodehouse, 18 Sir Claude Auchinleck, 19 Martinique, 20 Gloucestershire.

Entertainment

Your rating:	● 0-5	Buy a TV	● 6-10	Keep at it
	● 11-15	Join a quiz team	● 16-20	Enter a quiz show

1.   Which Irish presenter hosted TV's moral dilemma show *Do The Right Thing*?
2.   Which 1958 film musical featured the song *Some Enchanted Evening*?
3.   Which U.S. band had a top twenty hit with *Disarm* in 1994?
4.   Which British director starred in the 1993 film *Jurassic Park*?
5.   From which planet was the alien half of *Mork and Mindy* in the TV comedy series?
6.   On whose book was the 1988 film *The Accidental Tourist* based?
7.   What kind of car did *Inspector Morse* drive in the police drama series?
8.   Who entered the charts in 1965 with *I Left My Heart in San Francisco*?
9.   What was *George and Mildred*'s surname in the Seventies sitcom?
10. Who won a Best Actress Oscar for her performance as a rape victim in the 1988 film *The Accused*?
11. Who played David Addison in the Eighties U.S. comedy drama series *Moonlighting*?
12. About which British artist was the 1978 number one *Matchstalk Men and Matchstalk Cats and Dogs*?
13. Which famously scruffy garment did TV detective *Columbo* wear?
14. Which UK group had a number one hit with *Two Tribes* in 1984?
15. Which consummate British actor played the great writer in the 1991 film *Kafka*?
16. Who played the female half of *Terry and June* in the TV sitcom?
17. Which UK group released an album entitled *Elegant Slumming*?
18. Which of the Snow brothers co-presented BBC 1's *Tomorrow's World* alongside Philippa Forrester?
19. For his performance as an AIDS victim in which 1993 film did Tom Hanks win his first Best Actor Oscar?
20. Who played *Citizen Smith*, alias 'Wolfie' in the comedy series?

ANSWERS: 1 *Terry Wogan*, 2 *South Pacific*, 3 *Smashing Pumpkins*, 4 *Richard Attenborough*, 5 *Ork*, 6 *Anne Tyler's*, 7 *A 1960 Mark 2 Jaguar*, 8 *Tony Bennett*, 9 *Roper*, 10 *Jodie Foster*, 11 *Bruce Willis*, 12 *L S Lowry*, 13 *A raincoat*, 14 *Frankie Goes To Hollywood*, 15 *Jeremy Irons*, 16 *June Whitfield*, 17 *M People*, 18 *Peter*, 19 *Philadelphia*, 20 *Robert Lindsay*.

 # General Knowledge

| Your rating: | ● 0-5 | Join a library | ● 6-10 | Keep at it |
| | ● 11-15 | Join a quiz team | ● 16-20 | Join Mensa |

1. Which American actress starred in *Barbarella*, *Klute* and *Coming Home*?
2. Of which country of the former Soviet Union is Tbilisi the capital?
3. Which queen of Egypt was the mistress of Julius Caesar and Mark Antony?
4. In which century did Vincent van Gogh live?
5. Which British novelist wrote *The Collector* and *The French Lieutenant's Woman*?
6. With which musical instrument is Benny Goodman associated?
7. What is the U.S. name for a courgette?
8. What was the first name of the 19th century prime minister Gladstone?
9. Which patriotic song comes from Thomas Arne's masque *Alfred*?
10. What is the administrative centre of Hertfordshire?
11. Which 17th century English antiquary compiled the biographical anecdotes published as *Brief Lives* in 1898?
12. Who wrote the novel *The Vicar of Wakefield*, the poem *The Deserted Village* and the play *She Stoops To Conquer*?
13. Which Danish footballer scored the goal that won the Worthington Cup Final for Tottenham Hotspur in 1999?
14. Which actor plays Jack Geller in *Friends*?
15. Which Italian river burst its banks in 1966 causing disastrous flooding in Florence?
16. What form of skiing is also known as langlauf?
17. Which radioactive element has the chemical symbol At?
18. In which Central American republic is the volcano Irazu?
19. Who directed the films *The Wild Bunch*, *Straw Dogs* and *The Getaway*?
20. Which English-born poet wrote *Look, Stranger*?

ANSWERS: 1 *Jane Fonda*, 2 *Georgia*, 3 *Cleopatra (VII)*, 4 *19th*, 5 *John Fowles*, 6 *Clarinet*, 7 *Zucchini*, 8 *William*, 9 *Rule Britannia*, 10 *Hertford*, 11 *John Aubrey*, 12 *Oliver Goldsmith*, 13 *Allan Nielsen*, 14 *Elliott Gould*, 15 *River Arno*, 16 *Cross country*, 17 *Astatine*, 18 *Costa Rica*, 19 *Sam Peckinpah*, 20 *W H Auden*.

 *General Knowledge*

Your rating:	● 0-5	Join a library	● 6-10	Keep at it
	● 11-15	Join a quiz team	● 16-20	Join Mensa

1. Which queen of England was the daughter of Henry VIII and Catherine of Aragon?
2. Who was the first man to walk on the moon?
3. Which veteran American actor won a Best Supporting Actor Oscar for *Affliction*?
4. Which city in Massachusetts is the seat of Harvard University?
5. Which British novelist wrote *Room at the Top* and *Life at the Top*?
6. Whom did Margaret Thatcher succeed as leader of the Conservative Party?
7. What name is given to the salted roe of a sturgeon?
8. Who played Michael Faraday in the 1999 film *Arlington Road*?
9. Which king of the Huns was known as the Scourge of God?
10. Of which Eastern European country was Nicolae Ceausescu president?
11. Which Lancashire town was designated a new town in 1961 to relieve overcrowding on Merseyside?
12. In which 1513 battle was King James IV of Scotland killed?
13. Which Oscar-winning actress was born in Walton-on-Thames in 1935?
14. What sort of creature is a bushmaster?
15. Which American explorer was the first to reach the North Pole?
16. With which musical instrument is Claudio Arrau associated?
17. In which sport might you play a long jenny?
18. What was the former name of the country Burkina Faso?
19. Which British engineer designed the Clifton Suspension Bridge?
20. In which American state is the city of Tacoma?

 # General Knowledge

| Your rating: | ● 0-5 | Join a library | ● 6-10 | Keep at it |
| | ● 11-15 | Join a quiz team | ● 16-20 | Join Mensa |

1. Which England cricket captain was involved in an argument with an umpire in Pakistan in 1987?
2. Who was the Roman god of love identified with the Greek Eros?
3. By what name is a plant of the genus *Digitalis* commonly known?
4. In the American legal system, what does D.A. stand for?
5. Which British author wrote *The Pilgrim's Progress*?
6. In which U.S. state is the city of Chicago?
7. Which British actress won a Best Supporting Actress Oscar for her short appearance in *Shakespeare in Love*?
8. What is the sixth letter in the Greek alphabet?
9. Which British dramatist wrote *The Caretaker* and *The Birthday Party*?
10. What is the capital of Venezuela?
11. Which 1st century BC Roman poet was famous for his Odes, Epistles and Satires?
12. Who lost his world heavyweight boxing title to Gentleman Jim Corbett in the first championship bout fought under the Queensberry Rules?
13. In which TV show did the character Captain 'Howling Mad' Murdoch appear?
14. Of which country is the Tay the longest river?
15. Which former England cricket captain has the middle name Ivon?
16. Of which country is Sucre the legal capital?
17. Which House of Representatives committee was set up in 1935 to investigate subversive organisations in the United States?
18. Who became Roman emperor after the murder of his nephew Caligula?
19. Which Cubist artist made the abstract film *Le Ballet Mechanique* in 1924?
20. Which Shakespeare play features the characters Angelo and Claudio?

ANSWERS: 1 Mike Gatting, 2 Cupid, 3 Foxglove, 4 District Attorney, 5 John Bunyan, 6 Illinois, 7 Dame Judi Dench, 8 Zeta, 9 Harold Pinter, 10 Caracas, 11 Horace, 12 John L Sullivan, 13 The A-Team, 14 Scotland, 15 David Gower, 16 Bolivia, 17 Un-American Activities Committee, 18 Claudius, 19 Fernand Léger, 20 Measure for Measure.

 # *Entertainment*

1. The TV drama *The Rector's Wife* was based on which author's book?
2. Which *Wall Street* star appeared in the 1993 film version of *The Three Musketeers*?
3. Which group had hits with *Roxanne* and *Message in a Bottle* in 1979?
4. What was the newspaper called in the TV series *Nelson's Column*?
5. For which U.S. vocalist did *Rock and Roll Dreams Come Through* in 1994?
6. On which channel was *The Oprah Winfrey Show* initially screened in the UK?
7. What was the murder weapon in the 1992 film *Basic Instinct*?
8. Which 'Forces Sweetheart' is famous for singing *We'll Meet Again*?
9. What job did *Rosie* have in the former sitcom of the same name?
10. What kind of creature was Thumper in the 1942 animated classic *Bambi*?
11. Which weatherman leapt from Ireland to England on a giant floating map during TV's *This Morning*?
12. Which American crooner had a top five hit in 1969 with *My Way*?
13. Who played the male lead in the 1946 film *It's a Wonderful Life*?
14. Which UK boy band had a number one hit with *Everything Changes* in 1994?
15. Which actress received an Oscar nomination for her performance as a barrister in the 1993 film *In the Name of the Father*?
16. In which English city was the sitcom *Bread* set?
17. Which blonde screen idol had a 1964 top ten hit with *Move Over Darling*?
18. Which *Coronation Street* character was famous for her hot pots, served in The Rovers Return?
19. Who directed the 1992 film *Malcolm X*?
20. Which TV presenter had a 1964 number one with *Anyone Who Had a Heart*?

 *General Knowledge*

Your rating: ● 0-5   Join a library   ● 6-10   Keep at it
               ● 11-15   Join a quiz team   ● 16-20   Join Mensa

1. Which husband and wife shared the 1903 Nobel Prize for Physics with Henri Becquerel?
2. What name was given to a place of work in which all employees were required to be members of specified trade unions?
3. Which British author wrote *The Thirty-Nine Steps*?
4. In Jewish cookery, what is a kneidel?
5. Which London street between the Strand and Ludgate Circus became synonymous with the British newspaper industry?
6. What is the capital of Belgium?
7. Which canal was nationalised by President Nasser in 1956?
8. What nationality was Pop Artist Jim Dine?
9. Which English-born actress was twice married to actor Richard Burton?
10. In which country was media tycoon Rupert Murdoch born?
11. Which Austrian composer wrote the oratorios *The Creation* and *The Seasons*?
12. To which genus of plants does traveller's joy or old man's beard belong?
13. Which African lake was discovered by Sir Richard Burton and John Speke in 1858?
14. Who narrates Woody Allen's film *Radio Days*?
15. Which Turkish-born British engineer designed the Mini?
16. What sort of creature is a pipistrelle?
17. Who was Britain's first Muslim MP?
18. Which eccentric Italian film director was the surprise winner of the 1999 Oscar for Best Actor?
19. In what is Bounty Island, New Zealand, covered?
20. What is the largest asteroid or minor planet?

 **General Knowledge**

Your rating: ● 0-5   Join a library   ● 6-10   Keep at it
             ● 11-15   Join a quiz team   ● 16-20   Join Mensa

1. Which British novelist wrote *Silas Marner*?
2. What name is given to the symbol placed at the beginning of a musical stave to indicate the pitch?
3. Who played Daryl Van Horne in the film *The Witches of Eastwick*?
4. What part of the body contains five metatarsal bones?
5. Which English city is the administrative centre of Cumbria?
6. In what year did the French Revolution begin?
7. What name is given to a score in American football in which the ball is taken across the opponents' goal line?
8. What strait separates the Isle of Wight from Hampshire?
9. Which clipper ship built in 1869 is preserved as a museum at Greenwich?
10. British painter George Stubbs was famous for his studies of which animals?
11. Which Italian dramatist wrote *Six Characters in Search of an Author*?
12. What is the English name for Keffalinia, the largest of the Ionian Islands?
13. Which female British artist born in 1931 is associated with the Op Art movement?
14. What substance obtained from the sapodilla tree is used to make chewing gum?
15. Which toxic pale yellow halogen gas has the symbol F?
16. In which English county is the fishing village of Clovelly?
17. Which English composer gave up music and became an agent of Thomas Cromwell?
18. In which two cities are Cleopatra's Needles?
19. What is an oenophile?
20. Which Spanish film director made *The Discreet Charm of the Bourgeoisie*?

 *General Knowledge*

1. Which American novelist wrote *The Call of The Wild* and *White Fang*?
2. What is the UK's chief ferry port for the Continent?
3. Which saint is sometimes known as the Bishop of Hippo?
4. How many triangular points or chevrons are there on a backgammon board?
5. Which famous horror story was written by Bram Stoker?
6. Of which African country is Harare the capital?
7. What does a lepidopterist study or collect?
8. Who painted 1878's *Snow at Louveciennes*?
9. To which carnivorous mammal does the adjective vulpine relate?
10. What is the capital of Romania?
11. Which French New Wave film director made *Les Biches* and *Le Boucher*?
12. For which British contralto singer did Sir Edward Elgar compose his *Sea Pictures*?
13. Which corrosion-resistant alloy was substituted for silver alloy in British coins in 1946?
14. In which European country is the cathedral city of Breda?
15. Which king of England founded Eton College and King's College, Cambridge?
16. By what name was Italian baroque painter Michelangelo Merisi known?
17. Which German Nazi politician founded the Gestapo?
18. Which British actor played horror film director James Whale in the film *Gods and Monsters*?
19. In which year was singer Placido Domingo born?
20. Which Shakespeare play features the characters Sir Toby Belch and Sir Andrew Aguecheek?

Entertainment

Your rating: ● 0-5   Buy a TV   ● 6-10   Keep at it
               ● 11-15   Join a quiz team   ● 16-20   Enter a quiz show

1. How many Oscars did Steven Spielberg's 1993 film *Schindler's List* win?
2. Which hospital sitcom starred James Bolam and Peter Bowles as long-stay patients Roy Figgis and Archie Glover?
3. What was Bruce Springsteen's 1994 hit taken from the film *Philadelphia* called?
4. Who played Dr Beth Glover in the drama series *Peak Practice*?
5. Which UK vocalist released an album entitled *Brutal Youth* in 1994?
6. Which actor played the villain in the 1991 remake of *Cape Fear*?
7. Who presented the long-running darts quiz show *Bullseye*?
8. Who originally recorded the soul classic *Stand By Me*?
9. Which actor played Marcus Tandy in the ill-fated soap *Eldorado* and William Gilmore in the drama series *Anna Lee*?
10. Which *Romancing the Stone* star directed the 1992 film *Hoffa*?
11. Which Icelandic singer was *Violently Happy* to be in the top twenty in 1994?
12. What type of creature was *Beethoven* in the 1992 film?
13. Who sang the 1982 number one hit theme song from *Fame*?
14. Which *Coronation Street* character was played by William Tarmey?
15. Which late Canadian comic actor starred in 1993's *Cool Runnings*?
16. Who played the manor's new owner, Richard De Vere, in the sitcom *To the Manor Born*?
17. Which soul duo had a 1982 top ten hit with *I Can't Go For That (No Can Do)*?
18. Who played the troublesome Jimmy Corkhill in the soap *Brookside*?
19. In which British city was the 1985 Russian romance *Letter to Brezhnev* set?
20. Which female U.S. rap duo had a 1994 top ten hit with *Whatta Man*?

ANSWERS: 1 *Seven*, 2 *Only When I Laugh*, 3 *Streets of Philadelphia*, 4 *Amanda Burton*, 5 *Elvis Costello*, 6 *Robert De Niro*, 7 *Jim Bowen*, 8 *Ben E King*, 9 *Jesse Birdsall*, 10 *Danny De Vito*, 11 *Björk*, 12 *A St Bernard dog*, 13 *Irene Cara*, 14 *Jack Duckworth*, 15 *John Candy*, 16 *Peter Bowles*, 17 *Hall and Oates*, 18 *Dean Sullivan*, 19 *Liverpool*, 20 *Salt-N-Pepa*.

 *General Knowledge*

Your rating:
● 0-5   Join a library
● 6-10   Keep at it
● 11-15   Join a quiz team
● 16-20   Join Mensa

1. Which American poet wrote *The Song of Hiawatha*?
2. What name is given to the use of divining rods to discover subterranean minerals or water?
3. Which Swedish pop group's music inspired the West End musical *Mamma Mia*?
4. What is garam masala?
5. Which beetle takes its names from its well-developed mandibles that resemble antlers?
6. In which English county is the port of Harwich?
7. What name is given to any rod-shaped bacterium?
8. What measure is used to express the fineness of gold?
9. Who composed the 1812 opera *Tancredi*?
10. Which Wiltshire country house with a safari park is owned by the Marquess of Bath?
11. Which British novelist wrote *The Go-Between* and *The Shrimp and the Anemone*?
12. What is the chief mountain range of South Africa, also called Quathlamba?
13. Who played Det. Sgt. Tom Stone in police drama *Z Cars*?
14. In which city was the painter Francis Bacon born?
15. Which Jewish religious movement was found the Ba'al Shem Tov?
16. What is the most abundant lanthanide element?
17. Which actress won the Cecil B. DeMille Award at the 1969 Golden Globes?
18. Who was the elder brother of Hasdrubal Barca?
19. Which editor of *The Economist* wrote *The English Constitution* in 1867?
20. What is the state capital of Illinois?

ANSWERS: 1 *Henry Wadsworth Longfellow*, 2 *Dowsing*, 3 *Abba*, 4 *A mixture of spices*, 5 *Stag beetle*, 6 *Essex*, 7 *Bacillus*, 8 *Carat*, 9 *Rossini*, 10 *Longleat*, 11 *L P Hartley*, 12 *Drakensberg Mountains*, 13 *John Slater*, 14 *Dublin*, 15 *Hasidism*, 16 *Cerium*, 17 *Joan Crawford*, 18 *Hannibal*, 19 *Walter Bagehot*, 20 *Springfield*.

 # General Knowledge

1. Which British fighter pilot who lost both his legs in a flying accident was knighted in 1976?
2. What was the former name for Sri Lanka?
3. Which comedian wrote 1991 novel *The Liar*?
4. What was the name of the ship in which Sir Francis Drake circumnavigated the globe?
5. Of which Middle Eastern country is Baghdad the capital?
6. How many arms does a squid have?
7. Which Beatles song was voted the song of the century in a 1999 BBC survey?
8. What food is also called garbanzo?
9. Which indoor game is played with a shuttlecock?
10. Do stalactites grow upwards or downwards?
11. Which German travel guide editor published his first guidebook in 1829?
12. What is the quality rating for diesel fuel, similar to the octane number for petrol?
13. Which Russian novelist wrote *Crime and Punishment* and *The Brothers Karamazov*?
14. What was Karl Howman's character name in the TV comedy series *Brush Strokes*?
15. Which German city and port is at the confluence of the rivers Neckar and Rhine?
16. What name is given to the Japanese art of flower arrangement?
17. Which English mathematician conceived the idea of a mechanical computer that could store information?
18. What name is given to the official reports of debate in the British parliament?
19. Which Franco Zeffirelli film stars British Dames Maggie Smith, Judi Dench and Joan Plowright?
20. Ujpest is an industrial suburb of which eastern European country?

ANSWERS: 1 *Douglas Bader.* 2 *Ceylon.* 3 *Stephen Fry.* 4 *The Golden Hind.* 5 *Iraq.* 6 *Ten.* 7 *Yesterday.* 8 *Chick-pea.* 9 *Badminton.* 10 *Downwards.* 11 *Karl Baedeker.* 12 *Cetane number.* 13 *Fyodor Dostoevsky.* 14 *Jacko.* 15 *Mannheim.* 16 *Ikebana.* 17 *Charles Babbage.* 18 *Hansard.* 19 *Tea With Mussolini.* 20 *Hungary.*

THE TRIVIA QUIZ BOOK

 *General Knowledge*

Your rating:
- 0-5   Join a library
- 11-15   Join a quiz team
- 6-10   Keep at it
- 16-20   Join Mensa

1. Which British comedian was famous for his *Half Hour* on radio and TV?
2. What is the lowest pitched instrument of the violin family?
3. How many sides does an octagon have?
4. Who created the fictional detective Sherlock Holmes?
5. Which famous spa is in the Black Forest in Germany?
6. What name is given to an emission of water from the ground?
7. What name is given to the indigenous Polynesian people of New Zealand?
8. What part of the human body contains bones called metacarpals?
9. In which U.S. state is the tourist town of Redondo Beach?
10. What is the technical name for a squint?
11. Which Athenian lawgiver framed a notoriously severe code of laws in the 7th century BC?
12. In which 1066 battle did King Harold defeat his brother Tostig and King Harald of Norway?
13. Which cult author wrote the novel *Post Office*?
14. What is the ruling political party in Syria and Iraq?
15. Which optical disorder is known medically as diplopia?
16. What name is given to the leader of congregational prayer in a mosque?
17. Which Hollywood actress starred in 1987 film *Allan Quatermain and the Lost City of Gold*?
18. Which American dramatist collaborated with George S Kaufman on *You Can't Take It With You*?
19. What was the first synthetic plastic, created by Leo Baekeland?
20. Which French composer wrote the orchestral rhapsody *España*?

ANSWERS: 1 *Tony Hancock,* 2 *Double bass,* 3 *Eight,* 4 *Sir Arthur Conan Doyle,* 5 *Baden-Baden,* 6 *Spring,* 7 *Maoris,* 8 *The hand,* 9 *California,* 10 *Strabismus,* 11 *Draco,* 12 *Battle of Stamford Bridge,* 13 *Charles Bukowski,* 14 *Ba'ath Party,* 15 *Double vision,* 16 *Imam,* 17 *Sharon Stone,* 18 *Moss Hart,* 19 *Bakelite,* 20 *Emmanuel Chabrier.*

Entertainment

Your rating: ● 0-5   Buy a TV   ● 6-10   Keep at it
            ● 11-15   Join a quiz team   ● 16-20   Enter a quiz show

1. For which 1993 animated film starring Wallace and Gromit did Nick Park win an Oscar?
2. Which spoof DJs were played on TV by Harry Enfield and Paul Whitehouse?
3. What was the title of Steven Seagal's 1994 action movie, which he also produced and directed?
4. Which crooner had a top ten hit in 1982 with *I Wanna Do it With You*?
5. Which 1993 movie starred *Batman*'s Michael Keaton as a cancer victim?
6. From which country were the rock band INXS?
7. Which *Ghost* star did some *Dirty Dancing* with Jennifer Grey in the 1987 film?
8. Who had a 1965 hit with *In the Midnight Hour*?
9. Who starred as Danny opposite Olivia Newton-John as Sandy in the 1978 film *Grease*?
10. Which French fashion designer appeared in a kilt on Channel 4's *Eurotrash*?
11. Which member of the Fonda clan starred in the 1957 film *12 Angry Men*?
12. Which U.S. rock group had a 1986 hit with *You Give Love a Bad Name*?
13. Who played James Bond in 1974's *The Man With the Golden Gun*?
14. Who was the darts scorer on the quiz show *Bullseye*?
15. What was the favourite food of the *Teenage Mutant Ninja Turtles* in the 1990 film?
16. Who was the presenter of TV's *Mastermind*?
17. Which British group had a 1964 number one hit with *I'm Into Something Good*?
18. Which brothers starred as brothers in the 1989 film *The Fabulous Baker Boys*?
19. Who played Derek Wilton in *Coronation Street*?
20. What was the 1995 film about the 'fifth Beatle' Stuart Sutcliffe called?

ANSWERS: 1 *The Wrong Trousers*, 2 *Smashie and Nicey*, 3 *On Deadly Ground*, 4 *Barry Manilow*, 5 *My Life*, 6 *Australia*, 7 *Patrick Swayze*, 8 *Wilson Pickett*, 9 *John Travolta*, 10 *Jean-Paul Gaultier*, 11 *Henry Fonda*, 12 *Bon Jovi*, 13 *Roger Moore*, 14 *Tony Green*, 15 *Pizza*, 16 *Magnus Magnusson*, 17 *Herman's Hermits*, 18 *Jeff and Beau Bridges*, 19 *Peter Baldwin*, 20 *Backbeat*.

 # General Knowledge

Your rating:
- ● 0-5 Join a library
- ● 11-15 Join a quiz team
- ● 6-10 Keep at it
- ● 16-20 Join Mensa

1. Which British novelist and poet wrote *The Mayor of Casterbridge, Far From the Madding Crowd* and *Tess of the d'Urbevilles*?
2. What is the capital of the Isle of Man?
3. Which German composer wrote the *Brandenburg Concertos* and *The Well-Tempered Clavier*?
4. Who played Dan Conner in the sitcom *Roseanne*?
5. In the Old Testament, what was the name of the tower that was intended to reach heaven?
6. What sort of creature is an iguana?
7. Who founded the Scout movement in 1908?
8. What, politically, does UDI stand for?
9. Which island in San Francisco Bay was the site of a notorious maximum security prison?
10. Who wrote *The Admirable Crichton* and *Peter Pan*?
11. Which 13th-century English monk has been credited with the invention of the magnifying glass?
12. Who succeeded Mussolini as Italian prime minister and negotiated the armistice with the Allies?
13. In which South American country is the oil refining town of Moron?
14. By what name was the West German left-wing guerrilla group the Rote Armee Fraktion known?
15. Which of the Seven Wonders of the World was constructed by King Nebuchadnezzar II?
16. What name is given to rodents of the family *Sciuridae*?
17. Which famous English public school was founded by John Lyon?
18. In which year did artist Paul Cézanne die?
19. What was the site of the world's first fast breeder nuclear reactor
20. Which Charles Dickens novel features the character Rosa Bud?

ANSWERS: *1 Thomas Hardy, 2 Douglas, 3 Johann Sebastian Bach, 4 John Goodman, 5 Tower of Babel, 6 A lizard, 7 Robert Baden-Powell, 8 Unilateral declaration of independence, 9 Alcatraz, 10 J M Barrie, 11 Roger Bacon, 12 Pietro Badoglio, 13 Venezuela, 14 Baader-Meinhof gang, 15 The Hanging Gardens of Babylon, 16 Squirrels, 17 Harrow, 18 1906, 19 Dounreay, 20 The Mystery of Edwin Drood.*

 *General Knowledge*

Your rating:
- 0-5   Join a library
- 11-15 Join a quiz team
- 6-10   Keep at it
- 16-20 Join Mensa

1. Which popular revolt of 1381 was led by Wat Tyler and John Ball?
2. In which European country is the resort town of Spa?
3. Which Australian actress won the Best Actress award at the 1999 BAFTAs?
4. Who wrote *Uncle Tom's Cabin*?
5. Which district of the borough of Richmond-upon-Thames contains the HQ of the Rugby Football Union?
6. What is the largest living ape?
7. What name is given to an extended period of dry weather with a virtual absence of precipitation?
8. What type of birds' nests are used to make bird's-nest soup?
9. Which U.S. naval base in Hawaii was attacked by Japanese planes in December 1941?
10. What was Antonio Stradivari famous for manufacturing?
11. Which French army officer was falsely convicted of betraying military secrets and sent to Devil's Island in 1894?
12. What is the dog called in the book *Three Men in a Boat*?
13. Which Spanish golfer won his second green jacket at the 1999 U.S. Masters?
14. In which London park is there a statue of *Peter Pan* sculpted by George James Frampton?
15. Which Irish dancer was the mistress of Louis I of Bavaria?
16. What is the largest island in the Canadian Arctic?
17. What name is given to an abnormally low concentration of sugar in the blood?
18. Which former pop star created the 1983 children's sitcom *Luna*?
19. Which butterfly has brownish wings marked with large purple eyespots?
20. In which Cumbrian port was the first British nuclear submarine built?

ANSWERS: 1 *Peasants' Revolt.* 2 *Belgium.* 3 *Cate Blanchett.* 4 *Harriet Beecher Stowe.* 5 *Twickenham.* 6 *Gorilla.* 7 *Drought.* 8 *Swifts.* 9 *Pearl Harbor.* 10 *Violins.* 11 *Alfred Dreyfus.* 12 *Montmorency.* 13 *Jose Maria Olazabal.* 14 *Kensington Gardens.* 15 *Lola Montez.* 16 *Baffin Island.* 17 *Hypoglycaemia.* 18 *Mickey Dolenz.* 19 *Peacock butterfly.* 20 *Barrow-in-Furness.*

 *General Knowledge*

Your rating:
- 0-5   Join a library
- 11-15   Join a quiz team
- 6-10   Keep at it
- 16-20   Join Mensa

1. Which South African surgeon performed the world's first successful heart transplant?
2. A hurricane is categorised as force 12 on which scale?
3. Which singer does Dennis Quaid portray in the 1989 film *Great Balls of Fire*?
4. In which U.S. state is the Grand Canyon?
5. Which letter on a typewriter keyboard is between A and D?
6. What is the third largest of the Channel Islands?
7. Who captained the England team that won the 1966 World Cup?
8. What does 'entre nous' mean?
9. Which British novelist wrote *Brave New World*?
10. What sort of creature is a drill?
11. Which British satirical novelist wrote *Nightmare Abbey* and *Gryll Grange*?
12. In which battle was Henry III captured by the barons led by Simon de Montfort in 1264?
13. Which English composer's works include the ballet *Café des Sports*?
14. To which order of insects to ants, wasps and bees belong?
15. Which Lebanese port is also known as Sur?
16. Who was the last king of Italy?
17. Which father and son triumphed with Bobbyjo at the 1999 Grand National?
18. In which ocean is the Rockall Deep submarine trench?
19. Which American president founded the Peace Corps?
20. In which 1757 battle did Robert Clive defeat the Nawab of Bengal?

ANSWERS: 1 Christiaan Barnard, 2 The Beaufort scale, 3 Jerry Lee Lewis, 4 Arizona, 5 S, 6 Alderney, 7 Bobby Moore, 8 Between you and me, 9 Aldous Huxley, 10 A monkey, 11 Thomas Love Peacock, 12 Battle of Lewes, 13 Antony Hopkins, 14 Hymenoptera, 15 Tyre, 16 Umberto II, 17 Tommy and Paul Carberry, 18 Atlantic Ocean, 19 John F Kennedy, 20 Battle of Plassey

Entertainment

Your rating: ● 0-5 Buy a TV ● 6-10 Keep at it
● 11-15 Join a quiz team ● 16-20 Enter a quiz show

1. Who presented the various *Alright on the Night* TV specials?
2. Who had a top five hit in 1986 with *Sledgehammer*?
3. Which Australian vocalist formerly played Beth Brennan in TV's *Neighbours*?
4. Which *Alien* director made the 1991 road movie *Thelma and Louise*?
5. Which Nineties comedy series starred Patricia Routledge as Hyacinth Bucket?
6. What was the title of Disney's 1970 feline animation?
7. Who presented *Masterchef* on BBC 1?
8. Who played C.S. Lewis in Richard Attenborough's 1993 film *Shadowlands*?
9. Which office sitcom starring Clive Francis was created by the *Red Dwarf* team?
10. Which pop duo launched a musical *Liberation* in the charts in 1994?
11. Who portrayed the tragic hero of *The Elephant Man* in the 1980 film?
12. Who collaborated with South African musicians to produce his album *Graceland*?
13. Who played the heart-throb of TV's *Heartbeat*, PC Nick Rowan?
14. Which 1993 film about research into AIDS starred Richard Gere?
15. Who had a number one with *The Most Beautiful Girl in the World* in 1994?
16. Which 1993 thriller/road movie starred Brad Pitt and Juliette Lewis?
17. Who played Bruce Wayne and *Batman* in the classic TV series?
18. Which British band made the album *The Wall*?
19. Who played Sanjay Kapoor in TV's *EastEnders*?
20. Who directed and starred as the mysterious *High Plains Drifter* in 1972?

 *General Knowledge*

Your rating: ● 0-5   Join a library   ● 6-10   Keep at it
              ● 11-15   Join a quiz team   ● 16-20   Join Mensa

1. Which ocean did Sir John Alcock and Sir Arthur Brown fly across in 1919?
2. What was the stage name of English-born movie star Archibald Leach?
3. Which country won the last ever Five Nations Championship in Rugby Union?
4. What name is given to an instrument that measures atmospheric pressure?
5. Which famous megalithic structure is on Salisbury Plain in Wiltshire?
6. In which country did Gorgonzola cheese originate?
7. Who discovered the planet Uranus in 1781?
8. What is a lyra viol?
9. Which American novelist wrote *Little Women*?
10. What name is given to the New Testament accounts of Christ's life attributed to Matthew, Mark, Luke and John?
11. Which British novelist wrote *Titus Groan* and *Gormenghast*?
12. What name is given to the anti-Roman Catholic riots that took place in London in 1780?
13. Who directed the 1963 classic *The Great Escape*?
14. What is the capital and main port of Montserrat?
15. Which German city's china industry moved to Meissen in 1710?
16. Of which U.S. state is Albuquerque the largest city?
17. Which artist painted 1910's *Piano and Lute*?
18. What was the first name of the American circus impresario P.T. Barnum?
19. Which Croatian city is known as Ragusa in Italy?
20. What is the oldest U.S. military decoration?

 *General Knowledge*

Your rating:	● 0-5	Join a library	● 6-10	Keep at it
	● 11-15	Join a quiz team	● 16-20	Join Mensa

1. Who wrote *The Iliad*?
2. What was sought by alchemists for its supposed ability to turn base metals into gold?
3. Which king of Macedon was said to have cut the Gordian Knot?
4. By what name is American doctor and champion of euthanasia Jack Kervorkian popularly known?
5. Which acute infectious disease is caused by the bacterium *Salmonella typhi*?
6. In which zodiacal constellation is the red giant Aldebaran the brightest star?
7. Which American jazz singer was known as Lady Day?
8. In which country is the ancient city of Tarsus?
9. What name is given to the hereditary condition in which blood does not clot properly?
10. Who directed *The Maltese Falcon*, *The Treasure of the Sierra Madre* and *The African Queen*?
11. Which coastal resort in Suffolk is the site of an annual music festival founded by Benjamin Britten?
12. What name is given to electromagnetic radiation, the frequency of which lies between that of the violet end of the visible spectrum and X-rays?
13. Which actor, singer, composer and lyricist was once married to Joan Collins?
14. In which English county is the port of Gosport?
15. What are the scopae of a bee?
16. On which river does Barnsley stand?
17. Which member of the Bloomsbury Group wrote *Eminent Victorians*?
18. Which London borough was the site of a 1471 battle in the Wars of the Roses?
19. In which office environment was the 1983 sitcom *The Happy Apple* set?
20. Which Italian doctor was famous for the system of education she developed for small children?

 *General Knowledge*

Your rating:
● 0-5 Join a library
● 11-15 Join a quiz team
● 6-10 Keep at it
● 16-20 Join Mensa

1. Which Roman defence work was the northern frontier of Roman Britain for 250 years?
2. What name is given to the small bones that make up the spine?
3. In which South American country is the port of Valparaiso?
4. What name is given to the fertile low-lying area of England west and south of the Wash?
5. Which British chemist invented the miner's safety lamp?
6. In which country was the conductor Sir Georg Solti born?
7. Which Italian team did Manchester United beat to reach the 1999 Champions League final?
8. Who played artist Dora Carrington in the 1995 film *Carrington*?
9. Which nursing specialty is concerned with the care of women during pregnancy and childbirth?
10. What name is given to a pilchard less than one year old?
11. Which Czech-born British dramatist wrote *Rosencrantz and Guildenstern Are Dead* and *Travesties*?
12. Of which African country is Ouagadougou the capital?
13. Which French composer and member of Les Six wrote the opera *Christophe Colomb*?
14. What did artist Helmut Herzfelde change his name to during World War I?
15. Which Civil War general became the 18th president of the United States?
16. In which borough of Greater London is the former borough of Wimbledon?
17. What type of fruit tree is a mazzard?
18. Which 16th-century English dramatist wrote *The Old Wives' Tale* and *The Arraignment of Paris*?
19. What were the first names of Arthur Sullivan's collaborator W.S. Gilbert?
20. Which Canadian-born actress was a co-founder of United Artists with her husband Douglas Fairbanks?

Entertainment

| Your rating: | ● 0-5 | Buy a TV | ● 6-10 | Keep at it |
| | ● 11-15 | Join a quiz team | ● 16-20 | Enter a quiz show |

1. Which Channel Four comedy series starring Kelsey Grammer was a spin-off from *Cheers*?
2. Which reggae singer was the star of the 1972 film *The Harder They Come*?
3. Who had a 1958 top ten hit with *Good Golly Miss Molly*?
4. Which star of the 1990 Mike Leigh film *Life is Sweet* played Kevin Costello in the cricketing TV comedy series *Outside Edge*?
5. Which duo had a top five smash in 1994 with *Always*?
6. Who played *Doctor Finlay* in ITV's Nineties version of the medical drama series?
7. Which British teen idol recorded the 1971 chart-toppers *Get it On* and *Hot Love* with his band T. Rex?
8. Who played the man of steel in the TV series *The New Adventures of Superman*?
9. Who played Scarlett O' Hara in the 1939 Southern epic *Gone With the Wind*?
10. Which current affairs presenter and former newsreader fronted the viewers' complaints forum *Biteback*?
11. Which British female vocalist originally had a hit with *You Gotta Be* in 1994?
12. What type of animal was Brian in the children's programme *The Magic Roundabout*?
13. Which member of the Bridges clan starred in the 1993 movie *Fearless*?
14. Who played the well-loved buffoon *Mr Bean* on TV?
15. Which singer duetted with Willie Nelson on the 1984 hit *To All the Girls I've Loved Before*?
16. Which classic Korean War TV comedy featured Hot Lips, Klinger and Hawkeye?
17. Which action hero was the hard-hitting star of the 1993 film *Striking Distance*?
18. Who played the cantankerous *Chef!* of the TV sitcom?
19. Which group had a 1979 number one hit with *When You're in Love With a Beautiful Woman*?
20. Who starred as the young rebel in the 1955 film version of John Steinbeck's *East of Eden*?

ANSWERS: 1 *Frasier,* 2 *Jimmy Cliff,* 3 *Little Richard,* 4 *Timothy Spall,* 5 *Erasure,* 6 *David Rintoul,* 7 *Marc Bolan,* 8 *Dean Cain,* 9 *Vivien Leigh,* 10 *Sue Lawley,* 11 *Des'ree,* 12 *A snail,* 13 *Jeff Bridges,* 14 *Rowan Atkinson,* 15 *Julio Iglesias,* 16 *M*A*S*H,* 17 *Bruce Willis,* 18 *Lenny Henry,* 19 *Dr Hook,* 20 *James Dean.*

 # General Knowledge

Your rating:
- 0-5   Join a library
- 11-15   Join a quiz team
- 6-10   Keep at it
- 16-20   Join Mensa

1. Which British jockey achieved a record of nine victories in The Derby?
2. In which U.S. state are the volcanoes Mauna Loa and Mauna Kea?
3. Which Tottenham Hotspur player was voted Player of the Year and Footballer of the Year in 1999?
4. How many yards are there in a statute mile?
5. Which independent state in Rome is the seat of government of the Roman Catholic Church?
6. Of which African country is Mogadishu the capital?
7. What name is given to the fluid constituent of blood?
8. On whose play was the 1958 film *Cat On A Hot Tin Roof* based?
9. Which Spanish artist developed cubism with Georges Braque?
10. What is the length in yards of a cricket pitch?
11. Which hallucinogenic drug is derived from the Mexican peyote cactus?
12. What name was given to the skeletal remains uncovered in a gravel pit in East Sussex in 1912?
13. What, in defence, does MIDAS stand for?
14. What was the pen name of Marie Louise de la Ramée, author of *Under Two Flags*?
15. Which British birth control campaigner wrote *Married Love*?
16. What name was given to members of the Irish Republican Brotherhood?
17. What is the second largest and northernmost of the four main islands of Japan?
18. Which English actress born in 1874 founded a school of stage training?
19. Which Italian artist is best known for his portraits of Queen Elizabeth II and John F. Kennedy?
20. On which river does Merthyr Tydfil stand?

ANSWERS: 1 *Lester Piggott*, 2 *Hawaii*, 3 *David Ginola*, 4 *1,760*, 5 *Vatican City*, 6 *Somalia*, 7 *Plasma*, 8 *Tennessee Williams*, 9 *Pablo Picasso*, 10 *22 yards*, 11 *Mescaline*, 12 *Piltdown Man*, 13 *Missile Defence Alarm System*, 14 *Ouida*, 15 *Marie Stopes*, 16 *Fenians*, 17 *Hokkaido*, 18 *Italia Conti*, 19 *Pietro Annigoni*, 20 *River Taff*.

THE TRIVIA QUIZ BOOK

 *General Knowledge*

Your rating:	● 0-5	Join a library	● 6-10	Keep at it
	● 11-15	Join a quiz team	● 16-20	Join Mensa

1. Which American actress starred in the films *Jezebel*, *Dark Victory* and *All About Eve*?
2. What name was given to the Turkish empire founded by Osman?
3. What is the 23rd letter of the Greek alphabet?
4. In which Italian city is the opera house La Scala?
5. Which county cricket club has its headquarters at The Oval in Kennington?
6. What sort of creature is a merganser?
7. Which Indian religion celebrated the 300th anniversary of its founding in 1999?
8. How many gold medals did American swimmer Mark Spitz win at the 1972 Olympics?
9. Whose romance books include *The Ranch* and *The Ghost*?
10. What do the initials FBI stand for?
11. Which town in British Columbia is at the southeastern end of the Alaska Highway?
12. Who was the Roman emperor from 69 to 79 who ended the civil war and was deified after his death?
13. In which year did the TV show *Songs of Praise* first appear on our screens?
14. By what name is the fruit of the plant *Ananas comosus* known?
15. Which British dramatist and novelist wrote *This Sporting Life*?
16. What was the name of the Egyptian god usually portrayed as a falcon or with a falcon's head?
17. Which 19th-century French painter and illustrator was noted for his illustrations of works by Balzac, Cervantes and Dante?
18. In what part of the body is the pineal gland to be found?
19. What is the name of the former island penal colony at the entrance of Table Bay, South Africa?
20. What imperial unit of power is equal to 550 foot-pounds per second?

ANSWERS: 1 Bette Davis, 2 Ottoman Empire, 3 Psi, 4 Milan, 5 Surrey, 6 A duck, 7 Sikhism, 8 Seven, 9 Danielle Steel, 10 Federal Bureau of Investigation, 11 Dawson Creek, 12 Vespasian, 13 1961, 14 Pineapple, 15 David Storey, 16 Horus, 17 Gustave Doré, 18 The brain, 19 Robben, 20 Horsepower.

 *General Knowledge*

Your rating: ● 0-5   Join a library   ● 6-10   Keep at it
              ● 11-15   Join a quiz team   ● 16-20   Join Mensa

1. Which English merchant, who was three times mayor of London, is associated with a legend involving his cat?
2. By what first name was American jazz trumpeter John Birks Gillespie known?
3. How many are there in an ogdoad?
4. What name is given to the 102 English emigrants who sailed in *The Mayflower* and established the first settlement in New England in 1620?
5. Which French city near Paris is the site of an elaborate residence built for Louis XIV?
6. In which county is the industrial town of Doncaster?
7. Which lake in Germany, Switzerland and Austria is also called Bodensee?
8. Which metal whose symbol is Hg is used in thermometers, barometers and dental amalgam?
9. Who was the first gymnast to record a perfect score of 10 in international competition?
10. In which English county is the market town of Blandford Forum?
11. Which legendary Spanish aristocratic libertine inspired works by Byron, Molière, Mozart and George Bernard Shaw?
12. By what name is potassium hydrogen tartrate, which is used in baking powders, better known?
13. What was Steve McQueen's first name?
14. Who was forced from the throne in 1470 after falling out with the Earl of Warwick?
15. Which port on the island of Lewis is the administrative centre for the Western Isles?
16. In the Old Testament, who were the parents of King Solomon?
17. Which Frankish dynasty was founded by Merovech in the 5th century?
18. In which novel does the character Squire Allworthy appear?
19. Which castle in Belfast housed the parliament of Northern Ireland from 1921 to 1972?
20. What is the state capital of New Mexico?

ANSWERS: 1 *Richard (Dick) Whittington,* 2 *Dizzy,* 3 *Eight,* 4 *The Pilgrim Fathers,* 5 *Versailles,* 6 *South Yorkshire,* 7 *Lake Constance,* 8 *Mercury,* 9 *Nadia Comaneci,* 10 *Dorset,* 11 *Don Juan,* 12 *Cream of tartar,* 13 *Terrence,* 14 *Edward IV,* 15 *Stornoway,* 16 *David and Bathsheba,* 17 *Merovingians,* 18 *The History of Tom Jones,* 19 *Stormont,* 20 *Santa Fe.*

Sports

Your rating: ● **0-5** Wooden spoon   ● **6-10** Bronze medal
           ● **11-15** Silver medal   ● **16-20** Gold medal

1. Which sport is played by the Green Bay Packers?
2. Which famous horse did Lester Piggott ride to victory in the 1970 2000 Guineas?
3. In 2000, which team defeated Arsenal in the UEFA Cup final?
4. Which England defender's first names are Sulzeer Jeremiah?
5. How many times did Jack Nicklaus win the U.S. Open?
6. Which city hosted the 1952 Winter Olympics?
7. Who was the Premiership's top scorer of the 1999/2000 season?
8. In 1993, which British-born boxer defeated Tommy Morrison to become WBO heavyweight champion?
9. In 1998, which home nation were thrashed 76-0 by Australia's rugby union team?
10. In what year did football's first European championships take place?
11. Who beat Martina Hingis in the final of the 1997 French Open?
12. Which Canadian sprinter set a new 100m world record in 1996?
13. Which Yorkshireman was the first Test bowler to reach 300 wickets?
14. Who managed England's football team at the 1982 World Cup?
15. Which rugby league club beat Leeds in the 1994 and 1995 Challenge Cup finals?
16. In golf, how many strokes over par is a double bogey?
17. In which year did London host the Summer Olympic Games for the second time?
18. Which nation won football's European championships in 1972 and 1980?
19. Where would you find the baulk line?
20. Who was Formula 1 world motor racing champion in 1998?

THE TRIVIA QUIZ BOOK

 *General Knowledge*

1. Which English river passes through Tonbridge, Maidstone, Rochester, Chatham and Gillingham?
2. Who wrote *Sons and Lovers* and *Lady Chatterley's Lover*?
3. Where were the nymphs known as hamadryads supposed to live?
4. What name is given to plants that complete their life cycle within one year?
5. Which cotton fabric takes its name from the French city of Nîmes?
6. On what day is the Annunciation celebrated?
7. What is the name of the channel between Hampshire and the Isle of Wight?
8. Which domesticated member of the horse family is also known as an ass?
9. Who directed *Thelma and Louise*?
10. Of which U.S. state is Denver the capital?
11. Which British Restoration dramatist wrote *The Way of The World* and *Love for Love*?
12. What was the title of Robert Flaherty's pioneering 1922 documentary film of Inuit life?
13. Who composed the symphony *The Song of the Earth*, which was first performed in 1911?
14. What name was given to the Union of Austria with Germany in 1938?
15. Which French composer wrote the opera *Pelléas et Mélisande*?
16. What is the smallest and easternmost of the Great Lakes?
17. Which violent extremists of the French Revolution were named from their wearing trousers instead of knee-breeches?
18. What is the name of the delta district at the mouth of the River Rhône famous for its colony of flamingos?
19. Which British philosopher and pioneer of utilitarianism wrote *Principles of Morals and Legislation*?
20. What is the capital of Mozambique?

 *General Knowledge*

Your rating:	● 0-5	Join a library	● 6-10	Keep at it
	● 11-15	Join a quiz team	● 16-20	Join Mensa

1. Which UK government securities introduced in 1956 entitle the holders to participate in a prize draw?
2. What name is given to the compulsory enlistment of recruits for military service?
3. Which British group had a hit with *Bitter Sweet Symphony*?
4. What is the name of the large salty lake between Israel and Jordan?
5. Which U.S. thriller writer penned *The Long Goodbye*?
6. Who was the fourth wife of Henry VIII?
7. Which stringed instrument is featured in Rodrigo's *Concierto de Aranjuez*?
8. Which characters in Eastern European folklore are repelled by crucifixes, garlic and the light of day?
9. On which Cumbrian lake did Sir Malcolm and Donald Campbell establish world water-speed records?
10. Who played Lee Simon in the 1998 Woody Allen film *Celebrity*?
11. Which former world heavyweight boxing champion lost his title to Gene Tunney in 1926?
12. What is the classic literary language of the Hindu scriptures?
13. Which Russian-born stateswoman was prime minister of Israel from 1969 to 1974?
14. In which county of the Republic of Ireland is the seaside resort of Bray?
15. Which radioactive element has the symbol Pm?
16. Who was the last Stuart monarch?
17. Which American wrote the verse collections *Leaves of Grass* and *Democratic Vistas*?
18. In which constellation is Deneb the brightest star?
19. What was Mindy's surname in the sitcom *Mork and Mindy*?
20. Which Charles Dickens novel features the character Seth Pecksniff?

ANSWERS: 1 *Premium bonds*, 2 *Conscription*, 3 *The Verve*, 4 *Dead Sea*, 5 *Raymond Chandler*, 6 *Anne of Cleves*, 7 *Guitar*, 8 *Vampires*, 9 *Coniston Water*, 10 *Kenneth Branagh*, 11 *Jack Dempsey*, 12 *Sanskrit*, 13 *Golda Meir*, 14 *Wicklow*, 15 *Promethium*, 16 *Queen Anne*, 17 *Walt Whitman*, 18 *Cygnus*, 19 *McConnell*, 20 *Martin Chuzzlewit*.

 *General Knowledge*

Your rating: ● 0-5   Join a library   ● 6-10   Keep at it
              ● 11-15   Join a quiz team   ● 16-20   Join Mensa

1. Which English artist painted *The Leaping Horse*, *Dedham Vale* and *The Haywain*?
2. What name was given to a band of men employed to force men into the army or navy?
3. Which football manager led England to the World Cup in 1966?
4. With which athletics field event is Sergei Bubka associated?
5. Which Russian author's stories included *The Death of Ivan Ilyich*?
6. What is the capital of Denmark?
7. Which Berkshire village is associated with the Royal Military Academy?
8. Which snack item is named after former First Lord of the Admiralty John Montagu?
9. To which part of the body does the adjective sural apply?
10. Who is the young star of the BBC cookery programme *The Naked Chef*?
11. Which South African prime minister took South Africa out of the Commonwealth?
12. In which famous Anglo-Saxon epic poem does the hero slay the monster Grendel?
13. Which 1969 Samuel Beckett play lasts for approximately half a minute?
14. What name is given to the process establishing that a marriage is not legally valid?
15. Which British dramatist wrote *The Second Mrs Tanqueray*?
16. What is the capital of Costa Rica?
17. Who played Rocky Cassidy in t.v. drama *Boon*?
18. What branch of dentistry is concerned with the correction of malocclusion or badly positioned teeth?
19. Which London theatre was founded by actor Bernard Miles?
20. In computing, what does CPU stand for?

ANSWERS: 1 John Constable, **2** Press gang, **3** Sir Alf Ramsey, **4** Pole vault, **5** Tolstoy, **6** Copenhagen, **7** Sandhurst, **8** Sandwich (4th Earl of Sandwich), **9** The calf of the leg, **10** Jamie Oliver, **11** Hendrik Verwoerd, **12** Beowulf, **13** Breath, **14** Annulment, **15** Sir Arthur Wing Pinero, **16** San José, **17** Neil Morrissey, **18** Orthodontics, **19** The Mermaid, **20** Central processing unit.

Entertainment

Your rating: ● 0-5   Buy a TV   ● 6-10   Keep at it
                ● 11-15   Join a quiz team   ● 16-20   Enter a quiz show

1. Who starred as the *Top Gun* Maverick in the 1986 film?
2. Which husband-and-wife team had a number one hit with *I Got You Babe* in 1965?
3. Which satirical puppet show was co-created by Peter Fluck and Roger Law?
4. Which British group had big hits with *The Reflex* and *Wild Boys* in 1984?
5. Which cult U.S. cartoon show features Homer and Bart?
6. Who starred as the cop/shark hunter in the 1975 film *Jaws*?
7. Which late *Coronation Street* character was Weatherfield's mayor and was also awarded the OBE?
8. Who had a number one with 1994's *The Real Thing*?
9. Which actor played Yosser Hughes in Alan Bleasdale's Eighties TV drama *Boys From the Blackstuff*?
10. Who starred as the tough cop in the classic 1968 movie *Bullitt*?
11. The 1993 TV drama *Lipstick on Your Collar* was written by which English playwright?
12. Which Pink Floyd album reached the number one spot in 1994?
13. What was *The Lone Ranger*'s American Indian sidekick called in the TV western series?
14. The 1943 film *For Whom the Bell Tolls* was based on whose novel?
15. Who hosted the European TV quiz *Going For Gold*?
16. Which group had a huge hit in 1978 with *Y.M.C.A.*?
17. Which 1987 film starred Oliver Reed and Amanda Donohoe as a mis-matched couple voluntarily stranded on a desert island?
18. Who played surfing heart-throb Brad Willis in TV's *Neighbours*?
19. Who sang the 1958 adolescent anthem *Summertime Blues*?
20. Which French actor married Andie MacDowell for a *Green Card* in the 1991 film?

ANSWERS: 1 *Tom Cruise*, 2 *Sonny and Cher*, 3 *Spitting Image*, 4 *Duran Duran*, 5 *The Simpsons*, 6 *Roy Scheider*, 7 *Alf Roberts*, 8 *Tony Di Bart*, 9 *Bernard Hill*, 10 *Steve McQueen*, 11 *Dennis Potter*, 12 *The Division Bell*, 13 *Tonto*, 14 *Ernest Hemingway's*, 15 *Henry Kelly*, 16 *Village People*, 17 *Castaway*, 18 *Scott Michaelson*, 19 *Eddie Cochran*, 20 *Gerard Depardieu*.

THE TRIVIA QUIZ BOOK

 ## General Knowledge

Your rating:	● 0-5	Join a library	● 6-10	Keep at it
	● 11-15	Join a quiz team	● 16-20	Join Mensa

1. Which house in Gloucestershire, famous for its annual horse trials, is the family seat of the Duke of Beaufort?
2. To which political party did U.S. presidents Franklin D Roosevelt, John F Kennedy and Jimmy Carter belong?
3. What is the name of the Japanese dish consisting of small rice cakes topped with fish?
4. What is the English translation of René Descartes' famous statement "Cogito ergo sum"?
5. Which Argentinian footballer captained the team that won the 1986 World Cup?
6. In what year did Julius Caesar first invade Britain?
7. Which combat sport takes place on a piste?
8. Which British runner, famous for his rivalry with Sebastian Coe, won the 800m at the 1980 Olympics?
9. In which English county is the town of Burnham-on-Crouch?
10. Which Charles Dickens novel features the character Sam Weller?
11. Which Russian novelist wrote *One Day in the Life of Ivan Denisovich*?
12. What is the measure of a substance's compactness, equal to its mass per unit volume?
13. In which western series did Chinese cook Hop Sing appear?
14. What nationality was the conductor Ernest Ansermet?
15. Which German admiral, who made his name as a World War I U-boat commander, succeeded Adolf Hitler as German chancellor?
16. What sort of creature is a mudpuppy?
17. Which Anglo-Saxon kingdom was ruled by Penda and Offa?
18. Who created the puppet fox Basil Brush?
19. Which Scottish-born detective founded his National Detective Agency in the United States in the 1850s?
20. What name is given to the large stones used in building prehistoric monuments such as Stonehenge?

THE TRIVIA QUIZ BOOK

 *General Knowledge*

Your rating: ● **0-5** Join a library   ● **6-10** Keep at it
● **11-15** Join a quiz team   ● **16-20** Join Mensa

1. Which small independent republic is an enclave in Italian territory in the Apennines near Rimini?
2. What name is given to the variety of chalcedony used by Stone Age man for tools and weapons?
3. In which country was Arnold Schwarzenegger born?
4. What is the capital of Egypt?
5. Which branch of the armed services is represented by the initials RAF?
6. Of which county is Matlock the administrative centre?
7. Which American novelist wrote *The Maltese Falcon* and *The Thin Man*?
8. What was Gene Wilder's profession in the film *Bonnie and Clyde*?
9. Who wrote *The Merchant of Venice* and *Much Ado About Nothing*?
10. Which snooker player won the Embassy World Snooker Championship for a record seventh time in 1999?
11. Which Ethiopian emperor was known as Ras Tafari, or the Lion of Judah?
12. What name is given to a device that detects and measures nuclear radiation by counting the number of ionising particles?
13. Which Bohemian composer wrote the opera *The Bartered Bride*?
14. Which actress starred in the 1992 film *Bitter Moon* and married its director Roman Polanski?
15. Which Asian climbing plant contains the powerful insecticide rotenone?
16. What is the capital of Namibia?
17. Mireya Moscoso was the first woman president of which Central American country?
18. Who was Phileas Fogg's valet in the novel *Around the World in Eighty Days*?
19. Which leaf-eating monkey of Borneo is named for its long fleshy nose?
20. What is the administrative centre of Wiltshire?

ANSWERS: *1 San Marino, 2 Flint, 3 Austria, 4 Cairo, 5 Royal Air Force, 6 Derbyshire, 7 Dashiell Hammett, 8 Undertaker, 9 William Shakespeare, 10 Stephen Hendry, 11 Haile Selassie I, 12 Geiger counter, 13 Bedrich Smetana, 14 Emmanuelle Seigner, 15 Derris, 16 Windhoek, 17 Panama, 18 Passepartout, 19 Proboscis monkey, 20 Trowbridge.*

THE TRIVIA QUIZ BOOK

 *General Knowledge*

Your rating: ● 0-5   Join a library   ● 6-10   Keep at it
        ● 11-15   Join a quiz team   ● 16-20   Join Mensa

1. Which palace on the River Thames was built in 1515 by Cardinal Wolsey and given to Henry VIII?
2. Who wrote the operas *Cosi fan tutte* and *The Magic Flute*?
3. Which hell-raising British actor died in Malta in 1999 at the age of 61?
4. How long, in feet, is Gunter's Chain?
5. Which British actress starred in *The Prime of Miss Jean Brodie* and *A Private Function*?
6. Of which county is Winchester the administrative centre?
7. According to the New Testament, which angel announced to Mary that she was to give birth to Christ?
8. Who played the lead in the 1993 film *The Positively True Adventures of the Alleged Texas Cheerleader-Murdering Mom*?
9. Of which country is the Dáil Éireann the representative assembly?
10. Which Dutch artist painted *The Laughing Cavalier*?
11. Which former poet laureate's volumes of poetry include *The Hawk in the Rain* and *Crow*?
12. What is the capital and main port of Trinidad and Tobago?
13. *Stop Making Sense* is a film of a concert given by which pop group?
14. In which country is the city of Shiraz which gives its name to a grape variety used to make dark red wines?
15. Which British publishing company specialising in paperback books was founded by Sir Allen Lane?
16. Into how many constellations is the sky divided?
17. Which white mineral consisting of hydrated magnesium silicate is used for making tobacco pipes?
18. What name is given to the growing of plants in a liquid nutrient instead of soil?
19. Which artist said "Art is only a substitute while the beauty of life is still deficient"?
20. Of which African country is Porto Novo the capital?

Entertainment

Your rating:	● 0-5	Buy a TV	● 6-10	Keep at it
	● 11-15	Join a quiz team	● 16-20	Enter a quiz show

1. Which famous screen ape captured Fay Wray in a 1933 classic movie of the same name?
2. Which former *Blackadder* star presented the animation show *Stay Tooned!*?
3. Who had a top five hit in 1994 with a cover of *Sweets for My Sweet*?
4. What was Bernado Bertolucci's 1993 movie about Bhutan buddhists called?
5. Which BBC 1 anti-crime programme broadcast its 100th show in 1994?
6. Who starred as *Spartacus* in the 1960 film?
7. On which day could you have had an early *Breakfast With Frost*?
8. *If You Leave Me Now* was a 1976 number one for a group which shared its name with an American city. Which one?
9. Which animated, fur-clad character famously shouted "Yabadabadoo!"?
10. Barbra Streisand hit the charts in 1994 with which song from the show *Sunset Boulevard*?
11. In which decade was TV's *Heartbeat* originally set?
12. Who directed the nightmarish 1971 film *A Clockwork Orange*?
13. Who had a top five hit in 1989 with *Wind Beneath My Wings*, taken from her film *Beaches*?
14. Who replaced Richard O'Brien as host of TV's *The Crystal Maze*?
15. What was Manchester United's 1994 pop anthem called?
16. What were *The Flowerpot Men* called in the classic children's show?
17. Which *Ghost* star played a surgeon in the 1992 film *City of Joy*?
18. Which group had a 1980 number one hit with *Geno*?
19. Who played the over-anxious dad married to Mary Steenburgen in the 1989 family comedy film *Parenthood*?
20. Who plays Pat Evans in TV's *EastEnders*?

ANSWERS: *1 King Kong, 2 Tony Robinson, 3 C J Lewis, 4 Little Buddha, 5 Crimewatch UK, 6 Kirk Douglas, 7 Sunday, 8 Chicago, 9 Fred Flintstone, 10 As If We Never Said Goodbye, 11 The 1960s, 12 Stanley Kubrick, 13 Bette Midler, 14 Edward Tudor-Pole, 15 Come On You Reds, 16 Bill and Ben, 17 Patrick Swayze, 18 Dexy's Midnight Runners, 19 Steve Martin, 20 Pam St Clement.*

THE TRIVIA QUIZ BOOK

 *General Knowledge*

Your rating:	● 0-5	Join a library	● 6-10	Keep at it
	● 11-15	Join a quiz team	● 16-20	Join Mensa

1. Which Wiltshire market town was famous for carpet manufacture since the 16th century?
2. By what name is the veteran left-wing Labour MP who was the 2nd Viscount Stansgate better known?
3. What was Victor's wife called in the BBC comedy series *One Foot in the Grave*?
4. Who became principal conductor of the City of Birmingham Symphony Orchestra in 1980?
5. Which constellation lies on the zodiac between Cancer and Taurus?
6. What is the longest river in the Republic of Ireland?
7. What is the highest mountain in the British Isles?
8. Who is the author of *Desert Crop* and *Bondage of Love*?
9. Which major Egyptian port is at the Mediterranean entrance to the Suez Canal?
10. Of which Eastern European country was Alexander Dubcek leader?
11. Which British artist sculpted the four bronze lions in Trafalgar Square?
12. In which children's show did the quiz 'Double or Drop' appear?
13. Which English mountaineer's body was discovered on Mount Everest almost 75 years after his disappearance?
14. What was the adopted name of David Gruen, first prime minister of Israel?
15. Which British author wrote *The Outsider* and *The Occult*?
16. What sort of creature is a landrace?
17. In the Old Testament, who was the youngest son of Jacob and Rachel?
18. Which British film star and author died in 1999 at the age of 78?
19. Which is the largest of the United Arab Emirates?
20. Which Shakespeare play features the characters Orlando and Rosalind?

ANSWERS: 1 Wilton, 2 Tony Benn, 3 Margaret, 4 Simon Rattle, 5 Gemini, 6 River Shannon, 7 Ben Nevis, 8 Catherine Cookson, 9 Port Said, 10 Czechoslovakia, 11 Sir Edwin Landseer, 12 Crackerjack, 13 George Mallory, 14 David Ben-Gurion, 15 Colin Wilson, 16 A pig, 17 Benjamin, 18 Dirk Bogarde, 19 Abu Dhabi, 20 As You Like It.

 *General Knowledge*

Your rating: ● **0-5** Join a library ● **6-10** Keep at it
● **11-15** Join a quiz team ● **16-20** Join Mensa

1. Which American songwriter and composer wrote the songs *Night and Day* and *Begin the Beguine*?
2. Brisbane is the capital of which Australian state?
3. Which former presenter of *Animal Magic* died in 1999 at the age of 82?
4. Whose abduction by Paris led to the Trojan War?
5. Which Labour Party leader first became prime minister in 1964?
6. In which English port is Nelson's flagship *HMS Victory* exhibited?
7. What is the name for a Japanese woman whose profession is to entertain men?
8. Which writer was played by Daniel Day-Lewis in the film *My Left Foot*?
9. Which mountain has the faces of presidents Washington, Jefferson, Lincoln and Theodore Roosevelt carved into it?
10. Who wrote *Anna of the Five Towns* and *Clayhanger*?
11. Which English conductor was the original musical director of the Promenade Concerts?
12. What collective name is given to the chemical elements fluorine, chlorine, bromine, iodine and astatine?
13. Which German engineer is credited with manufacturing the first car powered by an internal-combustion engine?
14. Which co-founder of the Pre-Raphaelite Brotherhood died in 1882 in Birchington-on-Sea?
15. Which percussion instrument was popularised by jazz musician and bandleader Lionel Hampton?
16. What does the acronym GATT stand for?
17. Which Latin poet wrote the *Ars amatoria* and the *Metamorphoses*?
18. Which actress married director Renny Harlin in 1983?
19. Which British writer wrote the classic detective novel *Trent's Last Case*?
20. Who directed the films *La Strada*, *Casanova* and *Amarcord*?

ANSWERS: 1 *Cole Porter*. 2 *Queensland*. 3 *Johnny Morris*. 4 *Helen of Troy*. 5 *Harold Wilson*. 6 *Portsmouth*. 7 *Geisha*. 8 *Christy Brown*. 9 *Mount Rushmore*. 10 *Arnold Bennett*. 11 *Henry Wood*. 12 *Halogens*. 13 *Karl Benz*. 14 *Dante Gabriel Rossetti*. 15 *Vibraphone*. 16 *General Agreement on Tariffs and Trade*. 17 *Ovid*. 18 *Geena Davis*. 19 *Edmund Clerihew Bentley*. 20 *Federico Fellini*.

 *General Knowledge*

Your rating: ● 0-5   Join a library   ● 6-10   Keep at it
● 11-15 Join a quiz team   ● 16-20 Join Mensa

1. Which popular blue-and-white chinoiserie pattern attributed to Thomas Minton features a pagoda and figures on a bridge?
2. What name is given to a virtually barren area of land where precipitation is minimal and sporadic?
3. In which country of south-west Asia is the seaport of Abadan?
4. What is the common name for animals of the family *Felidae*?
5. Which royal residence includes St George's Chapel and the Albert Memorial Chapel?
6. What part of the body is affected by dermatitis?
7. Which American comedian was born Benjamin Kubelsky?
8. What is the name given to light rain whose droplets are less than 0.5mm in diameter?
9. Who was the lead singer of Irish group the Boomtown Rats?
10. Which Charles Dickens novel features the character Abel Magwitch?
11. Which former foreign secretary was instrumental in establishing Zimbabwe's independence?
12. What is the brightest star in the constellation Auriga?
13. Who composed the score for the 1981 film *Arthur*?
14. In which country did the board game pachisi originate?
15. Which Italian river is known as Tevere to the natives?
16. Who wrote *I Claudius* and *Claudius the God*?
17. Which actor played Henry in ITV sitcom *All at No. 20*?
18. What name was given to the two magistrates who held supreme civil and military authority under the Roman Republic?
19. Which river of Spain and Portugal enters the Atlantic at Oporto?
20. What sort of creature is a hamadryas?

ANSWERS: *1 Willow pattern, 2 Desert, 3 Iran, 4 Cats, 5 Windsor Castle, 6 The skin, 7 Jack Benny, 8 Drizzle, 9 Bob Geldof, 10 Great Expectations, 11 Lord Carrington, 12 Capella, 13 Burt Bacharach, 14 India, 15 Tiber, 16 Robert Graves, 17 Martin Clunes, 18 Consuls, 19 Douro, 20 A baboon.*

Entertainment

Your rating: ● 0-5   Buy a TV   ● 6-10   Keep at it

● 11-15   Join a quiz team   ● 16-20   Enter a quiz show

1. Which UK band had a number one hit with *Inside* in 1994?
2. On which channel was the intergalactic series *Babylon 5* screened?
3. Which star of *A Fish Called Wanda* appeared in the 1994 parental saga *Mother's Boys*?
4. Which tough Scottish cop was played on TV by Mark McManus?
5. Which British punk group recorded *Tommy Gun* and *Rock the Casbah*?
6. Which 1993 comedy sequel starred Charles Grodin and several troublesome St Bernards?
7. Which boy band had a 1994 top five hit with *Around the World*?
8. Who directed the 1972 film *The Godfather*?
9. Who had a top ten hit with *Arthur's Theme (Best That You Can Do)* in 1982?
10. Which 1988 movie featured Robert De Niro as a scruffy bounty hunter?
11. Which Irish singer spent *A Night in San Francisco* with his 1994 album?
12. Which member of the Who played *McVicar* in the 1980 film based on a true story?
13. Who presents the popular ITV quiz show *Who Wants to Be a Millionaire*?
14. *The Dead* was a 1987 dramatisation of *Dubliners*, by which author?
15. Which science and technology programme celebrated its 30th birthday in 1994?
16. Which soggy-sounding group had a number one smash with *Love is All Around* in 1994?
17. What was Grant Mitchell's brother called in TV's *EastEnders*?
18. Which British actor found Hollywood fame as the star of the 1994 film *Four Weddings and a Funeral*?
19. Who played *Sharpe* in various TV dramas?
20. *The Joy Luck Club* was a 1993 screen adaptation of which Chinese-American author's novel?

ANSWERS: 1 *Stiltskin,* 2 *Channel 4,* 3 *Jamie Lee Curtis,* 4 *Jim Taggart,* 5 *The Clash,* 6 *Beethoven's Second,* 7 *East 17,* 8 *Francis Ford Coppola,* 9 *Christopher Cross,* 10 *Midnight Run,* 11 *Van Morrison,* 12 *Roger Daltrey,* 13 *Chris Tarrant,* 14 *James Joyce,* 15 *Horizon,* 16 *Wet Wet Wet,* 17 *Phil,* 18 *Hugh Grant,* 19 *Sean Bean,* 20 *Amy Tan's.*